Anxiety and the dynamics of collaboration

AUP Titles of Related Interest

CONSULTATION IN RESIDENTIAL CARE
Children in Residential Establishments
R Silveira (ed)

CHILDREN NEED GROUPS
R Silveira and G Trafford

CARE OF THE ELDERLY
D J Hunter, N McKeganey and I MacPherson

COMMUNITY, NORMALITY AND DIFFERENCE
Meeting Special Needs
S R Baron and J D Haldane (eds)

CONTAINING CRIME
Community-based approaches
J McNeill and B Williams

MARITAL THERAPY
An inside view
Christopher Clulow

TO HAVE AND TO HOLD
Marriage, the first baby and preparing couples for parenthood
Christopher Clulow

ON CALL
Waren Colman

ANXIETY AND
THE DYNAMICS OF
COLLABORATION

Douglas Woodhouse

and

Paul Pengelly

ABERDEEN UNIVERSITY PRESS
Member of Maxwell Macmillan Pergamon Publishing Corporation

First Published 1991
Aberdeen University Press

British Library Cataloguing in Publication Data

Woodhouse, Douglas
    Anxiety and the dynamics of collaboration
    I. Title   II. Pengelly, Paul
    361.3

    ISBN 0 08 040912 1

Typeset by MS Filmsetting Ltd
Printed by Athenaeum Press Ltd,
Newcastle upon Tyne

Foreword

In 1970, well before our present preoccupation with the failures of communication and co-operation in child protection, I read with fascination the paper, referred to in this work, by Isabel (then) Menzies on the functioning of social systems in a hospital as a defence against anxiety. It was one of those rare, seminal pieces which cast new light on the processes and dynamics of one kind of institutional care. In 1979, I read Mattinson and Sinclair's *Mate and stalemate*. This (neglected) book was in the same tradition and seemed to me greatly to enlarge our understanding of the impact certain 'turbulent' families make on social workers.

This book is a worthy successor. Using material from a series of interprofessional workshops (and also quasi-professionals, as I must describe marriage guidance counsellors) on marital interaction and problems of collaboration, it examines the ways in which the dynamics between the couples impact on the professionals involved and affect their interactions. The groups comprised probation officers, social workers, GPs, health visitors and marriage guidance counsellors. The analysis of the impact of role on professional behaviour is particularly interesting and penetrating.

Will this book receive the attention which it deserves? Professionals in this country have a long standing ambivalent relationship with psycho-dynamic theory. In social work, which I know best, there has been a persisting unresolved dichotomy between the explanatory theories which stress external factors in the miseries and distress which clients experience and those which stress internal factors, whether individual or familial. It is alive and well at present in the child abuse debate! I have always regretted the intellectual intolerance of each to the other. At present, as difficulties and failures of professional co-operation with tragic consequences are constantly highlighted, most recently in the (post Cleveland) Rochdale Social Services Department, I am more than ever convinced that we must take heed of the hidden forces which pull us apart, or inappropriately together, when confronted with behaviour which disturbs us at deep levels. And what could be more disturbing than sexual and ritualistic abuse of children?

Those who have to cope with such phenomena have no time to indulge in the luxury of intellectual dogmatism. They must grab any theory which helps. I believe this book does help. All the sadder, therefore, to see that the one chapter which is incomplete is that concerning social workers in social services departments. It seems that the interplay of management and the workers taking part led to them being unable to come back and discuss the implications of the workshops for their role and organisational context as other practitioners did. I would like to think of this as idiosyncratic but fear it may be a frightening sign of the times, by which the potential sources of support and understanding are cut off by those under greatest pressure.

However, this is not a book about child protection. Indeed, as various enquiries have shown, preoccupation with marital work, a major focus of this book, actually carries some dangers; professionals may become so immersed in marital dynamics that other aspects of the family system are ignored. The strength of this book is that its account of the ways in which professionals get emotionally sucked into the lives of the clients or patients can be readily applied to a wide range of situations. Perhaps before long those who work with old people and their carers will be able to see the application of these theories to the development of 'care plans' for people at risk in the community.

We are indebted to the Tavistock Institute of Marital Studies for their patient commitment over many years to the development of these ideas, from which we have much to learn.

It would be good if, in these matters, the time were coming when we can acknowledge that, as Keats said, 'the Minds of Mortals ... leave each other in contrary directions, traverse each other in numberless points and at last greet each other at the journey's end'.

Olive Stevenson
November 1990

Contents

To Enid Balint
innovator, teacher and staunch friend
founder of the Family Discussion Bureau
(later the Tavistock Institute of Marital Studies)

Introduction

This book is primarily intended for those working in front-line social, health and counselling services—practitioners and managers at the 'sharp end' in the caring professions. It is about the nature of working partnerships which concern them: between practitioner and client or patient, and between practitioner and practitioner over clients and patients they have in common. The focus is on interactive processes, conscious and unconscious, not only within these relationships but also in the interplay between one kind of relationship system and another.

Any focus on professional practice has perforce to take account of the setting in which it takes place. The late Clare Winnicott observed many years ago that 'there is no such thing as case-work, only case-work in a given setting'. The term case-work was more in favour then than now, but it remains true that practice is conditioned by its environment: the service agencies in which it takes place, each with its characteristic institutional culture, each defined by and organised around the performance of distinctive tasks and the anxieties associated with them. If practice and its environment are interdependent, so too are practitioners and managers. Yet all too often in formal debate and in day-to-day experience they find themselves divided and in contention. Although what follows is predominantly based on case material contributed by practitioners, we increasingly realised that 'management' was a real if unseen presence in their practice. We believe that what we have to say is relevant, and we hope of interest, to managers and policy makers as well as to practitioners.

We should explain how we came to have access to this material and in what context. In the consultative document *Marriage matters*, a working party set up by the Home Office in association with the Department of Health and Social Security marshalled evidence from many sources to show, firstly, that marital stress could not be seen as the exclusive province of specialised services but had far-reaching implications for the work of a very wide range of social and medical agencies. Secondly, however, those giving evidence insistently drew attention to failures in collaboration between practitioners and agencies (Home Office/DHSS, 1979). One of us (DW) had been a member of the working party, the other (PP) had compiled the response of the Tavistock Institute of Marital Studies to the consultative document. When it became clear that events, political and economic, had overtaken the intended consultation process, we were stimulated to discover whether these two major findings—the impact of marital stress on community services and the problems of collaboration—could be investigated further. With the encouragement of our TIMS colleagues we pursued the matter and, late in 1982, after two years of discussion and negotiation initiated by us and an extensive search for funding, practitioners from five different agencies in one county embarked with us on a three-year study programme.

Fifty-four practitioners took part in all, including some who left and some replacements; thirty-four completed the full three years. They comprised general practitioners, health visitors, marriage guidance counsellors, probation officers and social workers. Other practitioners might appropriately have participated, of course, but these were the agencies we successfully negotiated with; in any case our resources would not have stretched to include more. As it was, health visitors were included on the entirely correct insistence of other disciplines. Having approached recruitment pragmatically, we and our participating colleagues ended up satisfied that these five made up a minimum sufficient sample of front-line agencies.

The practitioners were grouped in workshops of up to ten members. For the first six months, each discipline had its own workshop(s) except that, because of logistic difficulties, GPs and health visitors were combined in two 'primary health care' groups. After this 'in-house' phase practitioners were re-distributed to form mixed discipline workshops. Each of these contained members of all five of the participating agencies and, so far as possible, each was made up of people working in the same local district of the county; this increased the chance that members would have clients and patients in common and be able to present their work jointly for study and discussion. The mixed workshops ran for two years, leaving the final six months for collective evaluation.

At each fortnightly meeting a member presented for study their work with a current case; many cases were brought back at intervals so that the way they developed could be studied over time. The authors' role was to act as consultants and to record the work. Both of us attended all workshops during the in-house phase and for part of the mixed phase. After that we separated, each continuing with three of the six workshops but now with members taking it in turn to join us, sharing the task as 'co-pilots'.

There were two stated aims of the workshops. The first was to develop existing knowledge of how marital stress may be linked with problems that urgently preoccupy social and health services in the community (for example, delinquency, poor child care, emotional and physical ill-health); and to improve the capacity of key practitioners to respond in ways that help forward their own designated tasks—as doctor or health visitor, as probation officer, social worker or marriage guidance counsellor. Secondly, the workshops aimed to study and seek to improve working relationships between practitioners from different agencies and disciplines, since responsibility for work with a couple or family is necessarily shared in some of the most problematic cases such as child abuse.

The aims of the workshops incorporated the two dominant areas of interest for us arising from *Marriage matters*: problems in marital and family interaction and problems in professional interaction. In what follows we conclude that these two areas have important connections with each other, both in theory and in practice. Meanwhile, the aims also combined two principal motivating purposes: to develop understanding and to improve practice, i.e. research and training going hand in hand. Broadly speaking, the emphasis placed on these two purposes differed as between the practitioners (and their employing agencies) and ourselves; for them the primary motivation was the training component, for us the research. Each bore responsibility for realising their respective aims but, as a collaborative enterprise, the programme reflected the interdependence of the two purposes.

The complex processes involved in setting up the programme—and those within it once it was established as a 'temporary institution'—are largely beyond the scope of this book, interesting though they are technically. One important feature of them is referred to in chapter 9. In the main, however, we rely on the study of practice which was undertaken in the workshops and to which the central part of the book is devoted. The sources we have used are:

> — The accounts of their own cases which practitioners wrote up before and after workshop presentation;
> — The log which we (and our 'co-pilots') kept of each case JJ presentation and discussion;
> — The tape-recordings made of all workshop meetings and JJ other programme events.

So much reliance on case material faced us with the problem of preserving anonymity. That of the practitioners is safeguarded by the use of fictitious names; that of the agencies by omitting any reference to the area in which the study took place. The anonymity of clients and patients is also safeguarded by omitting any geographical reference, by the use of pseudonyms and, where possible, by disguising facts and circumstances. But there are limits to the latter; if one goes too far, essential material differs so greatly from reality as to make the dynamics false, and practitioners' work and responses false, too. To avoid this, salient features and psychological details have not been changed. This could mean that clients and patients recognise themselves in the unlikely event of their reading this book. As others have concluded (for example, Balint, 1964) the risk is unavoidable with any certainty. We shared the dilemma with the practitioners involved and what is written has been agreed with them. If, in spite of all the precautions, the book inadvertently causes resentment or distress to the people whose difficulties were the very stuff of learning in pursuit of better practice and inter-professional collaboration, we deeply regret it.

Working with us on the problem of anonymity was not the only or, indeed, the main contribution made by practitioners to the actual writing of the book. Not only was all the case material re-checked directly with them, but Part II as a whole was a joint endeavour. The complete drafts of all but one of its chapters were considered with those concerned and often amended and improved in the process. The exception is chapter 8; as we explain there, the social workers who took part were not available to work with us on preparing the manuscript. This effectively precluded us from using the case material they had contributed; the book is regrettably the poorer for that. We could not omit the social workers altogether, however, for their role is a crucial one in local service networks. So, despite the lack of supporting material and of their contribution to the drafting, we offer an appraisal of issues revealed in the work they presented taken as a whole (as we do with the other services). We also refer in chapter 9 to their contribution in collaborative cases with practitioners from other settings.

The reader should remember that the material relating to clients and patients was obtained in the context of the workshops and is told from the practitioners' point of view. Some of the examples show the practitioners getting into difficulties—the difficulties we wanted to study and they sought help with. The workshops afforded an all too rare opportunity for experienced and competent professionals to disclose predicaments, muddles and failures which were causing them concern, in conditions of containment for anxiety, support for learning and a reflective rather than a prescriptive climate. It is only by such means, we believe, that practitioners can develop their capacity to work and collaborate effectively with clients and patients or with colleagues. In writing this book we have had a similarly reflective and non-judgemental intention, seeking to understand what actually happened in our front-line colleagues' practice, in the workshop discussions and in the programme as a whole. In attempting a contribution from what we learned, we have kept in mind Kurt Lewin's oft quoted comment that 'there is nothing so practical as a good theory'.

All authors must complete a piece of work with a deep sense of gratitude to others. The nature of the collaborative programme which gave rise to this book ensured that we are indebted to more people than most writers. Many of those who were generous with their time and advice, and gave us active encouragement when, as novices and strangers to the area, we were setting up the programme, must be nameless. As with the practitioners and agency managers who joined us, to name them would be to endanger the anonymity of clients and patients which we were all committed to preserve. We could not have got started without them.

How much we owe to the practitioners who worked with us, especially those who helped in the preparation of the text, will be clear to the reader. That of agency senior managers will be less obvious. At the outset they made the programme possible by allocating scarce financial resources to it; their willingness to do so (along with the regional health authority) proved to be a decisive influence on other funding bodies. In spite of changes in government policies affecting statutory services, and other exacting pressures, a representative steering group managed the enterprise with us throughout (with only one change in membership). This was no sinecure; differences of view were often fiercely voiced, conflicting interests confronted, compromises reached in the interests of others. In this context we learned much about the practical management of institutional boundaries and the containment of anxiety in pursuit of agreed tasks.

Some major contributors to the work can be identified, however. Dame Rosemary Rue shared her incomparable knowledge of the National Health Service and encouraged and supported our efforts to involve GPs in the programme. The Marriage and Family Trust made a grant and enabled the local marriage guidance council (now 'Relate') to participate. The Tudor Trust helped to meet overall costs and the Home Office, which for many years has given financial support to the TIMS, made up the shortfall when fund-raising efforts were exhausted. We are also most grateful to the C L Cadbury Charitable Trust for a personal grant towards the book's preparation.

We are greatly indebted to our TIMS colleagues. They supported us in the work and carried the additional burdens which our absence entailed during a stressful period of change when our unit—no less than the agencies we were working with—had to face financial stringency and when requests for its therapeutic services were escalating. This demanded much forbearance, as did our preoccupation with the programme and its tensions which we inevitably took back to 'home base' with us.

Very special appreciation is due to Mary Walter, the programme secretary. From the planning stage, through the field-work to the completion of the manuscript, she contributed more than we had any right to expect. She not only administered the complicated arrangements which the programme entailed with foresight, tact and a full grasp of the task, she sustained us as only a first-class PA can. With endless goodwill, patience and skill she and Celia Dillon typed and re-typed drafts of the book. Meanwhile, invaluable service was rendered by Margaret Walker and the staff of the Tavistock Joint Library who always involved themselves with concern in the considerable amount of work they undertook for us.

We thank HMSO Publications Division (Copyright) for permission to reproduce the extracts from the Butler-Sloss Report on child abuse in Cleveland, and Sara Glennie, Sebastian Kraemer, Olive Stevenson and

Christopher Vincent for their valuable comments on the original draft of the Appendix.

Just how extensively we have drawn on earlier TIMS research and clinical publications and the thinking of others within and beyond the Tavistock will be clear from the text. That of two long-standing colleagues has been of major importance to us; both have been associated with the TIMS since its inception in 1948. To Dr J D Sutherland, with his deep understanding of the role of community services in the promotion of mental health in society, of the scientific status of psychodynamic theory and of the philosophy of care, we owe a special debt. So, too, to Isabel Menzies Lyth, especially for her seminal papers on the part played by anxiety and defences against it in the functioning of institutions. Mrs Menzies Lyth also acted as our consultant throughout the programme; she helped us to contain our own anxieties and reflect on our experiences in the course of it, and to gain some insight into the complexities of collaborative processes. We benefited greatly from discussions with both these senior colleagues and thank them for permission to quote from their publications. But the responsibility for what we have made of their work and that of the many others who have contributed to this book is, of course, ours alone.

Part I

POINTS OF DEPARTURE

1

Problems of partnership

The quest for effective collaboration between practitioners in different community services, in the interests of clients or patients they have in common, is as problematic as it is urgent.

Communication and co-operation prove most difficult to achieve when they are most needed. The disastrous consequences of grosser failure, in the field of child care in particular, have exposed the problem dramatically and given rise to great public concern. But as well as the periodic focusing of attention by demands that such failures be avoided in future—demands that are inevitably infused with irrationality—there has also been a continuing, less conspicuous, professional preoccupation with the collaborative difficulties to which the caring services are evidently prone. More than a decade ago the government working party referred to in the Introduction, reporting on the implications of marital stress for a range of community services, said:

> Time and again, through the comments of those giving evidence to us and through our own observations, the importance of collaboration between agencies has been emphasised. We have heard of inadequate co-operation at local level, amounting at times to suspicion, between ... agencies which ideally should be collaborating for the benefit of clients. We have heard of difficulties in making referrals between professional workers and misperceptions between workers in different professions and agencies ... Collaboration is never easy, which presumably is why it is more talked about than practised ... It requires a great deal of work and time; there are no short cuts and quite often collaborative attempts strike hidden reefs which frustrate the participants and cause disillusionment about future efforts (Home Office/DHSS, 1979, p. 55).

Judicial attempts to discover retrospectively what went wrong in the most tragic cases involving children have provided valuable information, and have sometimes implied that more is required than the progressive refinement of guidelines for practice and of administrative and legal procedures. But, like the inter-departmental review just referred to, they have contributed little to an understanding of the dynamic features of professional working relationships.

In the chapters which follow, derived from an inter-agency training-cum-research[1] programme, we aim to explore some of the 'hidden reefs' on which collaboration can founder.

PRACTICAL THEORIES

Our frame of reference in this study is based on experience gained in the Tavistock Institute of Marital Studies—from marital psychotherapy, from training and consultation work with practitioners in other settings and from previous research. The corpus of TIMS work and its theoretical lineage has been documented and fully referenced elsewhere (Woodhouse, 1990). It embodies the view that knowledge of interactive processes in marriage (i.e. the relationships of couples, legal or otherwise) is relevant to an understanding of interdependent relationships at other levels. The psychodynamic frame of reference seemed to us to offer a fruitful approach to the problems of partnership between helping agencies since it combined the clinical perspective of psychoanalytically-based therapy with couples and the social science perspective of open systems thinking. In both these perspectives theory is firmly grounded in practice.

Marriage and marital work—interactive models of problems in partnership

Marriage is a transference relationship *par excellence*. In marriage, the partners become a fundamental part of each other's environment. Each is both subject and object in their reciprocal attachment. By its nature, the relationship is a primary one; it is the most direct heir to childhood experience in adult life. Aspects of some of the earliest actual and phantasy[2] relationships of the partners are transferred by each onto the other. Their interplay ensures that unconscious[3] as well as conscious derivatives of the past are embodied in the relationship—but in a new and present dimension. Through the phenomenon of mutual transference, stress in marriage renders visible (and therapeutically accessible) conflicts and anxieties within each partner as they are externalised and acted-out in the relationship. Indeed, a critical advance in marital psychotherapy was to see that what the partners complain of, or are made anxious by, in each other is most often a projection of powerful but unwanted parts of themselves; that what is feared and rejected in the internal world of each, each tends to locate in the other. It follows that what is disowned and got rid of in this way is not lost, but is 'lived with' in the person of the partner.

By definition, both members of this system of relationships are in a similar situation. In marriage, the attachment of each to the other, which has both positive and negative aspects, can afford a psychic container within which conflict and anxiety, conscious and unconscious, can be struggled with, leading to a modification of defences.[4] In that case, the partners can increase their capacity to deal with internal tension and external stress; because of personal integration, there can be mutual growth. But the relationship system can also be one in which this maturational task is avoided or inhibited; each may so confirm the other's worst fears that defences against anxiety are reinforced, militating against emotional development and a collaborative engagement with life and its vicissitudes. From this systemic viewpoint, marriage can be seen as a paradigm of the struggle for creative relatedness in other human systems.

Practitioners also become the object of their clients' or patients' projections, good or bad. They, too, have transferred onto them feelings and attitudes arising from the unconscious as well as the conscious needs of those with whom they work. The practitioners' responses are bound to be affected—and this holds true even when, for whatever reason, they aspire to 'keep their distance' in professional encounters which are invariably of emotional significance to both parties.

Marital psychotherapy in which two practitioners collaborate in the therapeutic task has shown that the client couple's pattern of interaction (which embodies their defences against anxiety) influences the therapist couple's responses in the work and—of special significance in the present context—their own interaction. A simple example serves this introductory point. It is a commonplace in four-person therapy to find that, as it develops, one practitioner becomes convinced that the other is in some way colluding with one or other client, or otherwise behaving in a way that is detrimental to the work. The practitioner pair tend to respond to this conflict in their working relationship by 'fight or flight'. The institutional setting must exert such benign discipline as will contain the conflictual feelings and, more important, create a climate which encourages the workers jointly to be reflective and questioning. It is then frequently found that the therapists were unconsciously mirroring (reflecting) the client couple's interaction; that the timing of their differences and the way they were articulated were intimately connected with the couple's anxieties and defences (in the face of threatening change, for example)—anxieties which 'spoke to' those of the practitioners, but which neither they nor their clients could express in words. Instead of such responses merely being seen as attributable to unfortunate and avoidable technical difficulties, or solely to the practitioners' personalities, they often provide valuable clues to the clients' underlying dilemmas. Such a struggle by the practitioners to understand their own working problem frequently heralds a positive development in the therapy.

Applications in training and action research

Our approach was also shaped by TIMS work with colleagues from allied professions, both marital specialists and those whose tasks involve them with a wide range of problems which are linked (often in disguised ways) with stress and conflict in the family's nuclear relationship. Training programmes have repeatedly demonstrated that many 'non-marital' practitioners meet considerable difficulties in addressing the links between presenting problems and their clients' disturbed relationships, in ways appropriate to the setting of their work. Just as commonly, their agencies afford them little or no support in doing so—in spite of sponsoring their participation in the training. Conversely, marital specialists are prone to exclude non-marital issues, however relevant, from their work. And as the Home Office/DHSS working party discovered, collaboration between marital specialists and other practitioners can be every bit as flawed as collaboration elsewhere. The ambiguities are as clear as the reasons for them are obscure.

One piece of TIMS training work was particularly influential for us during the study. Over nine years of working with groups of social work supervisors, Mattinson (1975) developed a concept which threw light on unconscious processes in professional encounters, and on the permeability of personal boundaries. When supervisory problems were studied it was often found that unconscious defensive interactions between the worker and his or her client were being mirrored in the interaction between the supervisor and the worker —again unconsciously. This process, rooted in transference and counter-transference phenomena, was also found to be occurring in the supervisors' training groups themselves. Searles' (1955) term 'reflection process' was adopted to describe what was happening. The concept proved to have wider applications. A case-discussion group, for example, can also be a reflecting medium whereby psychological features in one relationship system—the clients'—are unconsciously conducted, via the 'bridging' worker, into another adjacent one—the group.

The immediate antecedent of the present endeavour was an action research project that traced dynamic links between clients, practitioners and their employing organisation. In their account of it, Mattinson and Sinclair (1979) chronicled the way clients employing the primitive defences of denial and splitting induced similar behaviour in practitioners together with a fragmented response by their agency. The same defences could also enter divisively into working relationships with practitioners from other agencies. The TIMS staff were working with clients alongside social work colleagues in a social services department. The evidence that accrued showed the organisation to be ill-adapted to treat a small but influential core group of married clients with severe relationship problems, a group which absorbed a disproportionately large volume of its resources, both psychological and material. These clients evoked ambivalent behaviour from social workers who wished to help, but feared being overwhelmed. Practitioner-client interaction then tended to reinforce the pattern of ambivalent attachments and the defences dominating the clients' lives. At the same time, the way the organisation functioned abetted practitioners in avoiding the kind of helping strategies appropriate to and urgently needed by this deprived and demanding group of clients. Indeed, the institutional framework, in association with the clients, in itself actually stimulated anxiety. It diminished practitioners' ability to address the clients' practical and emotional problems as interdependent, and to sustain the kind of reliable-enough relationship which alone held some prospect of enabling them to grow towards doing without social work intervention.

Mattinson and Sinclair drew on the now classic study of hospital nursing by Menzies Lyth (1970) to make sense of the interplay of social workers and their overburdened organisation. Earlier applications of a psychoanalytic approach to industrial relations (Jacques, 1951; 1955) had proposed that a major factor binding individuals into human associations is their need for defences against persecutory and depressive anxiety. Menzies Lyth developed this thinking to account for the stress evidenced and discussed by nurses in a general hospital in terms of their compulsive adherence to administrative and technical procedures, established attitudes and role relationships. She identified these constellations of behaviour as manifestations of 'socially organised defences' against the conflict and anxiety engendered by the nurse's task. An important feature of defences embodied in institutional procedures, she wrote,

> is an attempt by individuals to externalise and give substance in objective reality to their characteristic psychic defence mechanisms. A social defence system develops over time as a result of collusive interaction and agreement, often unconscious, between members of the organisation as to what form it shall take. The socially structured mechanisms then tend to become aspects of the external reality with which old and new members must come to terms (ibid., p. 51).

In her nursing study, and later, she described how membership of an institution has a marked effect on the personality development of those who work in it— for good or ill (Menzies Lyth, 1985). In passing, we note the parallels between her formulation of the psychic purposes served for individuals by membership of organisations and our view (above) of those served for the partners by the psycho-biological institution of marriage.

Her work was also in no way inconsistent with the experience of our own institution. We had become aware over the years that administrative and procedural decisions, as well as conflict and efforts to resolve it, could be as much bound up with work-related anxiety as they were with rational attempts to define and distribute roles effectively and to promote the staff's task performance. In the present study we came to rely extensively on Menzies Lyth's insights and tried to apply them to inter-professional and inter-agency relationships as well as the intra-agency processes with which she was primarily concerned.

Search of the literature revealed that, apart from some references by Mattinson and Sinclair, little attention had been paid specifically to the psychodynamic aspects of collaboration between practitioners and agencies in the field of care. However, two relevant papers were published when the fieldwork for this study was well on the way to completion. Not strictly 'points of departure' for the present work, they both proved valuable when it came to analysing our material and they call for mention here.

Hornby (1983) focused on problems of collaboration at field level due to the misuse of professional or agency boundaries for social defence purposes. As consultant to two local groups of social workers, one from a statutory, the other from a voluntary agency, she observed evidence of the doubts practitioners in each group had about their own capacity to help as much as the suspicions they entertained about the practice of their opposite numbers. Agency boundaries were invoked defensively in the face of such anxiety-provoking uncertainty. She pointed out that the defensive use of boundaries by practitioners not only prevented the working-through of anxiety at a personal level but also hindered the very collaboration that might have made their tasks easier. She showed that the problem could be eased through group discussion focused on working problems with a consultant, but echoed an important point made by Menzies Lyth and by Mattinson and Sinclair when she commented on the difficulty of resisting entrenched agency or professional defences, even for those practitioners who have developed mature ways of coping with personal anxiety as individuals.

Will and Baird (1984) wrote from the viewpoint of family therapists and, unlike the other authors cited, did not emphasise the part played by anxiety and defences against it at personal and social levels. They did, however, argue cogently the need for a systemic approach to what they called 'inter-professional dysfunction'. Using the case of a family with a school-phobic child, they illustrated the capacity of certain families to induce conflict in inter-professional relationships through what Britton (1981) described as 'complementary acting-out'. They pointed to the interaction of four sets of variables: 1, the personal, idiosyncratic responses of practitioners; 2, the divisive characteristics of clients which, 3, may be mirrored by the professional network; and 4, 'real professional vulnerabilities which provide lines of least resistance along which mirroring may occur' (ibid., p. 289). These vulnerabilities lay in differences of agency perspective related to task and responsibilities; differences in philosophy and values; and differences in status and prestige, not least those related to the pay and working conditions of the respective practitioners involved.

An open-systems perspective

Inherent in all the foregoing is a conception of the person as a dynamic and open system embedded in larger interacting ones with physical, emotional and social/cultural dimensions. We align ourselves with those from a wide range of disciplines [5] who, like Martin (1977, p. 55), have argued 'that living phenomena, and human life in particular, can most fruitfully be seen as a series of hierarchically arranged open systems and that 'this move or awareness that life phenomena can best be studied in an open-systems theory has been a major scientific breakthrough of the second half of this century'. Practitioners, like their clients and patients, are embedded in such open systems.

The motif running through our introductory themes is of interactive processes in that particular complex of systems in which client/patient, practitioner and agency/profession each play a salient part. The interplay of the systems in this complex is mediated by the practitioner who operates on the boundary between them and, figuratively speaking, faces both ways simultaneously—towards the client/patient system and towards the agency or professional system—influencing and being influenced by both.

Such a formulation highlights the densely textured relationships arising when inter-professional collaboration is attempted. There are clients'/patients' personal systems and the marital and family systems of which they are a part. Clients and patients interact with practitioners; together they constitute what, in Part II, we shall call the 'caring system'. Being mediators between client/patient and agency, practitioners introduce their agency/professional systems into the complex. And a further temporary system comes into being from the interplay of two or more professionals and their agencies when they are involved with the same client or patient. All these are subsystems of larger embracing ones of course, and ultimately of society, but for present purposes this completes the relevant schema. At each system level, new phenomena arise and a new and unique character emerges, but the components are interdependent; and there is, in fact, no clear demarcation between them. The capacity to manage boundaries which are indistinct and permeable is therefore crucial alike for individuals and for institutions.

The nature of anxiety

Given the prominent role ascribed to defences in what has been said so far, we should summarise our conception of anxiety, the subjective experience they are employed to ward off, before examining its influence on professional relation-ships and inter-professional collaboration.

Anxiety is part of the human condition.[6] Traced to their source, the roots of anxiety are to be found in the kind and quality of attachments in early infancy. Chaotic and threatening feelings within the infant can be rendered more manageable by the mother's intuitive responses—what Bion (1962, 1963) described as her function as a 'container' for the infant's feelings and her capacity for 'reverie', and Winnicott (1956a) called the 'holding' function of the 'good enough mother'. But if these primitive experiences are not sufficiently 'detoxified' in this way, through a relationship in which the infant's care conveys that it is loved for itself and as a whole, they may be exacerbated to a greater or lesser degree. Either the mother's internal preoccupations or noxious external events impinging on her and her baby may disturb the interpersonal process through which the child's emotional development is mediated.

Derived from mother-child interaction—that is, a function of relatedness—and with causal connections progressively rendered more complex by later experience, our internal worlds come to be characterised by feelings and emotions attached to figures both succouring and frustrating, benign and destructive. 'Good' and 'bad' are experienced as incompatible and mutually exclusive, so that what began as a unitary system is now divided; internal conflict ensues. No one is entirely free of it, and the pattern developed for managing internal conflict and its associated anxieties is decisive in structuring the personality. It determines the way we feel about ourselves and interpret our experience; it influences our interaction with others. Thus anxiety and its management does much to shape our lives and our relationships. Throughout, the internal interacts with the external; 'we have to keep in mind that all the later structures of any self that mediate a satisfying and fruitful life can be overwhelmed if the social milieu does not support the maintenance of that vital core' (Sutherland, 1980, p. 11).

Being in-built genetically for biological survival, the urge to seek and maintain interaction with others is characteristic of adults at all stages of life (Sutherland, 1989). It has been increasingly recognised that in our psychic inner worlds we are oriented to others from the very beginning. There are far-reaching repercussions of this increased insight. It has given rise, for example, to the realisation that 'an important element in the psyche is the *internal society* [our italics], comprised of images, concepts, memories and fantasies about people, in a great complexity of roles, functions and relationships' (Menzies Lyth, 1969, p. 61). Such a formulation links the psychological with the social.

To say that anxiety and defences against it have a major role in structuring the personality implies that they are at work at the deepest levels of the mind and that they are mainly unconscious. Accordingly, resistance to change is the rule. Change is inevitably feared if it is perceived as threatening an identity evolved in large measure as a means of coping with unconscious conflict and anxiety. However, since the defensive derivatives of anxiety in the inner world are manifest in the outer, particularly in human interaction, important aspects of them can become accessible to scrutiny and understanding. Therapeutic and much other experience confirms that we have a developmental drive and a psychic need to reunite what Laing (1960) called the 'divided self'. Potential may vary widely, but, given that effort can be sustained in a facilitating environment where conflict and difference are addressed rather than avoided, then defences can be modified and collusions (mutually reinforcing defences in relationships) can be ameliorated. More mature ways of dealing with anxiety can and do emerge.

If in the course of human development anxiety, conscious and unconscious, is inescapable, it cannot in itself be said to be pathological. We are indeed vulnerable without the capacity for realistic alarm, or if we are so defended that objective reality is denied. Freud is credited with a comment to the effect, 'happy are they whose anxiety works for them'. It is the propensity for unconscious anxiety and its associated defences to distort perception of the self, of others and of events, leading to inappropriate and ineffective responses to reality, that has to be reckoned with. So often, our anxiety works against us.

THE STATUS OF THE PSYCHODYNAMIC APPROACH

The theories that have informed us owe much to those who, like ourselves, have been enlightened professionally and enriched personally by what Guntrip (1971) called 'Psycho-dynamic science'. Its hallmark is the powerful role ascribed to unconscious motives in human behaviour.

But with different theoretical ways of conceptualising human behaviour so notoriously at odds, the relativity of theory has to be acknowledged. All theoretical formulations in this domain are relative to the field in which the generative data are collected. Theories which are developed in a given field will reflect that particular culture and the systems of thought prevailing in it. If they are to have any creative application for those in a different field they have to be appraised critically before being internalised imaginatively. Even if the field is an adjacent one, they have to be processed in this way before they can be successfully transferred. We attempt this task in the following chapters and share it with the reader.

We must also be clear that different kinds of knowledge, theoretical and practical, are relevant to different purposes and tasks. In this case, the purposes and tasks are those of practitioners and managers in the caring professions, which require of them an understanding of themselves as well as their clients or patients. As Sutherland (1980, p. 17) has pointed out, our understanding of the complexities of what happens in professional encounters with clients or patients, and between practitioners, has to be formulated 'in the best way we can to do justice to the phenomena and to be open to constant checking against fresh findings'. Herein lies the scientific component. As he observes, the goal of care, as of therapy, is not a part of science. 'It is an act of human concern. Its effectiveness, however, rests on the adequacy of our validated knowledge' (ibid., p. 18).[7]

This knowledge is to be judged both by the range of its applicability, and by its capacity to alert us 'to what to look for and provide ideas to help us understand events when they do occur ... [it has to] help read the situation' (Mattinson and Sinclair, 1979, p. 64). It must be of practical value to practitioners in helping them make sense of their complex and often bewildering experience: 'the principal criterion is whether the practitioner can make use of the new approach to enlarge his own theory of the situation he is in and to extend his competence' (Miller and Gwynne, 1972, p. 6).

Learning and time

Training and research in the field of human interaction have in common the need for time. Training which is not primarily concerned with imparting and assimilating facts or the acquisition of techniques, but with the evolution of changes in perception of 'self' and 'other' and in ways of working with clients or patients must afford the practitioner time—time to 'enlarge his own theory and extend his competence' (see also Balint, 1954, 1964; Woodhouse, 1967).

Meanwhile, for the researcher to distinguish what is actually happening from what is said or thought to be happening in relationships is invariably difficult. Menzies Lyth's (1986, p. 28) comment is pertinent: 'It is obvious that people do not say what they really mean even when they honestly and sincerely say what they consciously think'. As in the institutional consultancy she was discussing so in what practitioners say about their practice and their interaction with other practitioners; they cannot be expected to be absolutely open though they become increasingly so if the work goes well and trust is developed.

These were the main reasons for the duration and format of this interdisciplinary programme. It took time and emotional energy for practitioners to test out one another and ourselves in the learning environment, and be freer to reveal what was actually happening.

It was therefore only through the medium of committed relationships that we could expect to gain access to the very forces we needed to know about. We had to become involved in order to obtain crucial experiential data, and to be scientific by checking subjective against objective experience as they were reflected on constantly. This process is in line with Medawar's (1969) description of scientific reasoning as an exploratory dialogue between two aspects of thought which interact, the one imaginative, the other critical.

THE ROLE OF VALUES IN THE APPRECIATION OF EXPERIENCE

A further and broader contextual issue remains—the question of values. We noted earlier that the theories developed in a given field reflect the culture and systems of thought prevailing in it, that is to say its system of values. Sutherland's (1980) 'psychodynamic image of man' and his concept of 'care' best convey the TIMS philosophy and values which we took with us in the study programme. It could not be assumed that the participating practitioners and agencies would necessarily share them. A relationship of the kind and duration we were all to embark upon, involving an examination of practice, was bound to expose differences in the values that informed practice—differences between individuals and professional groups as well as between them and ourselves. The psychodynamic approach tends to raise mixed feelings and often contention;[8] whatever the intellectual and psychological strands of the debate, the values inspiring it are potent. In a series of papers concerned with the ecology of ideas, Sir Geoffrey Vickers (1968) observed that the structure and energies of man's inner world stem from his values; he uses his reason to serve and defend them, just as they govern what he called the mode of his appreciation. Having pointed out that science is a smaller and more peripheral part of human mental activity than we always remember, he concluded that this view

> is consistent with and seems even to require an unshaken faith in the power and duty of the human mind to make judgements of value—judgements that can never be validated, though they may sometimes be falsified, by appeal to any criterion other than another value judgement; faith qualified nonetheless, by the knowledge that such judgements can never be final (ibid., p. 50).

The big emotional and intellectual task of 'processing' ideas which we described earlier was bound to occasion challenges to personal and professional values. As they do in marriage, differences that were experienced as fundamental sometimes made it tempting to separate so as to live in peace. But collaboration requires the struggle with differences to be sustained, for if 'we take the side of the one to revile the other, we hurt the truth which comprehends them both' (Tagore, 1985, p. 44). We are doomed to stalemate unless we acknowledge our essential interdependence.

Notes

1 'Training-cum-research' was Michael Balint's term to describe his work with GPs (Balint, 1964). We applied it to this study programme, and particularly the case-discussion workshops which were its central feature (see chapter 3).

2   We follow the convention of using the word 'phantasy' to indicate unconscious processes and 'fantasy' to indicate conscious ones.

3   Freud designated mental activity as conscious, pre-conscious or unconscious. The depth to which such activity may be buried (the degree to which it is 'kept out of mind') varies considerably. In general, we use the term 'unconscious' without qualification.

4   We use the word 'defence' as it is applied in English psychoanalytic literature and discussion. Bettelheim (1983) points out that the original German *Abwehr* would have been better translated as 'parry'. 'This is closest to what Freud had in mind, because the phenomenon to which he referred consists of clever psychological measures taken to deflect or ward off unconscious content we wish to evade ... there is, in fact, no [successful] defence possible against ourselves' (ibid., p. 92).

5   Including physics, medicine and social science, sociology and social philosophy, as well as psychoanalysis and psychotherapy. See for example, Arden (1985); Bateson (1973); Capra (1982); Emery (1981a, 1981b); Emery and Trist (1972); Guntrip (1971); Jackson (1957); Jaques (1955); Jantsch (1980); Koestler (1964); Medawar (1969); Menzies Lyth (1988, 1989); Prigogine (1976); Sutherland (1980, 1983); Vickers (1968, 1983, 1984); Watzlawick (1967).

6   For a comprehensive review of the major theoretical contributions see Bowlby (1973, Appendix 1).

7   While a doctor's training, for example, is rooted in the 'hard sciences' (physics, chemistry, biology), the practice of medicine is generally regarded within and beyond the profession as an art.

8   The nervousness of social workers in using psychodynamic theory is discussed by Stevenson (1989a) when considering their lack of a coherent theoretical framework for assessment. They are not, of course, alone among the caring professions in these respects.

2

Problems in practice

Practitioners' problems often begin at the very start of a piece of work, but that is also the time when they may be least aware of them under the pressure of a mass of information and the need to decide what to do. Most practitioners will have had the experience of reaching some new understanding of a case later on and then realising, when they think back to how it began and re-read their original notes, that the clues were there from the start. In the study programme, as the workshops retrospectively examined the cases presented by members, it was likewise possible to see the early clues by which clients and patients indicated the connections between the problems they presented and other critical disturbances in their lives including their marital relationships. More difficult to discern were the constraints by which practitioners were given these clues and simultaneously prevented from following them up, or were sometimes put off the scent altogether. The more we did manage to trace these constraints, however, the more we saw that it was the same kind of constraint that was also operating to hamper practitioners' dealings with other relevant professionals.

In each of the four examples which follow, a piece of work is getting off to this kind of constricted start. The brief discussion of each example relies on hindsight for the sake of clarity at this stage; in later chapters we shall follow the much more uneven process of real-life learning as it took place in the workshops.

Open and closed: the couple with the spastic child

Miss Inskip, a health visitor, received routine notification of a premature birth. Jenny had been born at twenty-nine weeks and was to stay in the special care unit at the hospital for a month or so but Miss Inskip, following normal practice, visited the mother, Mrs Batchelor, at home. They had never met; not only was this Helen Batchelor's first pregnancy but she had still been working up to the time the baby arrived so had not attended antenatal preparation classes. She seemed to welcome Miss Inskip's visit and talked readily about her circumstances:

the pregnancy had been a planned one; she and her husband, Frank, had married young and were now in their early thirties; both had always worked full time, Helen as an academic secretary and Frank, an ex-soldier, as a security guard; he worked irregular shifts and was out at work at the time of the visit. They were buying their own house which Miss Inskip could see was spotlessly kept. Mrs Batchelor was going to the hospital every day to be with Jenny, and had learned to express her breast-milk to be fed to the baby in the incubator.

Interlaced with this positive factual information, however, was a theme of foreboding. Mrs Batchelor said she wondered if Jenny should have been born; she had had three haemorrhages during the pregnancy and took them as a sign that she was not meant to have a baby. The premature birth seemed to her to confirm this.

Miss Inskip was surprised; it was unusual for a mother to voice this degree of apprehension so openly at a first meeting and it put her on the alert. If she tried to focus the conversation on exploring these anxieties, however, Mrs Batchelor would change the subject. Miss Inskip therefore fell back on reminding her of the positive fact that Jenny seemed to be doing very well, and arranged three or four further visits before the baby was due to come home.

On these visits (with Jenny still making good progress) Mrs Batchelor expressed even more anxiety. She felt isolated in the village where she had never got to know anyone; she missed her parents, who had both died within the last five years; and she felt that her husband, though generally committed to her and the baby, would not give her the practical support she was going to need; in any case, neither of them had any experience with children. On the one occasion that Frank Batchelor was at home Miss Inskip's first impression was that he indeed expected the baby to be "a woman's job".[1]

As the time approached for Jenny to come home, Mrs Batchelor told the health visitor she could neither sleep at night nor face the day; she felt sick and her stomach was churning.

On the day of the planned homecoming Miss Inskip heard from the hospital that Mrs Batchelor had produced a series of reasons for postponing it, and had also repeated her worry that her husband would not support her. In the end the Batchelors, together, did fetch Jenny home and Miss Inskip visited the same day. She noticed that Mrs Batchelor had put Jenny straight onto a bottle rather than breast-feed her, but refrained from querying this change of plan. She felt, in fact, that Mrs Batchelor was already so anxious that if she "probed too much it would cause even greater anxiety", so she concentrated on making sure mother and baby were settled in together as well as possible.

During this period Miss Inskip herself was increasingly uneasy about the case. She was giving more attention and time than usual to it but had a constant sense that there was something more, or different, that she should be doing. She spoke to the Batchelors' GP and to her health visitor colleagues who were her primary support group; yet she continued to feel very unsupported, as if no-one could say what she needed to hear.

By the time Miss Inskip presented the case at the workshop, some twelve months after these events, Jenny had been diagnosed as having cerebral palsy —presumably from brain-damage at birth (see the further discussion of this case in chapter 6). But the spasticity had not begun to show until some time after Jenny came home, so that although of course it then seemed to confirm Helen Batchelor's fears it could hardly have been the source of them. The intense surge of anxiety that was already paralysing her at the beginning suggests that, for her, there was some special terror in exchanging her independence in a dual-career marriage for a more dependent role, with a totally dependent baby. Health visitors are familiar with the normal misgivings of women in making such a transition, but Miss Inskip was faced with a much higher level of anxiety than normal. It seemed to paralyse her in turn, so that whilst she devoted extra effort to the Batchelors she still seemed to have no extra space in her mind to consider the meaning for them of the baby's arrival in the context of their particular marital relationship—even though Helen Batchelor had clearly coupled Frank with herself as being unlikely to adjust to the transition easily.

It looks as if both the intense anxiety and the utter impossibility of exploring what it meant had been passed on to Miss Inskip by Mrs Batchelor's way of revealing her fears and then shying away from discussing them; being at the same time open and closed. In this light, we can see how in her dealings with other professionals Miss Inskip also seemed to have caught her client's feeling of being isolated and unsupported even though support was available.

In vino veritas

Mr Collins, a probation officer, undertook to prepare a social inquiry report for the magistrates' court concerning David Goodband, a married man of twenty-seven who had pleaded guilty to a charge of burglary. The police had told the court that Mr Goodband, very drunk, had entered a house and taken a handbag but had been discovered before he could escape; he had two previous convictions, for taking a vehicle without consent ten years earlier and for drunken driving three years earlier. Mr Goodband had said he was ashamed and felt he had a drink problem, and it was with that in mind that the magistrates had called for a report.

Mr Collins' first step was to interview Mr Goodband on his own; he found him a tense-looking young man who "completely unburdened himself" about his drinking and his life history. One of a large family, he had been treated violently by his mother, though he voiced no resentment towards her; in dissolving his parents' acrimonious marriage the divorce court had ordered that all the children be placed in care (in which they had already spent several periods). David had lost touch with them all except one brother, with whom he had eventually been placed at a residential school for five years until, at fifteen, he had gone to live with his remarried father. He had learned a trade as a fitter's mate for two years, and then served for four years in the RAF. He had always thrived on the disciplined life and set great store by authority (he still kept up a correspondence with his old headmaster). However, having returned to his trade and become a supervisor, he had got into the habit of drinking heavily after work with a group of work-mates amongst whom this was expected. He had stopped drinking since his arrest but felt he needed help to keep up this resolve.

He and his wife, Jacqueline, had met through being penfriends while he was in the RAF, and married soon after his discharge aged twenty-one. Three years older than David, Jacqueline had been widowed when her first husband was killed in an industrial accident. She had a daughter, now ten and legally adopted as their joint child.

At the end of the interview Mr Goodband said it had been "really helpful to talk to someone about all this". Mr

Collins felt encouraged, with a rare sense of a client who confided freely and seemed responsive to help. Before writing his report, however, he arranged a further interview with the couple together, at which he wanted to gauge how much strain Mr Goodband's excessive drinking might have caused in their marriage. He found Mrs Goodband concerned rather than rejecting, however, and both husband and wife welcomed his suggestion that (if the court agreed) a probation order would provide an opportunity to work at overcoming the drink problem.

Again Mr Collins was encouraged by their accord; it was a welcome contrast to the quarrelsome couples he encountered when undertaking welfare reports for the divorce court. He also learned that they had failed to conceive a child together but, after a lengthy course of preparation, had been accepted by the social services department as prospective adopters, though they expected to have to wait a year or two for a child to be placed with them.

The court duly made a probation order for six months. Mr Collins was then struck by a dilemma: when the time came for the Goodbands to adopt a baby, the probation service would be duty bound to disclose this new offence when the statutory enquiries were made, which could well spoil their chances. After struggling with this problem on his own, he eventually realised that it was the Goodbands rather than himself who should be worrying about it; when he put it to them, the couple decided to make a clean breast of the offence straight away and accepted Mr Collins' offer to accompany them to see the adoption social worker. At that interview both practitioners took the benign view that approval to adopt might only be temporarily suspended. In fact the adoption panel withdrew it altogether. This appeared to cause no bad feeling either between wife and husband or towards Mr Collins or the social services department. Instead, Mr Goodband got on with discussing how to stay away from drinking, and Mrs Goodband joined in most of his interviews.

As the probation order was about to expire, Mr Goodband was convicted of another offence of drunkenness, too minor in criminal terms to count as a breach of probation but a clear enough sign to Mr Collins that his chosen focus for work—the drinking per se—was too narrow to be effective.

At this point, Mr Collins brought the case to the workshop with the comment that he thought he had been "seduced". The group agreed, surmising that the couple—without conscious calculation—had implicated him in their absolute inability to allow bad feelings in their shared world. Since both David and Jacqueline Goodband had compelling reasons from their past experiences to keep this world safe and good, it was only in the outside world through his drinking and offending that David Goodband could register what had long been suppressed—his angry resentment at being so ill-treated earlier (perhaps Jacqueline's, too) and his sense of being inadequately equipped to carry the responsibilities he had now acquired. His further offence could similarly be seen as a sign of his disappointment and sense of loss at the ending of his relationship with the probation officer—again enacted in the outside world whilst face to face he professed himself quite happy. Mr Collins, representative of the outside world, might have got these issues explored and understood. He had indeed questioned whether the drinking had affected the couple's relationship, but was constrained by the determinedly 'good' marital climate from thinking about his question the other way round. Similarly, he could not follow through his own perception that the Goodbands must face the likely disappointment of their hopes of adopting, so that an unreal optimism coloured his dealings with the social worker and it was left to the more distant adoption panel to take the sterner view.

Which patient?
Which practitioner?

Dr Sanders, a general practitioner, was consulted by Alison Wright, a thirty-seven year-old woman who complained of feeling depressed and unable to cope at her part-time secretarial job. This was not the original beginning of the case but a re-opening or new episode; it was six months since Mrs Wright had last been to the health centre. This time she brought her nine year-old daughter, Lisa, with her; in fact she soon turned from her own problems to tell Dr Sanders that Lisa had started behaving strangely and refusing to go to school. Throughout the consultation Lisa sat on her mother's lap, and Dr Sanders noticed that she constantly sucked her thumb and from time to time would pat and stroke Mrs Wright's face.

Dr Sanders was aware of a background of previous episodes. Two and a half years beforehand Mrs Wright had started coming in sporadically with complaints such as tiredness, insomnia, heavy periods, stiff neck or shoulder, sinusitis, diarrhoea. Finding no physical illness and noticing that she seemed tense and anxious, Dr Sanders had asked several times if she was worried about anything (for instance her marriage) but with little response until after more than a year of this Mrs Wright had eventually disclosed that her husband, Bill, was having an affair with a girl of eighteen. He had in fact left shortly after that disclosure, though he would come round regularly with maintenance money. For some months Mrs Wright had kept up a stream of hurt protest either to the doctor or (in her absence) to the practice manager: she could not understand Bill's behaviour; she could not have been a better wife; and she would have him back at any time. Both doctor and practice manager had found this frustrating, because although they always started off sympathetically nothing they said seemed to make any difference to Mrs Wright, and they usually felt exhausted and irritated when she left. Then her visits had stopped.

Now Lisa was being presented as the focus of attention. Besides the school refusal, Dr Sanders thought that her regression to babyish behaviour indeed indicated some emotional disturbance; but she felt reluctant to "medicalise" the problem unduly (as she saw it) by making a psychiatric referral. So she thought of the health visitor attached to the practice, as someone well versed in children's problems, and asked if she would call and talk to Lisa in an informal counselling role. The health visitor agreed to do this, but gave up after two visits in which Lisa clung to her mother and would not be drawn into conversation.

In the context of the case as a whole, it seems likely that to present Lisa to the doctor, with her school refusal and her childlike clinging, was Mrs Wright's way of portraying the pain of abandonment which she was still quite unable to bear or deal with in herself. Like the earlier physical symptoms, the new 'symptom' of Lisa's behaviour was disconnected from its source. Almost certainly Lisa could not be helped to recover and resume her normal development except through her mother being helped to do likewise, but Dr Sanders was constrained from restoring the connection between symptom and source so as to address the problem in this way. To do so would have opened up

Mrs Wright's own pain, which had already seemed so untouchable and unhelpable on the previous occasions when she had shown it more directly. Perhaps, too, it was the same untouchable but pervasive horror of rejection that got through to the doctor when she asked her own health visitor to take on a task somewhat outside her proper function sooner than 'abandon' her patients to a more distant psychiatric agency. Here (like many other practitioners) Dr Sanders was seeking to invoke another professional not so much from a realistic hope of helping her patient as from a need to be released from her own dilemma: the conflict between a wish (and duty) to help Mrs Wright, and the painful fact that she wanted something that no-one could give her. We return to this case in chapter 9.

All the king's horses

Mrs Lambert, a marriage guidance counsellor attached to a primary health care practice, was telephoned at home "out of the blue" by a Mrs Cutler, who said she had heard of Mrs Lambert from a friend of hers who worked at the surgery, and would like to see her. Having checked that she was registered with the practice, Mrs Lambert offered her an appointment at the health centre, which she kept, together with a second a week later.

Maggie Cutler was forty-one, "short and thin, curly hair, Irish, arrived in a tracksuit, all busy, and she *never* stopped talking". She said she wanted a divorce from her second husband, Tom, who was six years older; Mrs Lambert asked why she had come to her rather than to a solicitor, and Mrs Cutler replied that she wanted advice first. However, she filled the first interview with a flood of detailed but disjointed information, without pausing for Mrs Lambert to do more than ask an occasional question to try and keep track. Amongst the information was that she had been married first for three years in her early twenties, and now for eleven years to Tom Cutler; she had rejected both husbands sexually, didn't blame the first for finding someone else but was critical of Tom's failure to keep on trying (she described him as an "old woman" and wondered if he was homosexual); her only sexual excitement had been with an apparently sado-masochistic lover between marriages; from the first marriage she had a son of eighteen and a daughter of seventeen, the former now a psychiatric patient for the past year; there was an eight year-old daughter of this marriage, and a mentally handicapped foster-daughter placed with her by the social services department. Family interviews had been set up at the psychiatric hospital that her son attended, but Mr Cutler had dropped out of these.

By the end of the first interview Mrs Lambert felt very disturbed and confused, and badly in need of some way of ordering both the information and her own thoughts. She rang the GP (who did not know Mrs Cutler had approached her) and got permission to look at the medical records on the family. These revealed a complex history of referrals concerning the boy from the age of three (when Maggie's first marriage was breaking up), mostly to the child guidance clinic and thought to have been prompted by the mother's worries as much as any serious condition in the child. Mrs Cutler herself had been referred to the visiting psychiatrist at the health centre, but after four or five sessions he had stopped seeing her and had written to the GP, "thank you for sending me this pleasant lady who has so much love to give". Mrs Lambert methodically wrote down all the dates, "trying", she said, "to tie it up".

She then spoke to the GP, voicing her concern and wondering about contacting the psychiatric hospital, where she knew one of the psychiatrists who also acted as consultant to the marriage guidance council. The GP suggested she might mention it to him if she saw him, then on second thoughts wondered if he should drop him a line himself. This was left unresolved, but when Mrs Lambert said she was also worried about Mrs Cutler being a foster-mother the GP told her vehemently not to "get the social services going".

In the second interview, Mrs Lambert elicited Mrs Cutler's side of the story concerning the previous medical history, including her view that the visiting psychiatrist had talked about everything except what she wanted, i.e. a divorce. This echoed her opening remark the previous week, but then she appeared to contradict herself by saying she thought it would be too tough for her to manage as a single parent, and Mr Cutler would probably refuse to leave. Eventually, she revealed that she had discussed her marital difficulties in her husband's presence with the social worker who handled the fostering arrangements; it was the latter who had suggested they seek help from marriage guidance, to which they had both agreed.

Mrs Lambert tried to clarify why in that case she had approached her individually, and concluded by suggesting that Mrs Cutler should now tell her husband what had happened, while she would write offering him an appointment for himself.

Afterwards, Mrs Lambert was full of doubt whether these moves had been correct or a foolish mistake. She was left just as confused as after the first interview; she also now felt she had more information than she could handle, and wished she had never looked at the medical records. At the same time she harboured a fantasy of convening a round-table conference of all the practitioners involved, where "all the bits could be put together".

Mrs Cutler's initial impact on Mrs Lambert was overwhelming. It was as if the client's agitation had passed straight through into the counsellor, just as Mrs Cutler had barged through normal procedures by ringing Mrs Lambert at home and seeing her without a referral from the GP. Struggling to recover her competence and get some bearings, Mrs Lambert herself trespassed over a boundary (as she later felt) by reading the medical notes. Her discussion with the GP seemed to pass the anxiety on to him; as she reported it, he became indecisive about the psychiatrist and agitated about social services.

When liaising with relevant third party practitioners thus seemed too difficult, Mrs Lambert sought to deal with the anxiety by turning back to her own metier of marriage counselling. Abandoning the effort to check out and evaluate her misgivings, she concentrated on trying to establish a 'correct' counselling structure. She took steps to include the most relevant third party of all—Mr Cutler—but for the moment this only raised further anxieties, again no doubt reflecting those of Mrs Cutler.

It was at that juncture that Mrs Lambert brought all the anxieties to the workshop where the attempt was made to contain and understand them. We subsequently learned the outcome. Mr Cutler kept his appointment, and with both clients' agreement Mrs Lambert consulted fully with the hospital psychiatrist and the social worker—who appeared not to have consulted each other about the Cutler family. She was then able to reach a clear decision that marriage counselling at this stage would be a diversion from the family interviews at the hospital, and closed the case.

*

We have not singled out these four cases to expose 'bad' practice but to illustrate the kind of predicament that can befall any practitioner, whether they notice it or not. These practitioners had noticed, and brought their cases to the workshops for study because they were troubled and curious about their experiences. At the time, however, it was precisely the capacity to be curious—to question and reflect on experience—that they were deprived of in their constrained response to their task with clients and patients, and their constrained approach to relevant liaison with other practitioners.

If it is useful to think about practice difficulties in this way, we need to go on to enquire what force or combination of forces is operating to produce such constraints in the practitioners, and what purposes this could be serving. We have observed that these constraints seem to arise out of the interaction between practitioner and client or patient from the moment they start to engage with one another, yet on a common sense view this runs counter to the client's or patient's best interests and the practitioner's best intentions. We need some practical way of construing events so as to find some meaning beyond common sense in such contradictions.

The way we have presented and discussed our four case examples might suggest that the practitioners were simply the victims of covert resistance on the part of their clients or patients. We have inferred, for example, that Miss Inskip came under the influence of anxieties that originated in Helen Batchelor; that Mr Collins was drawn—'seduced' as he put it—into the make-believe world of David and Jacqueline Goodband where bad feelings could not be known about; that Dr Sanders was caught up in Alison Wright's inability to bear her own affliction so that her attention was deflected onto nine year-old Lisa; and that Mrs Lambert's feeling of anguish and disjointedness was induced in her as a mirror image of Maggie Cutler's fragmented state of mind. We have also postulated that in each practitioner's dealings, or non-dealings, with other relevant professionals it was these same unseen influences, emanating from their clients or patients, which skewed their thinking.

But it would be an illusion to think of a practitioner as operating in a vacuum devoid of any influential relationships except that with the client or patient. It is a drawback of individual case reports that they can foster this illusion, since the main focus is necessarily on the clients and their world; even so, our four examples contain some fragments of information to remind us that practitioners have their world too. Miss Inskip was following the 'normal practice' of the health visitor service; she found Helen Batchelor's open apprehension 'unusual', implying a norm for mothers that training and experience led her to expect. Mr Collins was also struck by the contrast between the Goodbands and other more typical clients; and it was when he thought about the probation service's statutory obligations that he realised the couple's adoption prospects were in jeopardy. Unlike these two practitioners, who typically initiated the contact with their clients and were themselves activated by information from elsewhere, Dr Sanders was there to be consulted as Alison Wright chose; that conformed to the norms of general practice, but some of the more idiosyncratic aspects of her world were also apparent in the way her practice manager and the health visitor were used, and in her wariness of the 'medicalising' tendencies of other doctors. When Mrs Lambert received an irregular approach from Maggie Cutler she took at least some steps towards getting the position regularised; that these were only half-measures was not surprising, perhaps, since she belonged to one agency but had to adapt to the ways of another. Her rootedness in the marriage guidance world was also clear from the train of thought she followed when she talked to the GP about contacting the psychiatric hospital.

These, however, are fragments only, and at many points in the four stories there is no way of knowing whether the practitioners' reactions reveal more about their own characteristics or those of their respective disciplines. We shall in fact have little to say about the idiosyncratic personalities of individual practitioners; we take it for granted that these were influential, but it was not part of our purpose or theirs to examine them and—the important point—they are scarcely of general application. It is a different matter with the characteristics of a discipline; if these play a part in producing the constraints in practitioners that we have described—and especially if their influence, like that of the clients and patients, is partly hidden and unwitting—then we need some way of discovering them. We shall attempt this in Part II, where we take an overview of the whole set of cases contributed by each discipline.

In that overview we shall include the fifth discipline in our study, the local authority social workers, even though we are unable to describe their individual cases. Had we been able to include one in this chapter we could certainly have illustrated similar constraints, and a comparable predicament, to those we found in the other four.

A further feature of the four cases remains to be noticed. It both unites the four practitioners and at the same time differentiates them sharply as members of their respective disciplines; and it touches on issues that became crucial in our study. Each practitioner, under pressure and constrained as we have seen, sooner or later fell back on a particular focus for action. When the whole context of each case is considered, this focus invariably seems so narrow as to exclude important factors and inhibit effective work and effective collaboration. But from the practitioners' point of view when they were in the thick of it this focus on the contrary seemed the vital one. For Miss Inskip it was ensuring that mother and baby settled in together. For Mr Collins it was helping his client stop the drinking-and-offending behaviour. For Dr Sanders it was dealing with the symptom that was presented to her. For Mrs Lambert it was counselling the marriage, and for the absent social worker (as we shall see in chapter 8) it would doubtless have been protecting a child from harm at its parents' hands. For each practitioner it signified the heart of the job he or she was essentially there to do and remained accountable for. This leads us towards some of the core anxieties and the corresponding defences of each discipline which practitioners may be impelled to invoke, under pressure, to the point where there is no emotional or intellectual space for anything else.

It is hard to think about collaboration when you are defending the last ditch of your own professional identity.

Note

1   Double quotation marks are used throughout when reporting what was actually said by members of the workshops.

Chapter 3

Learning through experience

Regular group discussion of practitioners' current cases was the main source of shared learning in the study programme. Before proceeding to the core of the book, we consider briefly the use of this format as a vehicle simultaneously for training and research, and the nature of the data generated in this way.

Case-discussion groups have a considerable history (see for example Rosenfeld and Caplan, 1954; Balint, 1959; Irvine, 1959). They have their roots in the case conferences held in child guidance clinics and psychiatric hospitals and departments. Practitioners of all relevant disciplines have commonly taken part in diagnostic and treatment conferences which are an established part of the therapeutic work in such agencies—integral to a search for understanding of the complex processes of thinking, feeling, acting and interacting bound up in the difficulties which bring patients and their families to them. Since the 1920s when child guidance clinics began and the training of psychiatric social workers was established in Great Britain, the use of small group discussion has proliferated. Such groups are regularly programmed into conference events dealing with professional and technical matters, especially those addressed to members of the caring professions; they are also a prominent feature of much professional education in these fields. A range of different approaches has developed arising from the various theories and practices employed. As Professor Coplin pointed out in his introduction to *The use of small groups in training* (Gosling, Miller, Turquet and Woodhouse, 1967, p. 7), 'what one does with and to a group depends mainly on what one "sees" as the nature of group functioning, and this, in turn, depends heavily on what one has been taught to "see"'.

Whatever the approach, however, case discussion always provides an opportunity to make new associations between phenomena which, though present all along, have not been recognised hitherto. This gives the case-discussion group format a value not only for practice and professional education, but also for research—though Coplin's point must always be taken into account. Thus, it was in work with groups of supervisors (referred to in chapter 1) that Mattinson (1975) and her colleagues found the tendency for reported interactions between worker and supervisor to mirror those between client and worker. This 'reflection process' was recognised typically when the supervision was at its most difficult; when the work on the case was 'stuck' and student and supervisor also at an impasse. Here was evidence of open systems phenomena, unconscious defences against anxiety employed in one relationship system (client-worker) being carried over into and affecting an adjacent one (worker-supervisor). Mattinson further described the mirroring phenomenon occurring in the supervisors' groups themselves. We drew on this work in our own use of workshop groups of practitioners because a case-discussion group likewise has the propensity to pick up and 'reflect' dynamic processes of which neither the practitioners concerned nor their clients or patients are consciously aware.

Mattinson's work was an instance of small groups originally designed for a training purpose being developed as a research instrument. In the present case, the workshops were designed as training-cum-research groups from the start.

Our approach was also influenced by Balint's work with doctors (Balint, 1964; Courtney, 1979), Bion's explorations in groups (Bion, 1961; Pines, ed, 1985), the experience of our own institute (Pincus, ed, 1960), and the work of Rice (1965) and others on organisational behaviour and group relations training. From group relations training work, of which we both had experience, we drew the expectation that the way practitioners interacted in the workshops would also tend to be informative about unconscious as well as conscious processes at work in the institution, or network of institutions, of which they were members.

Unconscious processes in groups, as in institutions, tend to arise particularly as a defensive avoidance of work which engenders anxiety. If collaborative work is to take place in a group, each member is confronted with threats to his sense of 'self'. This sense of self, the view members have of themselves, of others and of their outer world, is their most precious possession. It is bound to be defended stoutly. But learning which involves more than the acquisition of factual knowledge calls for change in those views, a personal change that is emotional as well as cognitive. Such change tends to be experienced as threatening because it can mean facing loss, relinquishing what has been known and hitherto relied upon.

For this reason change is usually resisted, even when, consciously, it is earnestly desired; certainly there will be strenuous efforts to manage its impact and control its pace. The process of managing and controlling personal change makes for the individual's separateness from other members, which can be at variance with that part of his personality which desires to be 'at one' with others —to coalesce rather than engage in real interaction with them. In the latter state, differences may be denied and an attempt made to avoid internal conflict and anxiety by means of externalisation and projection. Phantasy prevails; salvation is felt to lie outside the person—to be gained by allegiance to 'someone who knows', through a miracle wrought by others or through uncompromising dispute which can have the quality of a 'fight to the death'. Insofar as these mechanisms are in operation, as they inevitably are from time to time, some of those in the group may be ill-used by their colleagues, and for this each member has to assume appropriate responsibility. What happens in a group is determined by the individuals that comprise it. But in the environment of the group and the relationships within it aspects of the person which are not normally manifest can be brought into play. Unconscious ideas and theories tend to be active which are at odds with the individual's conscious intention to observe, participate and collaborate with others.

However, alongside defensive anti-learning and anti-work tendencies, the drive towards interaction with the real world represented by the group and its task remains powerful. Survival depends upon it. The environment and associated practicalities may (and in this study often did) present big obstacles; but it is the unconscious inter-personal factors that mainly affect the individual's capacity to attend to the group's task and mobilise the co-operation, give and take and regard for people that learning and work with others demand. While these unconscious processes are inescapable, the way they are manifested and the degree to which they are explicit and intrusive depend on a number of factors, especially the size of the group, the admixture of the members' personalities, the nature of the subject matter being dealt with and the group's working structure. To sustain learning and work inevitably involves frustration arising from tension between opposing facets of the individual as he experiences them in a group. Conflict and growth are inseparable.

This view of processes at work in small groups conditioned the way the workshops were conducted. For learning and collaborative work to be possible, the climate had to be right. We made it our responsibility to see that the workshop groups offered sufficient containment for anxieties to be tolerated and, as far as possible, not acted upon unduly in the ways we have described. This entailed ensuring the boundary conditions of the groups, for example consistency of time, place and membership, facilitating the presenting and recording of cases by members and endeavouring to keep the task in the forefront of our own and members' minds. Rather than direct the discussions we sought to assist the process of learning for the practitioners and ourselves alike.

Practitioners were at the centre of things. Through their role in the intermediary caring system, they were the link, the 'conductor' as it were, between the client or patient system and the agency system. They were therefore subject to the influence of both, whilst at the same time exerting their own idiosyncratic influence on both. It was through their presentation of cases that the dynamic processes at work in client/patient and agency systems were transmitted to the workshops—the learning systems of which we were part. It was to their personal articulation of these processes that members individually and collectively responded. And because of their position on the boundary between client/patient and agency systems, they were potential or actual vehicles for collaboration within or between services.

The pivotal role of practitioners is emphasised because they governed the status of the material we shall be considering and effectively defined its parameters. The study was designed to ensure that practitioners selected cases for inclusion which gave rise to difficulty and caused them concern. Exclusions were very few, the main criteria being that the clients or patients were current ones, had active family relationships rather than being isolates and were a source of preoccupation.

There were marked variations in the material that presenting practitioners were able to contribute because their observations were relative to their setting and to their professional task—as well as to their individual approach, acuity and personality. A standard set of headings was devised to guide practitioners in completing a 'record of cases studied' but the use they made of these was inevitably diverse. There were variations too in the ways in which workshop members were stimulated by a case and its presentation and how far they were mobilised to work and learn—and to draw out the presenter in the process.

In presenting their practice for scrutiny, moreover, practitioners were bound to reveal hidden aspects of themselves and to talk about their work with varying degrees of self-awareness and anxiety. Even the most seasoned worker can lose, or fail to find, an appropriate way of relating to clients or patients at some times and in some cases; often this is because of personal resonances which may be conscious or deeply unconscious. But with each member centre-stage in turn, meeting by meeting, it was the case and not the member's personal difficulty that was addressed. Personal dilemmas were not ignored. They were communicated with implicitly through addressing the problems in the work, but practitioners were left to ponder the implications for them personally of what was discussed; in facilitating the groups' work we, acting as consultants, strove to maintain the boundary between the personal and the professional if and when attempts were made to breach it.

The presenters were also left with the responsibility of assessing the relevance of the groups' contributions for their continuing work on the case. Only they were in a position to judge the appropriateness of the comments made—for themselves, their clients or patients, or their service setting. The temptation to 'take over' the case had to be resisted, especially when the practitioner seemed to be longing to be rescued or hoping to get rid of responsibility. Inevitably, as will be seen in the chapters in Part II, this temptation was sometimes succumbed to, usually when the anxiety provoked by the material was such as to induce other members and ourselves to forget the rule of respect and support for the presenter's professional autonomy. Direct teaching was undertaken occasionally, but the overriding aim was to contain anxiety rather than dissipate it by explanation, and so to promote learning through experience.

Interpretations of a group's behaviour *per se* were rarely made, and only when it seemed determinedly diverted from work on the case. However, some group processes could be recognized and exploited in the service of learning—as when members in their interaction with the case material or the presenter unconsciously revealed, through the reflection process, some underlying dynamic operating in the client or patient, couple or family; or in the inter-professional relationships concerning the case.

The array of 132 cases practitioners contributed was rich in its diversity. It provided examples of processes operating within and between relationship systems in a range of problematic situations where interaction in marriage and the family, and in the professional network, had implications for the work of practitioners in the different agencies. At the same time, by offering a sizeable sample of their practice for examination, participants afforded access to important characteristics of the cultures of their respective institutions and disciplines.

What has been said so far explains why the chapters in Part II, the heart of the book, vary in complexity. With the exception of the one concerned with social workers, each begins with detailed examples of cases studied in the workshops which made a significant contribution to learning. Most are cases which were presented more than once, and so afforded an opportunity to check, correct and develop initial attempts to make sense of the working problems presented.

The series of cases contributed by the discipline in question is also surveyed as a whole in each chapter in Part II (and here we are able to include the contribution of the social work participants), the aim being to identify patterns of response to clients or patients, and to other practitioners and agencies, which emerged as characteristic of each discipline represented in the study, particularly in relation to its distinctive role and task.

A further point arises from the use of case material as basic data. When applying our own perspective to the variable material reported we shall inevitably perpetrate what Michael Balint once called 'selective attention and selective neglect'. There is no doubt that the material assembled can be interpreted in different ways depending on the framework of theory and values the reader brings to bear. As Martin (1977, pp. 56-7) has pointed out, 'case material however well documented and vividly presented, while often appearing convincing to those who practice within a given system of thought . . . never fails to leave completely unimpressed those who work within a different system of thought. The data so presented are simply not regarded as relevant [or are] interpreted entirely differently'. The point is similar to Coplin's (quoted at the beginning of the chapter) about relativity in the understanding of group phenomena. This is what perpetuates the tendency for literature in the field of human relations to preach to the converted and for mutual influence between schools of thought to be limited (Kubie, 1970).

These problems cannot be escaped, of course, nor overcome entirely. But they have to be addressed, however partial the solution. This is one reason why two or three cases are recorded in considerable detail from each of the four disciplines who made this possible; shorter accounts sometimes follow, to illustrate variations on the same theme, or important phenomena not observed in the earlier examples. Comment is distinguished from the practitioners' material and the workshops' responses. The intention is to convey the reality of the work—to allow clients or patients, practitioners and workshop members to speak for themselves as far as possible—particularly in the more extensive accounts where muddle and the 'two steps forward and one back' process, the real stuff of learning and practice, has not been edited out. Where follow-up material became available, it is included solely for the light it throws on the continuing development of interactive processes; we and the practitioners were not engaged in an outcome study but in an attempt to make sense of working problems as they arose.

Our aim in the five essays in Part II is to enable readers to share something of that experience and to leave them in a position to compare their own interpretations and conclusions with ours about the influence of dynamic factors on the interplay between client or patient, caring and agency systems.

Part II

PRACTITIONERS IN FIVE SERVICES

4

Marriage guidance

We begin this series of chapters with marriage guidance work because we came to realise that it afforded a crucial conceptual link between the two main focuses of our study. In the first place practitioners in this setting had marital stress and engagement with couples as their primary concern. In the second place, it became clear (see chapter 9) that inter-professional collaboration across the whole network of services was permeated with the same dynamic tensions concerning triangular relationships and third parties that we were studying at close quarters in the marriage guidance field.

Most people seeking help from marriage guidance counsellors are explicit that their difficulties are located in the couple relationship, or they have been helped, sometimes induced, to define them in this way by a third party. Over many years, attention has been drawn to the complexities that can attend such a definition or re-definition (Woodhouse, 1962; Clulow, 1985, chapter 2) and we meet them again in the work reported here. But those who cross the threshold of a door marked 'Marriage', however mixed their feelings, will inevitably locate their difficulties in the marital system and convey them to a practitioner who is expected to be able to respond to *this* way of communicating dis-ease— rather than the language of illness, say, or delinquency, or other social 'symptoms'.

Most of the counsellors taking part in the study practised in two settings: in their own counselling centres, and in health centres where they were attached to primary care practices. Cases were contributed from both settings.

The first example, like nearly half the counselling centre cases, came through what counsellors called 'the normal channel': a client had telephoned for an appointment. But the counsellor, Mrs Wakeford, was urged by the secretary to see Mrs Dolby without delay; she did so without the reception interview that was usually offered to those who might have to wait for an appointment.

The split lady—   The first session (like Mrs Lambert's in chapter 2) opened
what belongs where   in a way that puzzled Mrs Wakeford and seemed to her
and to whom?   more appropriate to a solicitor than a marriage counsellor. Mrs Dolby asked about the division of property in the

event of separation or divorce which she implied she had in mind. Complaints about her treatment by Mr Dolby and her daughter followed.

During the three sessions reported in the first presentation, Mrs Wakeford learned that Mrs Dolby had been married since her early twenties to a slightly older man, a life-long factory worker. Her daughter was now just twenty. Mrs Dolby volunteered that she had had a breakdown some months after the girl's birth, when she was a psychiatric in-patient for nearly a year and had a lengthy course of ECT. She remembered being depressed and sleeping most of the day, but could not otherwise be specific about what had gone on at that time nor how her then young baby had been looked after during her illness. There had been a second psychiatric episode three or four years ago which had been treated with psychotropic drugs by her former GP. She had taken these until earlier in the present year. Mrs Dolby said things were now so bad at home that she felt another breakdown was imminent. Her husband wanted her "to get more pills from the doctor" but she had resisted; "they're not the answer, are they?" She had gone to the surgery, however, and when her present GP suggested joint consultations Mr Dolby had attended with her. According to Mrs Dolby, marital counselling was recommended; the health visitor, who saw her often, also urged her to go to marriage guidance, offering to press for an early appointment if a delay was likely. In the event there was no contact between the primary care practice and the council at this stage. Mrs Wakeford had noted that it seemed as if the health visitor and the doctor looked to marriage guidance to "rescue everybody".

She described a well-groomed woman, tastefully but inexpensively dressed, whose main characteristic was the marked contrast between a "completely still, submissive body . . . and a lively, cheery, unmarked face"; Mrs Dolby said she was depressed but did not appear so.

Mrs Wakeford was impressed by her client in other ways, too. Mrs Dolby was sure that all the professionals, for example her doctor and the health visitor (and earlier, the hospital staff), were on her side; they had told her husband and daughter to rally round and not put pressure on her. She had stopped working after her first break-down but now had a "nice little job" where the people were sympathetic and "like a family". She saw herself as the unloved one in her own family, "which ought to be close and loving, didn't it?" Her husband was "bossy" and controlling; her daughter, always too quick for her, was contemptuous, expecting her mother to clear up after her. She rejected the food Mrs Dolby prepared, preferring to go and eat with her boyfriend—and she was "in cahoots" with her father. They "treat me horrible".

During a recent row, she had tried to frighten the pair of them by putting on her coat and walking out. When she came back after some hours, however, "no-one said a word". Mrs Wakeford noted that none of the family were ever referred to by name and that Mrs Dolby related to her "in a child-like manner as if to say, 'here is the problem, what are you going to do about it for me?' She's a determinedly helpless individual".

She also emphasised that her efforts to encourage Mrs Dolby to reflect on the part she might be playing in what was going on made "absolutely no impression". Most comments seemed to be taken by Mrs Dolby to imply the counsellor's agreement with her—and evoked a triumphant look; occasionally she seemed bewildered by what was said to her. Mrs Wakeford said it was difficult to remember the content of the sessions for some reason, but her overriding impression was of unusual irritation. She had worked with many clients who "push things out and into others, but they don't usually get me in the same way ... I can't work out why I was so irritated by this woman".

By the end of these interviews, Mrs Wakeford was convinced that she needed to see the couple together. Mrs Dolby readily agreed to an invitation being sent to her husband but was sure he would refuse it. At the time the case was first discussed, however, he had accepted but had not yet been seen.

Mrs Wakeford 'phoned the GP when she had formed her own impressions of Mrs Dolby; she felt that to have done so earlier might have distorted them, but now wanted "to get his picture of the marriage". The doctor predicted that Mr Dolby's story would be very different

from his wife's; there were voluminous case notes on Mrs
Dolby, a long-standing patient of the practice, but her
husband was indeed 'pushy' and controlling, and acknowledged no problem. The doctor confirmed many aspects
of what Mrs Dolby had said and Mrs Wakeford felt he
echoed his patient's view of the situation—perhaps
collusively so. He also explained that it was his practice
not to go beyond three counselling consultations with
patients. If he decided they needed additional help, he
tried to get them to someone who had more time than he
could afford.

The workshop formulated the idea that Mrs Dolby's breakdowns were each
associated with major transitions in her family life. The first had followed her
marriage and early pregnancy, the second her daughter's puberty; her present
disturbance was explicitly linked with the girl's sexual interests and flaunting of
her relationship with her boyfriend, as she approached the age at which her
mother had married. Interesting though this idea was, however, the discussion
was one-sided, focusing exclusively on the wife; the workshop log-book
recorded that there was "little room to reflect on the interaction in the marriage
and no acknowledgement that *both* partners had experienced social and
emotional changes". The group was much preoccupied with the possible
influence on Mrs Dolby's behaviour and relationships of her psychiatric illness
and treatment, including the recent sustained medication. Members displayed a
generally patronising attitude towards Mrs Dolby, and likewise towards the
counsellor.

According to Mrs Wakeford's record made for the study, however, this first
discussion left her with some important questions, the first being: 'How
realistic is the idea of working psychodynamically with her?' It had not
previously occurred to her to wonder if the client might be too psychiatrically
disturbed for this. True, Mrs Dolby had reported her history, but she had taken
it for granted that "if the GP said to them, 'you two go along and do some work
on your marriage' [Mrs Dolby] was capable of doing so". On the other hand,
Mrs Wakeford also noted, "what of a split within the marriage in which the wife
is the 'sick' one and the husband 'well'? What does each have invested in
maintaining this position? The possibility of such a split has to be kept in mind
to avoid colluding with it."

The case was discussed again after four joint interviews.
The counsellor reported that Mr Dolby seldom looked at
her, but was verbally challenging and aggressive. Sca-
thing to his wife at times, he brooked no interruption

from her or from Mrs Wakeford. Mrs Dolby "always back-tracked" in the wrangling that went on in the interviews, never stood up to him. In spite of the obviously fraught relationship, Mrs Wakeford became increasingly convinced that whatever happened, Mrs Dolby would never leave her husband. For her own part, she felt faulted and clumsy and was often drawn into contradicting him, realising at the same time that this was counter-productive. As with his wife in the single inter-views, she was very aware that her reactions to him were uncharacteristic of her. Mr Dolby stuck to his view of their situation: there was no problem except the one existing between his wife and his daughter. It arose because Mrs Dolby handled situations badly: she "blows things up"; the right way to deal with them was "to take the steam out of things . . . damp them down"—which he always had to do. It seemed to Mrs Wakeford that perhaps after all the GP was right about Mr Dolby. Alone with his wife in the earlier interviews she had felt, "poor man" to be married to such a woman, but in the flesh he was as pushy and controlling as his wife and the doctor had described. However, she also had glimpses of a different side of him, a less rigid attitude. For example, when she commented on how difficult he must find it always to be "the referee between your wife and your daughter", he readily agreed; but he "just had to keep things on an even keel". He also volunteered that he sometimes worried that the girl might have the same sort of breakdown as his wife; at another point he agreed with Mrs Wakeford that he felt the doctors blamed him.

These fleeting departures from his general demeanour were linked in the counsellor's mind with other remarks he had made about Mrs Dolby's "over the top" reactions. A brother of his had also had a breakdown at some point in the past; he was "a bit strange, needed careful handling". He felt it was intolerable that she made such a difficulty over this brother's visits and always complained bitterly that he only talked to Mr Dolby, never to her.

Mrs Wakeford began to see him as extremely anxious about madness which might erupt and overwhelm at any time if things were not controlled and handled in the right way. It seemed to her that "he was holding on like grim death". She felt the couple were tightly bound together, but that both were "at the end of their tethers". At a common-sense level it seemed incongruous that they went out together regularly. There seemed so little room for warmth; "they have no space for each other in their relationship". It was one of the bleakest she had ever encountered.

At the first joint session it had been agreed to have four more meetings and then review the work. When it came to the third of these, however, without any warning Mr Dolby declared it to be the last. They had had their four meetings; "things were quieter" and he saw no need to go on, though he did have some concern about their daughter. His wife could continue to see the counsellor— or someone else if she chose.

Mrs Wakeford felt she had to accept his foreclosure. She told them she would be glad to see them in future, but only if both of them wanted to explore the evident stress in their relationship. She did not think the offer would be taken up and wondered whether, by insisting that both came for counselling, she was in effect "dumping Mrs Dolby".

There was a somewhat half-hearted consensus in the workshop about the need for both to be seen and Mrs Wakeford was urged to get in touch with the GP again to "keep the door open for them to come back to MG", especially as the doctor had clearly seen a need for Mr Dolby (though apparently symptom-free) to be included in the work.

Like Mrs Wakeford, the group was defeated and frustrated by this defended and apparently impenetrable relationship. They gave up on it and on her. The log sheet described 'clarity on the pattern of interaction, the wife evacuating all responsibility into the husband and he all madness into his wife. But this very forceful projective system is totally unconscious leaving conscious interaction as a running dog-fight with no real communication . . . insight goes for nothing . . . there seems to be no way into the clients'.

Follow-up

Nothing more had been heard of the couple by the time the study ended two years later; there had been no further contact between Mrs Wakeford and the

GP. Even after such an interval, however, she remarked that the memory of the Dolbys' constricting effect on her remained vivid and immediate.

Comment

The Dolbys exemplify, albeit in an extreme and chronic way, the propensity for conflict within each of two partners to be externalised and acted out between them in their relationship. The behaviour of each partner highlighted one side of the conflict and each fuelled the anxiety of the other. As the workshop recognised, the patterns of the Dolbys' interaction was clear; each was the repository of what the other seemed most to fear and reject in themselves. Though split off and disowned, what was rejected was however an integral part of their respective personalities which continued to be contained in the relationship. This construction accords with Mrs Wakeford's conviction about their powerful emotional attachment to each other notwithstanding the pain and hostility in their lives together. We do not know the genesis of the shared conflict, but there were clues in the material that it was linked with deep-seated anxiety about sexuality and instinctual impulses. Then there was the related problem of managing relationships in the three-person family.

Recognition of the dynamic purpose underlying this troubled marriage was important. But to see that there was more to it than simply a well husband with an ill wife does not explain how Mrs Wakeford and the GP and primary care team were confounded by the entrenched system of defences against change which this couple had jointly evolved.

We need to go back to the way the case began. The couple got into counselling without the 'sender' and the 'receiver' communicating with each other. There was no negotiation between the primary care practice and the marriage guidance council, i.e. no transaction across the boundary between them; indeed, the primary care practitioners' involvement in the referral remained hidden until the work began, and Mrs Wakeford felt the case had been 'dumped' on her agency. This echoed the couple's pattern of interaction; the marriage itself was very much a 'dumping operation'. For their part, the practitioners kept one another at arms' length; being members of agency systems, each with its own ways of 'exporting' and 'importing' cases, their behaviour replicated the split in the Dolbys' relationship and their inability to communicate. Without knowing it, they re-enacted the couple's avoidance of acknowledging to themselves or each other their underlying feelings and motives. One party was relieved of a burden; having accepted it, the other was aggrieved and resentful.

It would be easy to be pejorative about this state of affairs, but that would only serve to perpetuate the blaming so evident in the case, transferring it to the GP and health visitor for their surreptitious way of getting rid of the problematic case and to the counsellor and the marriage guidance council for their unquestioning acceptance of it. This would be to ignore the anxiety raised by the powerful unconscious dynamic within the Dolbys' marital system to which the practitioners were exposed and by which their respective agencies were prone to be influenced.

Some idea of the power of the couple to influence others can be gained from Mrs Wakeford's interaction with them, and from the workshop's response to her and her clients. The working problem she most emphasised was her experience of not being able to be herself with them—of responding uncharacteristically in spite of her conscious intentions. Acutely irritated by Mrs Dolby, she behaved like the husband; faulted by and contentious with him, she was immobilised like the wife. In this predicament she was unable to use her considerable experience or the sensitivity demonstrated in her other work in the face of the couple's unconscious maintenance of the status quo. It was then difficult to give credence to the albeit fragile part of Mrs Dolby that sought to assume some responsibility for what was happening (witness her resistance to the further medication urged by her husband), or to respond to Mr Dolby's fleeting acknowledgements of his unease, and engage with him when he retreated defensively. Though different in their roles and training, and no doubt in their own personalities and attitudes, the Dolbys' doctor and health visitor will also have been subject to these influences.   The workshop was in like case. Mrs Wakeford found some of its comments illuminating but there was little evidence that they influenced her work; as a third party its influence was resisted. The group's responses reflected the couple's interaction too. There was a marked tendency to pronounce and demean, some members portraying a caricature of supervision, treating the counsellor in a denigrating way as if she was an inexperienced, helpless amateur who could not cope—or else members lapsed into despair. That is to say, they treated Mrs Wakeford as the Dolbys treated each other. Meanwhile, everyone was drawn into a restrictive climate and a preoccupation with individual psychopathology at the expense of looking at the interactive processes at work—in spite of the task of elucidating both marital and inter-agency relationships. Uncertainty was dealt with by rejection. Everyone, the GP, the counsellor and the Dolbys, tended to be blamed, disparaged or categorised.

Couples like the Dolbys test the personal boundaries, courage and endurance of practitioners as well as the capacity of agencies to provide a holding environment within which anxiety can be contained and mastered. When so much of their anxiety is unconscious, behaviour on the practitioner's part which conveys that their dilemmas have been recognised and understood is likely to be of as much therapeutic significance as what is conveyed to them in words. In this instance, the Dolbys' anxiety about three-person relationships— currently manifested in their difficulties with their daughter but likely to be rooted in earlier experiences—affected their three-way interaction with the counsellor, and probably with the GP earlier. But, constrained by the clients' anxiety from recognising the link, neither practitioner could respond in a way that would have spoken to the difficulty.

In the further three-way relationship between GP, counsellor and couple, the practitioners were likewise constrained from communicating effectively about the Dolbys. Here the constraints were exacerbated by their respective agency-determined views of their own and each other's roles.

Nevertheless, Mrs Wakeford's final piece of behaviour did convey that at some level she had understood the situation. Her specific offer to see the couple together in future, but not Mrs Dolby on her own, left her feeling anxious that she was 'dumping' Mrs Dolby. It seems clear, however, that she was *not* colluding with the dumping dynamic but counteracting it by making her own boundaries known—i.e. she would not accept Mrs Dolby being dumped on her.

A quarter of the study cases seen in marriage guidance centres came into counselling not by the normal channel but by a different and what may be called a personal route. They were not randomly allocated but were earmarked to see a particular counsellor. This might be at the request of a colleague or a practitioner in another agency who knew that counsellor; former clients might also recommend 'their' counsellor to their friends, or themselves ask to be seen by her again.

John and Emily Broadbent came via the personal route. In their mid-thirties, with three boys under ten, they had had a still-born baby girl a year or so earlier. Clinical difficulties had arisen in the final stages of labour; a hysterectomy followed the delivery. Thereafter, their relationship deteriorated and a marriage guidance counsellor friend had become increasingly anxious about them and their family. It was she who paved the way for them to be seen by Mrs Jameson, whom John Broadbent asked for by name when he 'phoned for an appointment.

Mrs Jameson described them as a good-looking and attractive pair and said how bothered about them her colleague had become. She felt the latter "had needed to get a bit of special treatment for them ... I knew it was going to be quite a sad case and felt apprehensive". Meanwhile, John and Emily were "the sort of couple any of us could know", a fact that made her anxious about bringing the case into the study. But members welcomed it; one said, "we've heard about a lot of clients who wouldn't have been our friends, so it will be much closer to us".

Ambivalent
attachments—the
creative destroyers

Mrs Jameson first reported her work with John and Emily after six meetings, in the course of which she gleaned an outline of their history and a description of their problems as they saw them.

John had been at boarding schools from an early age. His mother (his father's second wife after divorce) died soon after he and Emily began to live together a few years before they married. Just after their marriage, when he was taking his finals, his father died suddenly. He failed his exams and in spite of encouragement to continue his academic work he jettisoned it. Instead he took on a small, precarious enterprise, a creative one in a field in which his father had made a big reputation. Though he called his family "close" he described one in which feelings were seldom expressed, his father as a disciplinarian and his mother as 'distant".

Emily's parents divorced after years of discord when she was in her late teens, a year or two before meeting John. Both parents remarried, and except that her father was said to be overbearing and an "autocrat" whose word could not be gainsaid, he figured little in her story; her mother was not mentioned at all. A trained artist, Emily did occasional teaching—without much enthusiasm.

Both John and Emily had half-brothers and sisters as well as full siblings of which they were each the eldest.

Both agreed that in their early years together they had been "really good friends and close" with a mutually satisfying sexual relationship. They had been happy until the children were born. All the pregnancies were planned and it had been Emily's pressing urge to have children that led them to marry when they did—in spite of John's reluctance. He found babies difficult and said he felt increasingly "pushed out" by them. This had repercussions when their eldest son became seriously ill just before he was due to start school. During the boy's protracted treatment and convalescence, Emily was preoccupied with him and kept both his care and that of the younger ones very much to herself because she felt John had not wanted them in the first place.

When their third child proved to be a boy, however, it had been John who pressed to have another child. He wanted a girl to complete the family. So his feelings about the loss of their first and only daughter and Emily's hysterectomy were especially acute. Emily had also felt that it would be good to have a daughter. For John, however, the wish for a girl to "complete things" had become as insistent as Emily's to start a family earlier on.

When the work began, the Broadbents had been accepted as prospective adopters and were well into the procedure. To Mrs Jameson, everyone seemed to be moved by what had happened to them; like her colleague, the adoption agency seemed to have "fallen over backwards" to help.

The couple reported rowing endlessly; "we can't talk about anything". Money was short and a bone of contention. Emily resented John's giving up of a potentially lucrative career and felt swamped and constrained by him. For his part, John complained that "things have to be Emily's way, I don't signify"; Emily got the sympathy, "no-one listens to my feelings". And to Emily he said, "it's bad for you that you can't have more children, but what about me, I can't either". She was "worn out and put upon by the children", but would not let him help. She avoided being with him; "I can't get near her".

They were worried about adopting because of the conflict between them, but they were most reluctant to call it off. Mrs Jameson had the impression that John's wish for counselling was mainly to ensure that the adoption was not endangered and that he had "got Emily along to be sorted out".

It emerged that tension had become acute earlier in the year when Emily suspected John's relationship with a girl temporarily working for him. Their own sexual relationship, deteriorating ever since the children were born, then became even more difficult. Talking in one of the joint interviews about Emily's belief that it was a sexual affair, John said (and convinced Mrs Jameson) that it was not. Everyone was taken up with Emily; the girl was easy to talk to, she listened to him when he felt Emily did not.

Mrs Jameson emphasised the difficulty she had in joint interviews; they "interrupted each other and countered anything the other said ... they were like a pair of squabbling children", each trying to get their story heard by her; "it makes you want to bang their heads together ... say shut up and listen to each other".

They were also a confusing couple. Usually Emily was dejected and was for separating while John stood for the adoption and for them and the family to be together; but these positions were sometimes reversed, with John wanting to split up "because it's hopeless". There were also moments when they could be more reflective. For example, John had wondered what it was like for Mrs Jameson. As if reading her mind he had said, "if I were you I'd want to bash us both". Nonetheless, she felt he was out of touch with her and was uncertain whether he would sustain a commitment to counselling. Meanwhile, alongside her dejection and angry tearfulness, Emily said she felt "as if a cloud had lifted" since her son's recovery; she brought pictures of the children for Mrs Jameson to see. Her interest in her work had gradually rekindled and she now wanted to get back to it "for the first time in years".

Like Mrs Jameson, the workshop was divided between sympathy for and frustration with the clients; the same was true of members' responses to her. Efforts to understand the stress in the relationship between John and Emily were not sustained and there were recurring moves to weigh up the partners as individuals, to apportion responsibility and take sides. At one point a male practitioner laughed enigmatically, and to Mrs Jameson's sharp enquiry explained that John "came over as a spoiled brat"; she retorted that it was Emily who was the spoiled brat when they were together.

The loss of the baby and the emotional and sexual implications of Emily's sterilisation raised considerable feelings in the group. Some, notably the health visitor members, were moved by what had happened to the couple and critical of the medical staff involved. But it was the prospective adoption that preoccupied the group most. All were amazed and some highly critical that the procedure had been allowed to go forward. Members, especially those in the statutory services, drew prescriptively on their knowledge of the adoption process and procedures. This seemed to offer a basis for certainty amid the contradictions thrown up by Mrs Jameson's account. She made it clear that she, too, had serious misgivings about the adoption (and had drawn particular attention to the clients' own uncertainty about it), but she responded to her colleagues' reactions guardedly, as though the statutory workers present might not maintain confidentiality and thereby jeopardise the Broadbents' application.

During the discussion, Mrs Jameson mentioned a personal difficulty she experienced in working with the couple. Not only were they the kind of people she and workshop members might know, but their medical experiences evoked memories of her own and of people she knew well. Her technical problem, however, was uncertainty. The evidence suggested the loss of their baby had precipitated the couple into counselling; and this tragic loss must have been what had moved the adoption agency to "take them onto their books so readily". She had begun the work thinking "that all this had to do with not really having done the grieving". But increasingly she questioned this simple assessment; "there seemed such pressure to replace the lost baby", it was as if there was an extra dimension to it, "what's it all about? I feel I'm missing something obvious."

In the workshop too, when members were engrossed with the theme of the lost child, a social worker questioned the centrality of the event. She put it starkly: "I think the baby dying is a bit of a red herring—awful as it is". She thought the difficulties "went far back . . . why was his nose so put out of joint when the babies came . . . his ambivalent feelings about displacement were emphasised by the [eldest] boy's illness". Another member then commented that both were eldest children whose noses had been put out of joint by the arrival of siblings. The contradictory impulses of this attractive couple were also noted—alongside the drive to be creative there was also destructiveness which "the child's medical history and hers, and the death of the baby so dreadfully confirm". The workshop logbook recorded: "Mrs Jameson seemed . . . apprehensive and disorganised about this case . . . possibly because of her identification with them".

> The work with the Broadbents was reported again five months later. Towards the end of this period the acrimonious joint sessions had given way to separate ones. The couple's present resentments were now sometimes linked by both to their past experiences. John's preoccupation about being unable to father another child with Emily took him back to his family; he talked again of his parents, in particular what a martinet he felt his father had been and the desolation he experienced when sent away to school. Emily's continuing complaints about feeling controlled and restricted by John were associated with memories of her father who "always got his own way". Then, as though talking about the present rather than the past, she said she "had to get away, to escape".
>
> After several single sessions, John came unannounced to one of Emily's interviews. The practicalities of her

leaving him, which she had previously rehearsed with Mrs Jameson, were again aired but now with John there raising only desultory objections. Mrs Jameson said she had not planned it, but as the interview ended all three of them found themselves agreeing they should fix no further appointments; Emily was to telephone for one after she had moved out. John did not demur.

Telling the workshop about these interviews Mrs Jameson recalled that in an earlier joint meeting, when talking of the loss of their baby, John and Emily had mentioned someone who specialised in work with the bereaved. She had asked them whether they were implying that they would like to see this therapist. They replied, "well, we were wondering about it". There was a strong suggestion in this that referring the burdensome couple had been in Mrs Jameson's mind, but if so, she had made no move to do so.

Having heard nothing from Emily for five weeks and feeling in a quandary, she had written to them both to say she would be pleased to see them or, if they wished, put them in touch with someone else. The response was immediate. Emily 'phoned to say she was still with John even though things were no better, and asked for individual appointments, first for herself, then for John.

Emily had been seen just before this workshop meeting; "an entirely different kind of session; she was there because she wanted to be". She seemed genuinely grateful that Mrs Jameson had got in touch and, when reminded of the possibility of a referral, said, "yes, I know, but at the moment we both want to come back to you". She felt something had changed, "something has settled" and then added, "it does take time to grow up, doesn't it?" She seemed "more of her own person" to Mrs Jameson and from what was said about her exchanges with John and his reaction to her decision to stay (bitter complaints that she was "messing his life around . . . everything keeps changing"), she thought they "might be separating out a bit". At the same time, Emily said she felt it was impossible for them to trust and rely on each other ever again.

Mrs Jameson ended with a question about whether single or joint interviews would be best. At the moment she felt some individual work was needed. She had always believed Emily would want to come back to see her on her own, but was surprised that John did.

The logbook records that this time the counsellor's presentation was more typical of her; she was less fraught and more in command of her material. Members of the workshop also responded differently. Instead of 'taking sides' and the earlier question and answer mode of relating to Mrs Jameson, they were stimulated by the material and built on each other's contributions.

Three interrelated issues were explored. First, the way the couple had contrived and were allowed to get into counselling without negotiation. It was pointed out that "clients like these, who make a tremendous appeal, tend to make you feel a heel if you say, 'just a minute'; if you stop and think, assess, and observe before plunging in". Then there was the unplanned gap in interviews. This appeared to have enabled Mrs Jameson to get a more effective working distance from the clients. Finally, there was the couple's manifest conflict about being separate or together and its counterpart in the pattern of interviews and Mrs Jameson's uncertainty as between joint or single sessions.

> Mrs Jameson discussed the work for the last time after a further interval of three months. All the interviews had been single ones except the last she reported; Emily had been seen much more often than John. When he came on his own after the gap in the work it became obvious that single sessions had been Emily's idea, not his, and he reacted strongly against it. After what she called an angry "argie bargie", he reluctantly agreed to one further individual meeting. Beyond this, two points emerged: his anger with Emily, now expressed more directly, for "mucking things up" for him; and the fact that he had just accepted a well-paid temporary job in his original field of work which would improve their finances but would take him away from home for some months later in the year. He would be able to hire someone to keep his business going.
>
> The sessions with Emily continued in the more open mode she had established on her return. She talked about how long it had taken for both of them to feel ready to settle down and be parents; it was not only John who had been uncertain about it. It came out that an unplanned pregnancy had been terminated before they married; Mrs Jameson was taken aback by Emily's conviction that she had disclosed this in the previous joint interviews. Emily also mentioned increasingly frequent visits to her home

town. She saw both her parents, but the main impetus was to resume old relationships and make new ones from which she could get emotional support. In the workshop, Mrs Jameson drew a parallel between these and John's earlier relationship with the girl who had worked for him.

Emily was anxious that John should not know about the new relationships; Mrs Jameson felt "in a bind . . . now I wish I hadn't seen them separately". She agreed to keep the secret, however, but discussed its implications with Emily who said, "the time may come when I feel I ought to tell him, but not now; it wouldn't help".

Mrs Jameson did, however, feel free to mention the early abortion when John came again. He, too, thought they had mentioned it before and she had to hold on hard to her own conviction that it was not something she could possibly have forgotten. He said the decision not to have the baby then had been a joint one and recalled how devastating the termination had been for both of them, "much more than we realised". In this context, he stressed how close he felt to the boys and how he dreaded being separated from them, especially the eldest.

Notwithstanding the content of the session, Mrs Jameson said she still experienced John as distant; she felt sure he thought there was no point in seeing her alone.

At her last reported single interview Emily went back to the theme of "getting out" but wondered, "could I cope on my own?" She also brought a message from John: he would like to join her for the next interview. She said that he now seemed convinced that it would be best for them to separate.

The joint interview opened with agreement between them that a period apart would help. This prompted Mrs Jameson to share with them her perception of "their fused identity", that they had clung together "like babes in the wood" at the start of their relationship. It seemed that the advent of the children and their eldest boy's illness had heralded a major change. The stress of these events and then the baby's death were "all disasters that had come from outside" to complicate things.

To her surprise, John endorsed her comment about being "fused" and said he felt the "only way we can resolve anything is actually to separate". He did not really want this but could see no other way forward. John was in fact unusually prominent throughout the interview, and referred again to their plan to adopt which had by now been halted. He still believed that to have adopted a girl would have made all the difference; at the time he had deeply resented Emily's withdrawal of their application in spite of his objections, but now realised "it isn't on".

They agreed to go away and consider the details of what parting would involve and then come back and discuss them. Mrs Jameson pointed out that both evidently had very mixed feelings about it—otherwise it might well have been managed earlier. She included herself when she told the workshop, "it seemed a relief to all of us to be together". A further joint appointment was fixed for the following week, but there was no plan to continue beyond that.

Mrs Jameson's presentation was again clear and business-like; she mentioned that she was coping with worrying illness in her own family, and revealed more of her own part in the interviews than previously. The striking feature of the workshop was the way other people also drew on their own experience as they worked with her. One member, seeing the probable link between the early abortion and the couple's marked reaction to the death of their daughter, recalled a painful loss she had sustained as a teenager which she thought "was quite done with—till it got triggered off again years later". Several others followed suit.

The discussion also reviewed the probable outcome for John and Emily of what seemed to be a shared difficulty, underlined by the way they had shown themselves to be alternately in touch with opposite feelings. A health visitor said, "it's as if both needed to be there for a complete statement to be made". But members echoed Mrs Jameson when she wondered "whether they will find a balance between them . . . I suppose my dominant feeling at the moment is that they will split up".

Follow-up

At follow-up three years after Mrs Jameson's final presentation we learned that the couple had parted, Emily moving to accommodation nearby with the children. They were in touch with each other, however, and the boys often stayed with John.

Both had made other relationships, but to Mrs Jameson's surprise John had sought further help from her two years after the first spell of counselling ended. He said he was not ready to commit himself to someone else until he understood better his part in what had gone wrong in his marriage to Emily.

Comment

The Broadbents are representative of a substantial group of couples finding their way to marital agencies—those for whom a comfortable emotional distance from each other is difficult to achieve. Closeness becomes invasive and stultifying, engendering hostility; but separateness represents abandonment and augurs frightening isolation. Their lives together tend to be characterised by a painful, for some interminable, search for a degree of proximity that might offer containment of the primitive anxieties inherent in either extreme (cf. Freud, 1921; Mattinson, 1975, chapter 2).

As Lyons (1973) points out, there is of course nothing exceptional in couples being 'at one' at the outset of the many sided, even paradoxical commitment of marriage—quite the reverse. But John and Emily (like many couples in similar difficulty over the management of psychological boundaries) found it hard to grasp and exploit the developmental opportunities afforded by such regression. What Mrs Jameson was able to learn of their respective histories made it clear that their parental attachments could not have made it easy to form flexible and trusting ones with each other; nor did their parents' marriages afford them a sustaining internal image of mediation between creative love and destructive hatred.

In this case, too, it is helpful to go back to the beginning. The Broadbents' shared problem of managing psychological boundaries was reflected in their entry into counselling—without pause on the threshold, as it were. Indeed, it was as if there was no agency boundary to be negotiated. Differences were obliterated. They were also treated as if they were one, an entity to be rescued from the disruption occasioned by their recent loss. Everyone was induced to 'fall over backwards to help'; being 'people like us', they merited special treatment. Because of their appeal, any pause to question and reflect (i.e. to be emotionally distinct from them) induced guilt, as if to do so was to lack compassion and was tantamount to rejection.

There was nothing in Mrs Jameson's account to suggest that either John or Emily consciously set out to influence potential helpers in this way; their influence was strong and pervasive nonetheless. The marriage guidance council's intake arrangements left it open to such unconscious persuasiveness. The adoption agency also seemed to have overlooked factors one might expect to be taken into account when assessing a couple's suitability. Mrs Jameson's identification with the Broadbents' experience of hospitals and their ill child added to the time and emotional effort it took for her to regain her customary stance. The powerful unconscious processes dominating the couple's inter-action also inevitably influenced their interplay with her. Their angry competiti-veness in the early sessions showed how uncertain both were about being listened to in their own right as individuals in the threesome interviews. Later they unconsciously collaborated to demonstrate the opposite sides of their shared dilemma. John was 'right out' (cold, distant), Emily 'right in' (confiding secrets to Mrs Jameson). The two sides of the defence against their anxious conflict being thus split between them, Mrs Jameson was hard-pressed to work with the ambivalence of both partners in three-person counselling, the customary marriage guidance model.

The follow-up throws further light on the couple's problem about managing threesomes. Contradicting her experience of him, John Broadbent sought help from Mrs Jameson for himself. This suggests that throughout he had longed for but could not allow himself a close relationship with the counsellor while he was sharing her with Emily. Separately, he could achieve it.

Most counsellors also had part-time attachments to primary care practices. Over a third of their cases were seen in doctors' surgeries or health centres. The example chosen was atypical in that the counsellor in question was new to general practice, having just replaced a well-established colleague, but it shows important features of attached counsellors' work and interprofessional relation-ships as well as being of interest in its own right.

The elderly two year-olds   James and Barbara Curtis were in their late sixties, married for almost forty years with grown-up children and grandchildren. Barbara's mother, in her nineties, had recently moved nearby and was the only surviving parent. James and Barbara had been frequent attenders at surgery though James was the main patient; he had a long medical history with numerous clinical investigations. His medical notes were said to describe him as hypochondriacal and subject to "anxiety depression".

There had been tension between them for years, with at least one period of separation. Shortly after James Curtis had been made redundant, Barbara had left home to live with one of their grown-up daughters—who later mediated her return, not least because of her father's extreme reaction to the separation.

The present episode began when Barbara attended surgery and complained of James' sleeplessness, his reluctance to take the prescribed sleeping tablets and his shouting at her during the night. This consultation followed a crisis with Barbara's mother who had called out a series of duty doctors and involved neighbours while the couple were away on holiday.

They were referred to Mrs Rogers soon after she had joined the practice by a doctor who "rolled his eyes saying, 'good luck to you' ". He and his colleagues clearly despaired of Mrs and Mrs Curtis. Mrs Rogers felt that the invitation so soon after her arrival to take on an apparently unrewarding elderly couple with chronic marital difficulties (and, as she quickly learned, considerable previous experience of individual psycho-therapy) must be in the nature of a test.

The couple readily accepted Mrs Rogers and at once settled into single interviews. A sardonic note in the workshop logbook records, 'no evidence of them feeling rejected [by the GP] ... but then they seem to have collected therapists and eaten them for breakfast'. Both, but Barbara especially, launched into florid accounts of their unsatisfactory sexual relationship and both laboured their dissatisfaction with each other in this respect from the beginning of their marriage.

When at one point James said angrily that he would not continue unless his wife revealed to Mrs Rogers how she demeaned him sexually, the counsellor suggested joint interviews. They agreed, but were very ill at ease in the threesomes for some time; problems with Barbara's mother now came a close second to their sexual preoccupations. Barbara Curtis portrayed herself as "hopelessly trapped" between the competing demands of her mother and her husband; James Curtis complained of a "combination of demanding women".

Their early lives had been disrupted by the war, Barbara's even more obviously than James'. When her parents divorced she, the oldest child, was the only one who stayed with her father and his new wife, being used as a go-between who was quizzed for information by each parent about the other. Her mother later got custody of her and consequently she escaped the fate of her father and step-mother who were both killed in an air raid. She would almost certainly have died, too, had she stayed with them; and she also lost several other close relations in the war.

James as a young child had developed an extremely close relationship with his mother during his father's absence on active service, and shared her bed until Mr Curtis senior was demobilised. His mother conceived almost at once after his father's return, and several more children were born in quick succession.

What they told her about their past and their relationship, though vivid and moving, often struck Mrs Rogers as rehearsed. She experienced Barbara as "pleading, like a little girl", and James as a "knowing, clever but petulant small boy". It was hard for her to believe they were grandparents.

Throughout these sessions, Mrs Rogers focused her work on the couple's sexual relationship which she linked to their early experiences with their parents. Once established in joint interviews, they never missed a session. She found them dependent, pessimistic and defeating clients.

Nonetheless, Mrs Rogers resisted the workshop's almost unanimous doubts about this couple's potential for change and about the truth of their sometimes lurid stories from childhood. As against her approach, other members emphasised the couple's present reality, their advanced years and the problem of coping with a difficult elderly relative. A conflict between optimism and pessimism was evident in the exchanges between members and Mrs Rogers. "Do they really want to get better ... carrying a grudge against each other" (senior probation officer). "There are positive things ... an improvement in spite of a couple of storms ... she didn't realise he actually loved her ... signs that they're dealing with the old mother better" (counsellor).

In subsequent presentations, other tensions became apparent, for example James and Barbara found breaks in the sessions at holidays very difficult to tolerate. After some evidence of improvement, Mrs Rogers, mindful that "the doctors don't expect me to see people for years ... look for something short-term", changed to fortnightly interviews as a move towards ending her work with the couple. Their reaction was dramatic, "a tremendous response, and back to square one". So she reverted to weekly sessions. Each successive holiday break was heralded by deterioration and hostility between them and towards her, followed by relief at the resumption of counselling and then some encouraging, if slight, development. How could she balance what she felt was an appropriate response to the clients' evident fear of change with what she felt the primary care practice demanded?

In fact, there had been no protest from the practice about the continuing counselling but the question was a live one in the workshop, particularly for members from probation and social services who were again sceptical. As one of them put it, "thinking about the use of resources . . . what are seventy year-olds expecting in the way of sex-life anyway . . . can't help thinking, why don't they pull themselves together?"

The actual response of Mrs Rogers' medical colleagues was surprise and relief that she had held onto the couple. One of them commiserated with her, "my heart sinks when I see them going into your room"; implying, Mrs Rogers thought, "sooner you than me". And jokes were made about Mr and Mrs Curtis over coffee which she found distasteful. In the workshop she identified the problem of how to have a constructive dialogue with the practice GPs —to keep them in touch with her work with their patients without endangering the privacy of the counselling relationship. She wondered if she would ever manage to achieve this with most of the doctors in the practice.

Though gradual, with many ups and downs, her reports showed a definite improvement in James' and Barbara's relationship over the twelve months during which the case was discussed in the workshop. Mrs Rogers described interviews that became progressively more robust, she being more brisk with them and they more direct with her and each other, though both partners were depressed at times. They were gradually able to relinquish their *idée fixe* about their sexual relationship; it improved, albeit fitfully. They reported that James became orgasmic for the first time for some years; Barbara was able to initiate intercourse on occasion. When her mother again "turned on the manipulation" Barbara vented her fury, but this time James was more accepting and constructive, maintaining that they must not let his mother-in-law upset their relationship.

Mrs Rogers' final presentation came after a long holiday, the prospect of which created even more anxiety than usual. Her confidence in the real changes she believed had taken place was so shaken that she gave them her home 'phone number and alerted the GP. In the event, they neither 'phoned her at home nor consulted the doctor. When counselling resumed, they were "strikingly better" and in the following interviews, both talked about Barbara's mother's depression, the losses the old lady had had in her life and her death which was inevitably approaching. Barbara said that, difficult as she had always been, her mother's vitality had helped her to survive losses, too. This led them to talk about the end of their own lives and Barbara to reflect sadly on the guilt and anxiety that had bedevilled them.

The possibility of finishing was actually raised by Barbara soon after they came back after the break when she was feeling optimistic. James at once became depressed and, Mrs Rogers felt, regressed too. When last discussed in the workshop, however, the ending phase had in fact begun; the frequency of interviews had been reduced as a prelude to termination—without protest from the clients.

Mrs Rogers made it clear that she had learned a lot from Mr and Mrs Curtis. They had become important to her and she liked working with older people. Ending would be a loss for her as well. Some of her workshop colleagues remained unconvinced of her resolve. Said one, "you keep saying it's got to stop ... you can be seduced into thinking more will happen ... why not give them a firm ending date now and stick to it?" The discussion again revealed marked variations in personal attitudes as well as some specific agency differences about ending work with clients and patients. For example: "rejoice that things are better ... my inclination is to cut my losses" (senior social worker); "we don't 'finish' with clients, not in this way" (health visitor); "they get better, or they think you're no good, so it resolves itself ... I don't have the experience of having to prepare people to do without me" (GP).

Mrs Rogers' workshop colleagues remained pessimistic about the extent and permanence of change the couple had achieved because of their histories and their age. One of the GPs commented that, from the point of view of the primary care practice, the outcome had to be judged by the frequency and content of subsequent surgery consultations.

Follow-up

There was one further contact with Barbara Curtis a year after counselling ended. Having visited her GP she asked to see Mrs Rogers to thank her for her help (she said she was happier and more relaxed in her marriage than ever before) and to tell her that James was just as difficult as ever! Feeling there was no real distress, Mrs Rogers resisted the implied invitation to open things up again and they parted warmly.

The couple's relationship with the practice then changed; they transferred to another GP in the medical team. James Curtis' attendance at surgery sharply declined, while Barbara continued to consult about six times a year. The new GP thought her hypochondriacal and dealt with her firmly but sympathetically; he felt at ease because, as he put it, "I do not feel particularly threatened by her attendance at surgery". A resurgence of marital stress occurred just before the follow-up and was voiced to the doctor in a joint consultation, but he contained it without involving Mrs Rogers.

Comment

When we consider the reported changes in Mr and Mrs Curtis' relationship— evidently real even if there were periodic relapses, three points seem important.

First, the referral had ensured that James and Barbara were treated as a couple, seemingly for the first time, and they had mainly been seen together. This is not always the technique of choice but it was helpful in this instance because of the nature of their defences against anxiety: denial, splitting and blaming. The threesome interviews evoked a central problem for them in view of their histories, their long-established pattern of interaction and their current situation with Mrs Curtis' elderly mother; but this, too, was potentially helpful provided it could be addressed directly in the course of the work. Mrs Rogers found herself able to do this more effectively than Mrs Wakeford with the Dolbys or Mrs Jameson with the Broadbents.

Second, the change in the counsellor's focus. In spite of the often critical atmosphere, Mrs Rogers could allow herself to be influenced by the workshop. She began, as she had to, where the clients were but came to see that, in the couple's definition of their problem as essentially sexual, a more central issue for them was avoided. This was their fear of living in the present and their propensity to hang onto and concretise their past grievances in terms of their sexual relationship as a way of avoiding the shared present experience of loss and sadness and the missed opportunities in their lives together. Their traumatic early experiences, though formative, were less important as explanation (which, when offered, only supported James' penchant for defensive intellectualisation and self-analysis) than as evidence of wrongs that could not be righted.

The third point to be noted was Mrs Rogers' growing awareness of the mutual importance of her relationship with her clients. Young enough to be their daughter, she was able to sustain confidence in the capacity of her elderly clients for change and to survive their angry despair. The past, which could not be altered, was confronted in the present where there was at least a possibility for them to have some influence over what happened. Conflict between the extremes of pessimism and optimism, idealisation and denigration was a central dynamic for James and Barbara. They maintained the grudge that, but for the other, their idealised fantasies could have been realised. To relinquish them meant facing what each most feared: that their sadness and defensive anger about what had been lost would be overwhelming. They had to be 'held' and helped to continue the struggle to accept that what was possible was good enough—to achieve realistic optimism.

In the inter-professional relationships Mrs Rogers and the practice were specially vulnerable to the couple's unconscious projections since their own situation was inherently conducive to mutual perceptions that were split along the same lines of idealisation versus denigration. The counsellor felt treated as 'wonderful (but amateur)' and regarded the doctors as 'insensitive (but awesome)'. Mrs Rogers' newness in her role and her understandable wish to acquit herself well, on her own behalf as well as that of her agency, can only have added to the problems that inevitably have to be worked through when counsellors or psychotherapists are introduced into general practice (Brook and Temperley, 1976; Graham and Sher, 1976; Wilson and Wilson, 1985). She was determined to protect her relationship with the clients and critical of the doctors' disparagement of them. But she also knew that, as a part-time attached counsellor from a voluntary organisation, she had limited authority and that it was the doctors, not herself, who carried ultimate responsibility for the couple. On the doctors' side, their reported comments and their obvious relief that the troublesome patients were being contained by the counselling can be seen as a measure of the anxiety they felt—unlike the later doctor to whom the couple transferred, who by contrast did not feel threatened.

In the workshop Mrs Rogers attracted envy as well as criticism of the level of work she was undertaking. The extremes of idealisation and denigration were again reflected in the responses of practitioners from other disciplines; dialogue was often as difficult there as she reported finding it with the doctors.

COUNSELLORS, THEIR CASES AND THEIR SETTING

The counsellors

Besides working in two very different settings, they were distinguished from other participants in a number of ways. Although they all elected to take part in the study programme, they were also in effect selected, being almost the whole of the group of trained and experienced staff deemed eligible by their agency. All were part-time (though the volume of work most of them undertook was considerable); and they were volunteers in the sense that they received fees only for hours contributed above an agreed minimum which was unpaid. A grant from a charitable trust covered the cost of the time they put into the study. Some undertook teaching work with other organisations and professional groups, for which they had trained in their own organisation. Two had also trained as marital sex therapists, one of them practising this technique in a local psychiatric hospital on attachment. One became a marriage guidance tutor (supervisor) during the study. All were women who were or had been married and their varied background experience included education, commerce and the arts.

The cases

The counsellors contributed just under a fifth of the total of cases, proportionately more than any other discipline. There was a wide range in terms of the clients' age, socio-economic status and duration of marriage. Most clients presented their problems explicitly in terms of the marital relationship and ostensibly wanted to work at them, even if they were just as uncertain and ambivalent about change as those of other practitioners. In two-thirds of the cases, for example, only one partner (usually the wife) initially came for help and in a quarter only one partner was seen during the work reported. Meanwhile, the psychopathology encountered was varied and could be severe—as the foregoing case studies indicate.

The main source of counsellors' working problems, however, was not the degree of individual disturbance but the nature of the couples' interaction. From the very start counsellors were confronted with overt marital stress that had its roots in the shared emotional preoccupations of couples; they had to appreciate that there was an unconscious meaning and purpose to what one partner expressed on behalf of the other. Such processes stemmed from anxiety and their essentially defensive nature was observable in each of the preceding cases, as was the influence of the marital system on the interaction between clients and counsellors—the caring or helping system.

The setting

This local marriage guidance council was the only non-statutory organisation represented in the study and by far the smallest. While virtually autonomous and self-financing, it was a constituent member of the National Marriage Guidance Council which carried responsibility for counsellor selection, basic and some further training and the maintenance of standards of practice nationally.[1]

As a core group of the local council's most experienced and assured practitioners, these counsellors were in a position to influence its practice and procedures. But they themselves were also inevitably subject to the enduring influence of the organisation's history and traditions.

This history began in 1938, a product of the church's concern for marriage and the family. The organisation became notable for its success in developing a national service based on volunteers and, especially from the late 1960s for its efforts to promote and maintain the skills of its counsellors.

In 1979, however, the report of the Home Office/DHSS working party on marriage guidance drew attention to the strain for the organisation of trying to maintain its base in voluntary service at the same time as it increased its technical competence (Home Office/DHSS, 1979). For example, the 'service would benefit immensely by the retention of those experienced Counsellors whose sole reason for leaving is to go into agencies where they are paid'—and, we would add, acknowledged as professionals. Commending the extensive programmes carried out nationally and locally, the working party also commented:

> the paucity of resources creates difficulties beyond the obvious ones. Inadequate financial support for the work tends to engender a lack of self-esteem and confirms uncertainty about the standing of the work in the eyes of others. It militates against close working links with other agencies ... it reflects what is sometimes felt to be the paradox of the rival demands for confidentiality and co-operation (ibid., p. 34).

Soon after our study took place a review of the organisation led to major changes in its management and public stance, especially at the centre. Whatever the impact of these changes on the institution's culture, however, one of the crucial factors determining its behaviour and mode of functioning will always be the nature of its major task—working with couples experiencing stress in their relationship. That remains even though environmental pressures, relationships and techniques associated with carrying out the task may alter over time, indeed are bound to do so.

CHARACTERISTIC DILEMMAS IN MARRIAGE COUNSELLING

Boundaries and their management

At the level of persons and their relationships, we have seen from the case examples how difficulties arose because psychological boundaries between the partners were blurred. Far from being distinct, as they might superficially seem, each was relating not so much to a separate person as to someone who was effectively part of themselves; to a greater or lesser extent, each was a receptacle for the other's unwanted self. Seen in these terms Mrs Dolby, for example, not only carried her own 'madness' but her husband's as well, while he bore all responsibility for attempts to contain it; each may be said to have had a 'double dose'. It was when Mr Dolby sensed that the work threatened the defensive blurring of psychological boundaries unconsciously agreed between him and his wife that he withdrew from counselling. Meanwhile, the power of this couple to dissipate personal boundaries could be gauged by the influence they exerted on Mrs Wakeford. Long after the work ended, she retained the vivid memory of being invaded and of not being able to be herself when with them. We also saw that the quest for separateness was the major element in the Broadbents' developmental struggle, and how Mrs Jameson had to 'get back inside her own skin' before she could interact effectively with them.

A marriage guidance council is itself an open system. The human problems which account for its existence and which it must import in order to function are therefore certain to exert a major influence on its behaviour. The management of boundaries and the kind and quality of the transactions across them are central issues for the agency as a whole just as they were in the counsellors' cases.

Crossing the threshold

As a voluntary organisation, marriage guidance is free of the specific obligations carried by statutory services; there is no compulsion to admit and work with prescribed categories of case. Although it is a specialised agency its stated aims, tasks and objectives ensure that so long as clients present with complaints arising from relationship problems (usually, but not exclusively with a partner)[2] they satisfy the criteria for admission. Freedom to "discriminate for or against clients", as one counsellor put it, is abjured and in its own way this agency's external boundary was just as permeable as those of the others we consider.

We have seen that clients got into counselling in different ways: via the normal marriage guidance procedure; through personal referral; and through referral by health centre staff, usually doctors. Clients in the first category might have a lengthy wait and be offered a reception interview in an effort to hold the situation until they could be seen.[3] These interviews were not intended as the basis of an initial assessment, however, and some counsellors emphasised that they preferred not to read the record of them, at least until they were into regular sessions. In all three categories, counselling began before a formal assessment was made in every case brought into the study except one—a health centre case known to involve transvestism.

We are not concerned here with value judgements; as Clulow (1985) points out, it is debatable whether and to what extent procedures should be allowed to define agency boundaries. Our purpose is to describe what we found, i.e. the primacy of the individual counsellor over institutional procedures at the point clients crossed the agency's external boundary.

Thus, Mrs Wakeford agreed to see Mrs Dolby, who had avoided the waiting list and a reception interview, with no inkling of the nature of the difficulty she was to encounter nor of a referrer's involvement, hidden until her work was under way. Mrs Jameson was free to accept the Broadbents as a special case and did so because of her colleague's anxiety about them. Though vulnerable to pressure because new to health centre work, Mrs Rogers, like other attached counsellors, was bound to discharge her agency's contractual obligations to the practice by accepting whatever clients were sent to her. Mrs Lambert (chapter 2), who was well established in her health centre, went further. Having once made sure Maggie Cutler was a patient of the practice, she did not hesitate to involve herself with a hitherto unknown client who had made a direct and unconventional approach to her without the prior involvement of the responsible GP.

The counsellor thus had the leading role on the agency's external boundary. In the virtual absence of a procedural threshold, clients' uncertainty, stress and conflict were channelled into the organisation immediately and exclusively via the three-person counselling relationship. In marriage guidance work this pattern is established even if only one spouse attends; with whatever conscious awareness, absent partners are a preoccupation for both client and counsellor since they are an integral part of the disturbed relationship with which the work is concerned.

Tensions in triangular relationships

As we said at the start of this chapter, the management of triangular relationships and the presence of third parties were issues which permeated inter-professional collaboration. They affected all agencies, as we shall see in later chapters, but they were central for the marriage guidance council and its practitioners. It is in the context of three-person relationships that we must explore what we saw as the major focus of anxiety in the counselling task of marriage guidance.

The crucial role in personality development of the child's experience of three-person relationships has long been recognised. Winnicott (1956c, p. 318) summarises the position as follows:

> At the root of neurosis proper is the triangular situation, the relationship between three people as this first appears in the child's life. Boys and girls develop differently at this stage, but there are always two triangles, that based on the heterosexual position and that based on the homosexual position. It can readily be seen that there is great complexity here.
>
> From all these possibilities Freud singled out for study the Oedipus complex and by this term we signify our recognition of the whole of the problem that arises out of the child's achievement of a capacity to be related as a human being to two other human beings, the mother and the father at one and the same time.
>
> It is just here that the major anxieties arise because it is precisely here that the instincts are maximally roused, and in the child's dream, which is accompanied by bodily excitement, there is everything at stake . . .

Marital partners bring to their relationship conscious and, more potently, unconscious residues of their first experience of triangular relationships and the way these were managed, and of themselves in relation to their parents as an interacting pair. The aspects we would emphasise are the child's original longing for exclusiveness and intimacy with one parent and consequent anxiety about the reactions of the other; and its envy, anger and fear arising from being excluded from their shared intimacy. Thus, third parties and the problem of discrimination loom large; someone is always in danger of being left out, or of being kept out. The reader will remember the different ways these themes were re-enacted in each of the cases we have reported.

We see at once that the dominant counselling mode in marriage guidance replicates the primary triangular relationship and how it is that objective features of the work are capable of stimulating feelings in practitioners which are rooted in their own personal experience. This situation is unavoidable (see for example, Balint E, 1959; Bannister, Lyons, Pincus, Robb, Shooter and Stephens, 1955; Sutherland, 1955; Woodhouse, 1967 in relation to marital work). Elements of early ambivalence, impulses both to split and to anneal the parents' relationship as well as to intrude upon it, along with fears of their retaliation, remain alive in practitioners as well as clients; they may be active at unconscious, near conscious or fully conscious levels of the mind. Such a complex of inner-world experience leads practitioners to evolve psychological defences against the ensuing anxiety. It is here that the setting, including the socially organised defences embodied in its culture, comes into play, objectifying and interacting with practitioners' anxiety and their personal defences against it (cf. chapter 1).

The triangle of referral

People seldom seek help with marital difficulties without a third party being involved, and this was certainly true of our marriage guidance series of cases. Only three of them were truly self-referred—as far as the practitioners could tell. Mrs Wakeford's experience with the Dolbys and their hidden referrer was not exceptional. The technically justifiable insistence by the marriage guidance council that clients apply personally for an appointment could give rise to a collusion between referrer and counsellor to avoid contact between them, as we shall also see from the work of health visitors (chapter 6). Also avoided was the vital question in any referral: in whose interests is it being made? This question is vital because each of those involved, the client, the referrer and the receiving agency, has vested interests at stake in the transaction (Clulow, 1985, chapter 2). All share a common problem in the management of deep-seated feelings evoked by exposure to pain and distress. Efforts to be relieved of these feelings can involve defensive manoeuvres that have led one of us to call referral 'the point of maximum dishonesty' (Woodhouse, 1977).

Unravelling this 'dishonesty', facing up to differences between the parties in the triangle of referral, may involve conflicts of interest. When we considered the organisation's boundary management, we noted the absence of intake and assessment procedures that might support counsellors in mastering the anxiety of confronting such conflict. As a result of avoiding it, a legacy could be carried into the counselling work and the caring system. An example of this was Mrs Wakeford's resentment that her agency and therefore herself were expected to rescue those who had instigated Mrs Dolby's application. Both Mrs Jameson's and Mrs Rogers' work was also affected by the absence of initial assessment. The negative effects of avoidance were most evident when the clients' predominant defence was splitting and denial, and it is remarkable how the agencies concerned were then prone to re-enact the clients' defence (cf. Mattinson and Sinclair, 1979)—with painful results for the counsellor.

Despite such secondary effects, however, so widespread was this avoidance of initial assessment that it has to be understood as a socially organised defence (Menzies Lyth, 1970) against the anxiety inherent in confronting differences and the scrutiny of the vested interests of third parties, with its potential for conflict.

Dealing with this anxiety more directly is also complicated by other factors. For example, as a branch of the national organisation symbolising concern for marriage, a local marriage guidance council is open to influence not only from its clients, but also from others in the community including other professionals. Their attitudes will be coloured by what they feel about marital conflict and breakdown—including distress, confusion, ambivalence, rejection and denial. The agency and its counsellors will be the targets for projection of these feelings insofar as they are not consciously acknowledged (see Menzies Lyth, op. cit., for analogous processes relating to hospitals and Miller and Gwynne, 1972, to institutions for the disabled).

When such projections suffuse the process of referral to the agency, part of its task must be to do what it can to ensure that those concerned take back responsibility for what is truly theirs—to avoid collusion. Paraphrasing comments made to us, the view seemed widely held that as a voluntary organisation largely dependent on external support and goodwill marriage guidance needs must respond to the demands made upon it. Behind this seemed to lie the untested belief that to exercise authority and discrimination at the point of referral was to endanger the survival of the agency. An analogy may be drawn with the common fantasy in marriage that an overt expression of difference may lead to conflict which will threaten the relationship. In fact, the reverse is generally true so long as the anxiety involved can be contained.

The triangle of collaboration

Clients confront counsellors with the paradox expressed in the title of Skynner's (1976) book, *One flesh: separate persons*. Some of the working problems arising from the paradox were apparent in the case examples at the beginning of this chapter, none more obvious than Mrs Jameson's uncertainty about whether to see the Broadbents separately or together. Their marriage demonstrated that to be confidently separate, but in relationship, means acknowledging that destructive and creative impulses co-exist in oneself as well as in the other, and carrying responsibility for this knowledge in the interests of a co-operative enterprise. Early experience which has failed to foster basic trust (Erikson, 1965), interacting with current external stress, ill fits a person to sustain the tension involved. Clients bring the burden of this emotional and moral dilemma into their relationship with counsellors who in turn experience it in the work. Thus, when Mrs Jameson saw Emily Broadbent on her own she was left troubled by the secret Emily shared with her but wished to keep from her husband. *The marital relationship itself* is in fact the source of the 'rival demands for confidentiality and co-operation' which the marriage guidance working party (Home Office/DHSS, 1979) thought were bedevilling counsellors' attempts to collaborate with other practitioners.

In the collaborative triangle of the couple, the counsellor and another practitioner or agency there is an interface at the boundary between two different working worlds. What to communicate to and what to withold from those who may be benign collaborators or threatening intruders? In practice, third parties were seldom actually in evidence in the counsellors' reported work. We found that joint work with a practitioner from another agency was reported in fewer marriage guidance cases than in those of any other discipline. All but one where it did occur were seen in health centres. Other practitioners were known to be involved with counsellors' clients in half the cases seen in marriage guidance offices, but there were only two instances of a counsellor getting in touch with them during the work reported—Mrs Wakeford's contact with the Dolbys' GP was one of them, and the other is discussed in chapter 9.

There was no case where the other practitioner got in touch, and this reciprocal tendency was confirmed by cases from the other disciplines in which practitioners evidently steered clear of working relationships with marriage guidance counsellors. This colluded with the counsellors' defensive isolation and will also have defended the other practitioners against the testing of phantasies about destructive intrusion into the 'secret' relationship of couples and between counsellor and client. Mutual support of the defence avoided work at the task of discovering what, in any given instance, would have been a realistic balance between confidentiality and co-operation.

Summary

As a specialist marital agency, the marriage guidance council's task involves its counsellors very directly in a universal human dilemma: the management of triangular relationships.

Marital partners create a primary relationship which is the most direct heir of childhood experience in adult life. Whatever other legacies influence their interaction for good or ill, those arising from the first three-person relationship have a major and distinctive role. The child's struggle towards emotional maturation through real and phantasy relationships with two parents remains unconsciously if not consciously alive in all of us—practitioners as well as clients. The study confirmed that the oedipal situation and its derivatives invariably give rise to primitive feelings and unconscious anxiety in practitioners engaging directly with marital stress and that these are a salient characteristic of the work.

Among the variables influencing practitioners' task performance, some stemming from clients, some from the worker's personality, the capacity of the setting to facilitate and contain the work and its associated anxiety is critical. But when members find the need to defend themselves from task-related anxiety the organisation gets used for this purpose, the defences being embodied in the procedures and policies evolved and sustained by succeeding generations of practitioners.

Ramifications of the tensions involved in triangular relationships in marriage guidance work forced themselves on our attention in the course of the study programme. Organisational patterns were revealed through the cases counsellors brought into it, patterns which came to be understood as institutionalised defences against the anxiety inherent in three-person interaction. They could lead to avoidance or denial, militating against counsellors' mastery of relevant anxiety; and they could be detrimental to inter-disciplinary collaboration, especially when collusively reinforced by the socially organised defences employed by other agencies. They also served to exacerbate counsellors' characteristic uncertainty between the conviction that they could claim a distinctive competence in the marital field and the experience of fragility because of part-time membership of a voluntary organisation.

Notes

1   Local marriage guidance councils contribute financially to the parent body and are represented on its various management and policy committees. Working within nationally agreed policy and with advice available from the centre, local councils nevertheless vary considerably in their operational arrangements and the technical support available to and called on by counsellors. Not all offer reception interviews, for example, and at the time of the study this particular council's links with primary care practices were more extensive than most.

2   The title '(National) Marriage Guidance Council' was made subordinate to a new name, 'RELATE', early in 1988.

3   Waiting lists naturally arise when demand for service outstrips supply; this marriage guidance council had one for almost all of the study. They are, of course, an implicit way of controlling an agency's boundary, reducing demand because of the tendency of would-be applicants to drop out before being seen; reception interviews were introduced to offset this.

5

General practice

General practitioners mostly brought cases to the workshops where marital difficulty or family stress was presented to them explicitly, or where a symptom turned out to be a 'ticket of entry' which soon took second place or was dropped when the relationship problem came into the consultation. In other cases patients proffered conditions which, though of concern medically, seemed to the doctor to be in some way functional in the pattern of their relationships. All these cases exemplified ways in which marital difficulties and related family problems impinge on the work of GPs and the issues these raise for primary care practices. Very few concerned professional collaboration, and we shall consider the significance of this later in the chapter.

Dr Jane Browne, the senior of two GPs in a rural practice, contributed the first of our examples. Perhaps because of the nature and location of the practice and her technique and personality, she knew a great deal about the history and personal relationships of the patients she presented, more than was usual for GPs in this study.

The couple with migraine

Dr Browne said she thought her case relevant to the study for several reasons: Mr and Mrs Bergman had each been seen individually by her for medical reasons, "then suddenly it shifted; there was a crisis in their lives together. In the past they had each been referred for specialist medical help; this time the husband needed to be referred to a psychiatrist to protect him and to protect me from the fears I had about the state he was in, but the marriage work stayed 'in house' . . . the husband presented himself as in need of medical attention, but it is really the relationship that needs attending to."

The Bergmans had become her patients some years before when they came to the locality because of Mr Bergman's work. Both were in their thirties, Mrs Bergman being the older by a few years; before marriage she had had a long-standing relationship from which she had a daughter, now adolescent. Mr Bergman had become a time-consuming and worrying patient. But Dr Browne found them a nice couple, describing him as "gangling and boyish in the relationship" and with herself; his wife had "a very nice face, though plain; a dumpy little mother" but an attractive woman.

Mr Bergman had suffered from migraine since childhood; it had interrupted his schooling and had affected and been affected by his relationship with his parents. For some two years the condition had brought him to the surgery increasingly often, the headaches more and more severe and he more and more desperate. Dr Browne had at one stage referred him to a specialist migraine clinic. She liaised closely with the clinic over the management of her patient's condition which, however, went unrelieved in spite of drugs prescribed at the maximum dosage. The attacks frequently kept him from work; Dr Browne had also noticed that they were worse when he was at home and especially at weekends.

Mrs Bergman had become pregnant a year previously in spite of being fitted with a long-term intra-uterine coil. The GP had picked up that Mrs Bergman felt she had "trapped" her husband by conceiving. She had explained to the doctor that he was firmly convinced that an hereditary factor in his migraine condition precluded their having children; the marriage had been entered into on that understanding. Because of this she made him the arbiter about whether or not the unexpected pregnancy should continue. He urged a termination and, with mixed feelings on Mrs Bergman's part, an appointment was arranged with a consultant gynaecologist. The decision was pre-empted, however, when the pregnancy was found to be located in a fallopian tube and a life-saving operation was performed to end it.

The therapeutic abortion and the sterilisation which followed had been a great upset for Mrs Bergman and involved much uncertainty, clinical and emotional, which was onerous for both patient and doctor. From her presentations it was clear that Dr Browne had seen the Bergmans through the medical complexities with much care and concern.

The family's life had then increasingly come to revolve around Mr Bergman's migraine and his wife's preoccupation with it—his medication, the demands it led him to make on his wife and step-daughter and the restrictions it imposed on their lives; there was little beyond the headaches and his work. Dr Browne knew that Mrs Bergman was often fearful that her husband would do himself an injury or that, if thwarted, the violence "inside his head" might erupt in violence in the home; she felt she and her daughter were at risk. Dr Browne was aware from what she knew of their backgrounds that physical violence as well as violent emotions in close relationships had played a big part in both their histories. Mr Bergman had been repeatedly thrashed by his father until he grew strong enough to defend himself. His mother had reacted to his migraines with anxious and intrusive control. For her part, Mrs Bergman had regularly been knocked about by the father of her daughter and this was eventually what led to her leaving him. In many ways, it seemed to Dr Browne, important aspects of the earlier experience of both partners were somehow at work now in their present relationship.

As she said at the outset of this first report, as far as she was concerned the marital difficulty became overt suddenly. It was as if Mrs Bergman had had enough; in effect, the statement she was making to her husband was: "I will continue to be your wife but not your nursemaid". She told the doctor about events which seemed to have led up to her outburst; there had been no protest about them at the time, yet they implied a "tremendous negation of [her] importance; it was as though she was there to service him but not the other way round". For example, when she went into hospital for the sterilisation, he delivered her there and then left; when she was away convalescing he did not 'phone her as promised, even though he knew she would be anxious about him.

After her outburst, however, the balance of their relationship apparently changed. There followed times when Mrs Bergman might well have left. Dr Browne doubted that she would, but while she herself was obviously fearful of what might happen if she did leave, her husband was increasingly convinced she would go and became very depressed.

One afternoon, Mr Bergman came to the surgery having left work in tears. So beside himself was he and so anxious did he make Dr Browne that she asked for and got an immediate psychiatric appointment for him. The fact that another patient of the practice had recently committed suicide added to her anxiety. Mr Bergman was then seen in the psychiatric unit as an out-patient for some weeks, his wife, too, on occasion. The content of these consultations was not reported, but the stated aim was to "sort out how to manage the migraine"; Dr Browne and her male colleague conferred on the 'phone from time to time. Both practitioners told the patients that they would be talking with each other. The GP said she did not invariably do this, but instinctively felt she should in this case. For her, a major function of the contact with her colleague was to contain her anxiety about the potential suicide risk (Mr Bergman later confirmed that he had indeed seriously considered suicide). She was enormously grateful for the psychiatric unit's immediate and supportive response. But she was at pains to emphasise that, though there was shared responsibility, their contact with each other did not amount to joint treatment. She said she was unclear how it came about that she continued her marital work with the couple rather than attempting to transfer this as well to the psychiatric unit, as she might well have done. It "just seemed natural that I should ... which was odd considering that I referred him in some fright myself".

Dr Browne's description of her patients and her own experience with them readily involved members of the workshop; the *résumé* above results as much from their interplay with her as from her opening account.

There was another GP in the group whose experience led him to be very pessimistic about the treatment for migraine and discussion focused on the influence of this chronic and resistant symptom on the couple's relationship with each other and with Dr Browne. Four themes emerged. First, there was the shared anxiety about intense hostility in personal relationships which had been violently experienced by both partners. Second, it was found helpful to think in terms of an emotional purpose being served for both partners by Mr Bergman's symptom and to move away from the idea of a long-suffering wife being pushed beyond endurance by her husband's excruciating pain and demanding behaviour. As one member put it, it was as if "*both* of them have violent headaches; Mrs Bergman has married hers". The third theme concerned the way the established pattern of their relationship was disturbed by the unlooked-for pregnancy and its sequel. The fourth had to do with the nature of Dr Browne's relationship with the couple. She had survived much anxiety and uncertainty, had stuck with them and felt positively towards them. Meanwhile, she and her colleague at the psychiatric unit had not undertaken joint therapy: each had maintained a different focus. She saw their relationship in terms of containing her anxiety about the suicidal risk. However, their partnership seemed to have effectively conveyed mutual trust to the couple.

> Dr Browne reported again seven months later. Mr Bergman stopped attending the psychiatric unit in spite of her strong recommendation that he should continue— made in the face of his protest that it was so much easier to talk to her. He developed a "false bonhomie" in the joint sessions with her and when she took this up with him he was able to tell her that he did not want to go on with these either; Dr Browne accepted this. He then made it clear that he felt both he and his wife should stop, but Mrs Bergman insisted on taking up the doctor's offer of weekly sessions for herself and came some half-dozen times before an agreed ending.
>
> Dr Browne said the previous workshop discussion, highlighting how Mrs Bergman colluded with her husband, helped her to "get to grips" with the situation in this phase of the work. She asked herself what it might mean "that a nice, warm lady gets herself into a persecuted predicament twice; instead of being a passive comforter I felt I could say, hold on". The minutiae of what went on in Mrs Bergman's interplay with her husband, and her part in it, were gone into. She was able to survive the anxiety generated by his sometimes frantic reactions when, with the GP's support, she opposed his injunctions and demands.
>
> In response to a question Dr Browne said she had never feared Mrs Bergman would withdraw from her. She was "basically fair-minded, so even when the going was rough she seemed to feel I was a benign figure". And as it turned out Mrs Bergman's increasing independence, for example in financial matters, did not bring about the disasters her

husband prophesied. But it was very difficult at times not to be drawn into taking sides, especially as Mrs Bergman seemed to be "the more normal one".

Neither had been seen in surgery for some time and although Dr Browne did not know "how good their relationship is now", the clear inference was that the migraine must be less troublesome.

The presentation and workshop discussion was lively like the previous one. One member commented, "it seems as if by working with her you have treated the migraine". The positive atmosphere was no doubt in part created by what seemed a good outcome of the work and of the group's contribution to it. However, some members ruefully compared the GP's working situation with their own. A health visitor contrasted the doctor's freedom and authority over the use of her time with the constraints she felt herself to be under; a probation officer noted the voluntary element in the doctor-patient relationship, so different from the compulsory nature of his clients' relationship with him. He felt "a greater responsibility [on me] in terms of what a given person can cope with . . . [my clients] don't have the choice not to see me . . . you were free not to chase him; you could shift the equilibrium through her".

Follow-up

Two and a half years after the final workshop presentation, Mr Bergman's migraine had not disappeared but was less onerous, its management being satisfactorily maintained; he was now working well. The couple's relationship had greatly improved; they had moved house but were still registered with the practice and in contact with Dr Browne.

Comment

The underlying features of the Bergman's relationship had much in common with others brought into the study. Recognition of the couple's shared unconscious preoccupation was a key to understanding the roots of the tension between them and of their collusive pattern of interaction. In this, through the defence of projection, each reinforced the other's basic fear—that the aggressive impulses associated with a struggle for personal autonomy would degenerate into destructive violence; autonomy could be achieved only in this frightening and unacceptable way, leaving one isolated.

Before she brought the case to the workshop Dr Browne had already sensed that important aspects of the past experience of both Mr and Mrs Bergman were perpetuated in their present relationship. At that stage, however, the dynamic at work was not appreciated, nor the creative potential of the conflict between them. Meanwhile, Mr Bergman's worsening condition induced in the doctor anxiety similar in kind and intensity to that engendered in his wife—he might kill himself. This focused her attention on him, the threatened and threatening patient. At that stage her anxiety allowed her little freedom to develop her intuitive insight that the violence in the past of both partners was an important part of their marriage. Later she was able to see that Mrs Bergman's propensity to be a victim, to deal with her own unconscious violence by projecting it into her partner, exacerbated Mr Bergman's condition. It should be noted that the pattern had begun to alter spontaneously but, by her questioning response to Mrs Bergman's behaviour and by the containing relationship she afforded, Dr Browne fostered further change in the balance of unconscious forces in the couple's interaction with a positive effect on Mr Bergman's migraine.

This GP could be open and was very much in touch with her anxiety. It is notable that the psychiatric referral, though a defensive move, also helped to contain it; neither the primary patient nor his wife were got rid of. They and their worrying problem were not rejected and Dr Browne felt she should and could continue with them. Then she resisted Mr Bergman's seductive efforts to separate her from her male colleague, and did not press him to stay in the work with her. Thereby she probably avoided a symbolic repetition of the cleft stick which was his childhood pattern—to be caught between his father's harsh treatment and his mother's anxious intrusiveness. Dr Browne's directness seems to have enabled him to be straightforward with her about his wish to withdraw and she was not put out about it. But she recognised his wife's wish to continue and supported her capacity to grapple with her own and their shared problem.

Work with one partner does not always engender change in the marital system, comprised as it is of the couple's interpenetrating personalities. It did so in this case and at least two factors are likely to have been significant. There was the basic integrity of Mrs Bergman's personality, the 'fair-mindedness' which the doctor recognised and which must have helped her resist the tendency to take sides. Then there was the confidence built up between her and *both* patients. She had proved herself to be a trustworthy care-giver, not least during the threatening clinical emergency which had disturbed the marital system's previous state of homeostasis (Jordan, 1968), that is, the pregnancy and its sequel.

A critical and unpredictable medical event had also disturbed a couple's established relationship in the next case—an event of an even more fundamental kind. Dr Joyce, who introduced the case, was an older practitioner, senior partner in a large suburban practice located in a health centre which was a focal institution in the area. He brought it during the early phase of the study when the workshops were composed of members from the same setting. The GPs and health visitors were meeting together.

A matter of life and death

A new episode in Mrs Dixon's long-standing relationship with Dr Joyce (and her even longer one with the practice) had begun a few weeks before the first presentation. She consulted Dr Joyce complaining of sleeplessness. Her rest was indeed disturbed, but he was not surprised that she was soon telling him about problems in her marriage. Though Mr Dixon was also on Dr Joyce's list, a woman partner had seen him in a series of psychiatric emergencies some months earlier which indicated that the relationship was in difficulties. With the marital problem now explicit Dr Joyce offered fortnightly consultations at the end of surgery for Mrs Dixon to talk about the situation. There had been four meetings to date.

The couple were in their mid-thirties and had married some ten years earlier. Mrs Dixon had entered marriage with a severe congenital condition considered to be untreatable and with a life-expectancy not much beyond middle age. She had, however, attended ordinary school and then was able to do sedentary work; she had been sterilised on medical grounds before marriage. By contrast, Mr Dixon was strong and physically active, much taken up with sport at which he excelled.

The critical medical event had occurred some years earlier. After one of Mrs Dixon's regular hospital checks, the consultants had reviewed her condition and decided that advances in knowledge and technique made surgical intervention possible. The result: a virtually complete reversal of her hitherto untreatable disability. However, shortly afterwards, when Dr Joyce had just taken over her care, she had contracted a series of grave but apparently unrelated illnesses. She survived these with what was clearly very considerable clinical help and moral support from him, recovered steadily and was back at work after a few months. Mrs Dixon inevitably became a special and gratifying patient. Her health was regularly monitored by Dr Joyce and she had continued well. A rosy-cheeked, plump girl, she was somewhat overweight but he did not share her worry about it. He had met her husband after her operation and during her subsequent illnesses and had been "greatly impressed by his care and concern ... nothing seemed too much trouble for him".

Following his wife's full recovery, however, Mr Dixon had changed his occupation as well as life-style. The pattern of their marriage altered too; he was increasingly away from home, especially in the evenings. This had seemed to go without remark by his wife who, as far as Dr Joyce could see, accepted the new pattern as simply due to his change of employment and an extension of his sporting activities.

The fact that Mr Dixon began a long-standing affair during this time had only emerged when the practice became involved with him following two serious suicide attempts; this was when he was seen by Dr Joyce's partner, Dr Ward, because of what she described in the notes as "hysterical fugues". Both doctors had concluded that the overdoses had been a "reaction to his double life". Dr Joyce also knew of an "extremely morbid reaction" to his elderly father's death not long after the couple were married.

Mrs Dixon herself had gone to see Dr Ward during the time her husband was attending—at first unaware of his involvement with another woman. In the course of his presentation in the workshop, Dr Joyce saw from the case notes that when this had been revealed Dr Ward had recommended them to seek help from marriage guidance. It was clear that they had not done so and he now thought it odd that Mrs Dixon was apparently not incensed about her husband's affair, either then or later.

In their current fortnightly meetings Mrs Dixon told Dr Joyce her husband had now left home. He returned each week for a couple of hours, but he was uncommunicative, unwilling or unable to do the urgent practical jobs he had committed himself to; the house was in a mess because of things he had started but left unfinished. She had obtained a legal separation and filed a divorce petition, but nothing more had been done about it. Dr Joyce felt sure she was very much in two minds about ending the marriage and would not proceed with the divorce if Mr Dixon "made any sort of positive move . . . she says it's up to him".

They talked about ways to get Mr Dixon to attend surgery; though living away from home he remained a patient of the practice. So, as it was Dr Ward who had seen him in the emotional crisis, Dr Joyce discussed with her the idea that Mr Dixon should be offered the opportunity to see her in sessions which would parallel his own with Mrs Dixon. Along with his concern about the marriage, he was worried about Mr Dixon's emotional state. How depressed was he; what risk was there of a further and maybe successful overdose?

Although the proposal was agreed, both doctors—but especially Dr Ward—were doubtful whether Mr Dixon would accept it. Noting his colleague's view that Mr Dixon was "better off on his own . . . that he was fed up with responsibility", Dr Joyce added, "but this doesn't fit in"—because, by all accounts, the woman with whom he was having an affair was also someone who needed a lot of support.

The presentation was mainly factual; it was difficult for the workshop to get a sense of the feeling tone of Dr Joyce's relationship with Mrs Dixon. There was no continuity in the consultations; "she starts each session afresh . . . no developing theme . . . I feel I haven't had everything yet . . . she appears outgoing but I don't think she has told me the [full story]". The interplay in the group was also stilted. The health visitors mainly asked questions; the other GPs generally made statements.

From the fragmentary workshop discussion, it was clear that members were perplexed by the incongruity of the Dixons' relationship. They were at one with Dr Joyce who thought it "strange that a macho type should link up with a cripple". They also wondered about the fact that in spite of being on Dr Joyce's list he went to Dr Ward in the crisis and that Mrs Dixon followed him to her. The doctors' obvious differences of view and attitude, as well as their apparently limited communication, were remarked on. This led one GP to say that "when they have free access to any doctor they can play games with us". But he later acknowledged that denial was to be expected in Mrs Dixon; "how could she possibly understand his wish to take his own life when her experience has hitherto been that life may be taken away from her?" There was general agreement about the dramatic impact of the change from 'ill' to 'well' and that its implications for the marriage had been difficult for the doctors to recognise;

but when the notion was put forward that there must originally have been an unconscious meaning and purpose in this couple's unlikely choice of each other, it was ignored. Dr Joyce then voiced the fear that if Mr Dixon did resume contact with the practice and the couple were addressed as a pair, there was a danger of "pushing him over the top".

It was some months before the case was heard about again and by then Dr Joyce was part of an inter-disciplinary workshop.

> Having recapitulated his first presentation, he reported that there was "a bit of a battle" when Mr Dixon saw Dr Ward; he was adamant that he did not need any help, and had not been seen since.
>
> Mrs Dixon continued to come regularly. There were no further moves towards a divorce, but the doctor came to believe the marriage was at an end; she had made another relationship and seemed to be settling into it. Because of where Mr Dixon was now living, it looked as if he was bound to move to another practice. The sessions with Mrs Dixon were largely taken up with practical issues; the question of the division of the couple's assets loomed large and Dr Joyce said he was mainly concerned with Mrs Dixon's plans for an independent future.
>
> He was disappointed at this outcome. He had believed there was a possibility of reconciliation—but having recently heard it rumoured that Mr Dixon had constantly had affairs from early in the marriage he now felt his optimism had perhaps been ill-founded. His own notes, made for the study, reflected both disappointment and self-criticism. "I think of her as an extroverted, outgoing girl who gets on well with everyone ... but I've always had reservations ... that there's something she's been keeping back ... an impression difficult to put into words that we've never truly understood each other, or perhaps it is that I've not understood her ... whether she's been able to tell me what's really been going on ... that's my doubt."

A sharp division between the robust and the tender came out in this workshop's response to Dr Joyce and his presentation. There were those who were tough ("there *isn't* all the time in the world") on what they saw as his passive reactive stance and his paternalism; others reacted more sympathetically and were protective of him. Stimulated to respond in different ways, the two factions failed to reconcile or relate to each other's perspectives.

Some members could well imagine that the potentially fatal condition diagnosed in the early months of her life was bound to have affected the development of Mrs Dixon's personality and her mode of relating to others. It must have influenced the way her parents and family treated her and she them— and Dr Joyce's relationship with her seemed to have been affected too. His presentation again suggested that she managed to get herself treated as special; so much had happened over which she had no control. Members also commented on her apparent inability to communicate with Dr Joyce in a "rounded way"—to express "the other and darker side" of what he had seen only as an extrovert personality. But as in the first workshop discussion, the group did not pick up and develop ideas that were mooted about the marital dynamics, for example that the relationship represented an unconscious attempt to deal with a shared problem about survival.

With the marriage assumed to be over and her husband out of the picture, members were exercised about Mrs Dixon. The way she seemed to "keep things out there" led a marriage guidance counsellor to "worry that she won't have learned emotionally" from her experience or through the consultations about her part in what had happened. In response, Dr Joyce said of her, "but there is no self-blame attached at all".

Led by a few members (the majority falling silent) the climate became increasingly strained, critical and directive. A referral elsewhere for psychotherapeutic help was considered but thought to be contra-indicated, Mrs Dixon having been Dr Joyce's long-time patient and firmly lodged in the practice. Instead, Dr Joyce was urged to be more active. Efforts were made to persuade him that it need not be destructive to recognise with her what the change in her health and life might have meant in her inner world and in her marriage, that it "can be a relief if the unspeakable can be said".

A note in the workshop logbook asked: "why was this case brought [back]? Perhaps an unconscious or even conscious wish to change something at the same time as feeling (and making us feel) up against a brick wall".

Follow-up

The case was followed up more than two years later. Mrs Dixon's special consultations had ceased not long after the last workshop presentation and she had not been seen in surgery for more than a year. Dr Joyce was surprised to see from the case notes that she had not even been for her periodic check-up which she had never missed in the past. Mr Dixon was now registered with another practice. It was assumed the couple had parted permanently.

Comment

It is difficult to be sure about the dominant dynamic in the early primary care workshop. Members of the two health professions were guarded with each other in an unfamiliar situation. The stilted atmosphere may have been more a response to this than a reflection from the case and its presentation. Whatever the process, it had the effect of distancing members from Dr Joyce and his dramatic and anxiety-laden material. Only late in the discussion was some attempt made to understand the couple's relationship and the practice's problem in treating them. The doctor's feelings were avoided.

When the mixed discipline workshop became involved, the presenting problem had changed. Mr Dixon was thought to be out of the picture and, convinced that the marriage had ended, Dr Joyce focused on Mrs Dixon. Members followed suit. In this well-established group a reflection of the dominant defences employed by the patient—denial and splitting—was clearly enacted. Some members were critical of Dr Joyce, others gentle and protective. What the two sides stood for seemed to be incompatible and in this they also paralleled the two doctors who were out of touch with one another. And, as if it were intolerable for a senior doctor to be bewildered and at a loss, his self-criticism, uncertainty and no doubt naive disappointment received scant attention. The anxieties prevailing in the two groups may have been different, but the result was similar. As in Dr Joyce's consultations with Mrs Dixon, there was an avoidance of the 'darker side' and a failure to open things up. Although there were some helpful ideas about the probable genesis of Mrs Dixon's way of relating and about the doctor-patient relationship (getting herself protected and being treated as special), the group dealt with the GP's problem and its own anxiety by assailing him with advice and explanation. This raised his own defences and he became like a 'brick wall'. There is an echo here of Dr Joyce's interaction with his patient who, advised in a paternal way, was not able to tell him what was 'really going on'.

Taken together, the two workshop discussions epitomised the emotional problem of reconciling differences and coping with contradictions. In this case these were posed in the starkest terms—life and death, the basic preoccupation of doctors as well as patients, one that is embodied in the practice of medicine.

The picture of the Dixons and their relationship is a shallow one, especially their history before this episode, but there can be no doubt that their attachment to each other had unconscious as well as conscious purposes for each of them. At deep levels of their personalities, managing anxieties about life and death must have been their major shared preoccupation. The enigma of 'a macho type linking up with a cripple' is explicable if it is seen as an attempt by each, through their relationship, to keep in touch with the ultimate pole of difference in the other—she with life that from her birth had been under threat; he with mortality, a 'darker side' of him visible in his prolonged morbid response to the loss of his father as well as his extreme reaction when, with her illnesses cured, his wife ceased to be a suitable receptacle for his projected anxiety.

As far as we can tell, the marriage 'worked' with illness and health distributed between them as they originally were. Mr Dixon's earlier affairs (and they were only hearsay) might be understood as part of a manic defence against his anxiety about death. But the transformation wrought by Mrs Dixon's surgery and her recovery from the subsequent illnesses (themselves perhaps not unconnected psychologically with the great change that had taken place) caused a fundamental shift in their relationship. Mr Dixon literally found himself married to a woman other than the one he had originally chosen—and then had an affair with another damaged woman. For her part, Mrs Dixon not only became a new woman; within two years she was living, not with an apparently lively, active man, but with a deeply depressed one who attempted to destroy himself. Notwithstanding her new-found physical wellbeing, the change involved a significant psychological loss for both partners—of established ways of relating to each other and themselves. *Both* were faced with the emotional problem of what to do with the aspects of their personalities which they had hitherto split off and projected onto each other, even though this apparently proved more of a threat to Mr Dixon than to his wife.

The fact that their interdependent defences were no longer of mutual emotional value had gone unrecognised. Therein lay the big problem for Dr Joyce and the practice. If the Dixons are conceived of as 'two halves of a whole', *both of whom* were struggling with powerful and primitive feelings related to living and dying, then the disparate reactions of the two doctors can only have served to confirm for them in the outer world their anxiety about communication between conflictful aspects of their inner worlds.

It is relevant to compare the Dixons with the Bergmans, especially in the rigidity of their respective mutual defences. When Mr Bergman withdrew, there was enough flexibility for Dr Browne to work with his wife to influence and support developmental change in the marital system. This was not so with the Dixons; their defences were more rigid and extreme in the face of an even more basic anxiety. The fact that Dr Browne had some inkling of the relevance of her patients' earlier experience to their interaction and to the symptoms presented (and that she was not overwhelmed when the couple's defences were in disarray) was important. By comparison, the nature of the Dixons' attachment to each other had been much harder for the doctors to appreciate and, as one workshop member observed, "the trail was pretty cold" by the time Dr Joyce initiated an attempt to relate to them as an interacting pair.

Whilst there were obvious differences between the doctors concerned in these two cases (and in their responses to anxiety at a personal level) the differences between the two practices, in their structure and organisation, were also highly significant. Dr Browne and her colleague in their rural practice each saw their own patients, departures from this regime being minimal. In the busy suburban health centre where Dr Joyce and Dr Ward worked, by contrast, the administrative policy of patient access to any doctor, especially in emergencies, rendered the practice system particularly open to unconscious influence from the Dixons. It was prone to reflect their pattern of interaction, a dynamic based on keeping things separate.

In the two preceding cases, much of our interest was in the marital interaction set up by the spouses' complementary unconscious preoccupations. Dr Browne's case showed the therapeutic advantages of thinking in terms of a 'shared illness'; Dr Joyce's, some of the difficulties for doctors in adopting such a view. The GP series however also included cases in which only one patient presented problems concerning intimate relationships. These focused attention more directly on important aspects of the doctor-patient relationship. One such case was brought into the study by Dr Roberts. He felt the difficulty was "a continuation of previously presented family problems".

The anorgasmic young woman

Angela Samson, in her early twenties, was one of several sisters who had all had difficult relationships with their mother, and whose parents vehemently disapproved of the men they eventually married.

Dr Roberts had first got to know Angela when she sought contraceptive advice during a rebellious adolescence, and later when she became pre-maritally pregnant by her future husband. Her parents had been his patients for many years; her mother, who had been disgusted and ashamed about the pregnancy, was currently a frequent attender at surgery with various resistant somatic symptoms.

Having in due course married and moved away Angela was now back home, with her marriage broken up, and once again Dr Roberts' patient. At consultation, she complained of being anorgasmic except by masturbation.

He decided against referring her for specialist help with her sexual problem because she was now unattached. Instead, he offered her a series of extended consultations at fairly lengthy intervals to "explore more deeply her attitude to her sexuality and her parents [and] her feelings about having to come back [home]". She talked frankly and thoughtfully about her own marriage and that of her parents.

By the end of the series of consultations, Mrs Samson's divorce had been granted (with satisfactory access to the child), she had begun a new steady relationship in which intercourse was enjoyable and she was orgasmic for the first time ever. She had got a home of her own and now had her daughter with her, a move which Dr Roberts had supported.

The notes he made for the study included the following assessment: "the case appears to have closed itself. It is also of interest that her relationship with her mother has improved considerably and her mother's relationship with me is much less defensive; she seems to have benefited from Angela's new-found independence. The case was simplified by the fact that Mrs Samson solved many of her own problems and only required support and encouragement to gain greater awareness and independence. The fact that she formed a new and more satisfactory relationship with a man reinforced this progress; intervention on the practitioner's part was minimal."

The workshop was notable for the way members invoked conflicting theoretical models when discussing Angela Samson's psycho-sexual development. And just as Angela had to struggle to disentangle herself from her family so, along with Dr Roberts, the group found it hard to distinguish between the two; they were intimately connected yet separate. As members wrestled with the concept of permeable personal boundaries in family relationships, especially between Angela and her mother, one asked, "who is the patient here then?"

But the issue that loomed largest arose from Dr Roberts' tendency to exclude himself in his report. A suggestion that he underestimated his influence on the outcome of the consultations, in which he had in effect 'prescribed himself', was challenged forcefully: "Where is the proof that we do anything? . . . there is no way of quantifying [Dr Roberts'] contribution or her improvement." That led back to the problem of personal boundaries, this time between practitioners and their patients and clients. Another medical member voiced the fear of an unmanageable burden if "things were opened up"; for the non-medicals, the fear was of "encouraging dependency".

Follow-up

Two years later Angela was remarried and had made no significant calls on the practice. Her mother was strikingly better and her attendances less frequent.

Comment

Like Dr Roberts, the workshop tended to focus on and speculate about the close interaction between Angela Samson and her mother, especially the fact that the latter's 'illness' (the quotation marks are Dr Roberts') seemed to have remitted as Angela became more independent. But the most striking feature of the workshop discussion itself was the lack of mutual influence between the group and Dr Roberts. For example, his work with Angela had ended by the time he presented it—a *fait accompli*. Unlike the earlier examples there was therefore no chance of affecting it. Meanwhile, details of the consultations were neither given nor elicited; members were content to accept the sexualised material couched in broad terms and responded to it theoretically—they kept at an emotional distance from it.

It was when Dr Roberts' view of his role in the consultations was questioned that the group came to life and revealed the underlying anxiety; evidently it lay in precisely that issue of reciprocal influence across permeable personal boundaries which members had ostensibly been so interested in as between Angela and her mother, i.e. when remote from themselves. Our own view remains that the doctor's contribution was far from 'minimal' in this case. Unlike her parents, he showed from the first that he was not threatened by Angela's 'bad' feminine sexuality, and he did not reject her by referring her elsewhere. In spite of his struggle to distinguish what belonged to her and what to her mother, he related to her in her own right; and he demonstrated positive concern towards her. Angela, who had chosen to come back as his patient, obviously responded to this and their work together proved mutually rewarding.

Dr Roberts' overt reason for having the case discussed was to gain a better idea of 'the family problem' and of the connection between the presenting symptoms of mother and daughter. But perhaps another important reason was to test out uncertainty about taking an explicitly psychotherapeutic role with patients. He had no doubt about investigating the private intimate problems the patient presented to him. But, having done so, he was most reluctant to acknowledge his personal influence and potency in engendering change.

Drawing attention to the importance of Dr Roberts' relationship with Angela Samson enabled the initial defensive response of the workshop to give way to an expression of members' underlying anxiety about personal involvement with clients or patients, especially the widespread medical fear of 'opening things up'—a telling phrase with its echo of surgical intervention.

Dr Roberts' uncertainty about the psychotherapeutic value of his consultations and, by implication, about the potential of the doctor-patient relationship in this regard, was by no means unique in the GP series of cases. For example, another doctor gave an account of work with a widow in her eighties. Having established that nothing organic accounted for the symptoms she complained of, he said the patient made it plain that "she wanted to talk more widely than the purely physical so I thought, let's give it a go and see where it takes us". The presenting symptom having cleared up completely, he brought the case to the workshop during a succession of fortnightly, half-hour sessions, the longest sustained contact he had yet had with a patient. The sensitive old lady used the consultations to review with him her life, her family and her marriage. His report made it clear that he asked questions reflectively and in an involved way, sometimes drawing attention to inconsistencies. In effect she 'rewrote her story' as her life approached its close. Yet he, too, was at pains to minimise his contribution, saying that he "gave very little direction or comment . . . I was just a listener and [to his workshop colleagues] I'm largely her mouthpiece here". Passivity was not typical of him judging by his other work.

THE DOCTORS AND THEIR CASES

Doctors in the study came from urban and rural primary care practices ranging in size from single-handed ones to large partnerships. They also varied in training and experience from those relatively new to general practice to those nearing retirement, the majority being in mid-career. Ten GPs participated, seven throughout, and they contributed twenty-nine cases, just over one fifth of the total. They had responded as individuals to the invitation to join the study programme. Whatever else led them to do so, they all had a particular interest in the part played by relationship problems, especially marital stress, in their work. In the main, they were doctors who defined their role in general medical practice broadly. In this sense they were probably an unrepresentative group.[1]

As GPs they lived with a particular kind of uncertainty. Several contrasted their work in primary care with hospital medicine, with its emphasis on the quest for precise diagnosis and speedy treatment. By contrast the GP has usually to bide his time. Because he is involved with the whole person rather than specific bodily systems, the many variables—constitutional, emotional and social—in the genesis and unfolding pattern of disorder usually preclude speed and precision.

The dilemmas and working problems raised by the cases previously discussed were echoed in different ways throughout the GP series. Basically they came about, like those of practitioners in other settings, because unconscious internal conflicts had been externalised and acted out in marital and family relationships. Difficulties arose in all professional settings when tensions emanating from the inner worlds of those within a relationship system combined with stress in the outer world to overwhelm the resources of one or both partners. But people going to doctors had defined themselves as *patients* and usually made an initial presentation which qualified them as such. In only two cases was there no obvious 'ticket of entry' in the form of a symptom and in one of these the patient opened the consultation with the remark, "I'm not sure whether I should be here or at marriage guidance".

We should note here, too, that many of the presenting problems in the episodes doctors brought into the study were serious and of real concern. Besides the first two cases discussed earlier, there were others involving suicide risks or attempts, clinical depression, psychotic breakdown, addiction and serious violence. Forty per cent of GP study cases were of this sort. Although those taking part were bound to want to discuss their most worrying and perhaps dramatic cases, the figure suggests the salience of anxiety-provoking situations in the work of GPs, coming as they did from a wide range of primary care practices.

Patients presenting initially were mainly adult women; a few were men, and there were two couples who first attended surgery together. In only one case was a marital difficulty first revealed through the treatment of a sick child—though there were children under eighteen in all but three of the patients' families. This is not to say that children were not affected by their parents' difficulties or were inactive in their family systems, but the young were rarely prominent in the reported material or the work. The focus was on the adult patient(s) who consulted.

BOUNDARIES AND THE MANAGEMENT OF ANXIETY IN GENERAL PRACTICE

In their study cases the GPs were generally involved in long-term, if episodic, relationships with patients. As we have seen, policy in their practices varied as regards patient access to particular doctors, but the doctor-patient relationship was most frequently a continuing one; and it could be for life. A move away from the practice area or death were the most likely reasons for severing it. In spite of GPs' autonomy and control *within* their work, which contrasted with that of most other practitioners, work patterns were unpredictable. Indeed, it sometimes seemed that the external boundaries of their agency systems eluded efforts to manage them because of the pressure from patients. Excusing his late arrival and early departure from a workshop meeting one GP commented, "ours is an 'on demand' service". Doctors in the study varied as to how much they evidenced this primacy of patient demand, and other practitioners, too, were sometimes absent when they had to choose between calls on them from their agencies and the requirements of the programme. But only doctors were 'bleeped out' of their workshops and had meetings disrupted by 'phone calls which were invariably responded to.

This was, then, a group of committed GPs who made a ready response to patients and, as we have seen, not only in medical emergencies. However, they generally had limited knowledge of patients' social histories and personal lives in spite of their special interest in marital stress and the relational context of illness and, for some, a psychotherapeutic bent. What we called the 'shallow picture' Dr Joyce had of the Dixons' background and marriage was not exceptional. Getting involved with emotional stress could threaten established boundaries between doctor and patient. One GP explained his doubts about going into a woman patient's marital difficulties (which seemed to be related to the condition she was presenting) by saying that they were bound to meet out of surgery because he regularly passed her house when walking his dog. This had apparently been easy to manage when the focus was on her physical ailments.

Somatic and emotional disturbance tended to raise different issues for doctors; treating physical illness was 'safer'. It should be remembered that practitioners in other disciplines were also attempting to extend the range of their practice and were faced with doubt and uncertainty in doing so. Any of them could feel threatened by involvement with their clients. The workshop discussions of Dr Roberts' work with Angela Samson and of the case involving the elderly widow were only two of the occasions when the issue was made explicit. But it was an issue that had special connotations for doctors.

A medical dilemma: conflict between 'closeness' and 'distance'

All practitioners tend to evolve a comfortable mode of relating to clients or patients according to their personalities, and the way they experience anxiety in inter-personal relationships generally and professional relationships specifically. There is, however, an element in the relationship between doctor and patient that distinguishes it from that of most other practitioners with their clients. By virtue of their role in the treatment of physical illness, doctors are sanctioned to have direct contact with and to intrude into their patients' bodies. For them, there can be closeness of a kind very few practitioners, except nurses, may enter into. Doctors thus have to manage a special boundary between themselves and patients—and by their training, especially initial training in hospitals, have been schooled to do so. As Menzies Lyth said of the work of nurses, the doctor's task is liable to stimulate 'strong libidinal and erotic wishes and impulses which may be difficult to control', as well as a whole gamut of powerful feelings evoked by the treatment of illness and the patient's search for cure. The objective reality of the work has the capacity to stimulate unconscious phantasies that 'exist in every individual in the deepest and most primitive levels of the mind' (Menzies Lyth, 1970, p. 46).

From the medical student's introduction to medicine and clinical practice the distinction between him or herself and the patient has to be strenuously maintained in the interest of professional detachment and to avoid personal identification.[2] It is true that, by comparison with medical students' concentrated experience of acute and serious illness in hospital, that of doctors in general practice is diversified by the array of patients and conditions they treat ranging from infants to the elderly, from the well to the ill, from grave to trivial ailments, from routine consultations to life-threatening emergencies. But early professional training is formative. Even though more recently qualified practitioners may well have been more exposed to human relations issues and the emotional aspects of illness in their training than their seniors were, the psychological as well as the functional imperative to maintain a firm boundary between doctor and patient is enduring. The imperative has its roots in the treatment of physical illness in individual patients, and in traditional medical science, including psychiatry, with its reductionist rather than systemic frame of reference (Sutherland, 1980).[3] The boundary makes for emotional distance between doctor and patient; it helps to create conditions in which the encounter may be depersonalised.

At the same time, the doctor's relationship with the patient is also an exclusive one. One indication of this for us was the high level of concern some GPs expressed about confidentiality, especially early in the study; one case was withdrawn on this account. As far as we know, it was only doctors who talked with patients about their wish to discuss their material in groups which included those from other professions. The boundary around the doctor-patient relationship and the preservation of its exclusiveness becomes a personal as well as a professional responsibility.

Singular conflict and tension is thus built into the relationship which embodies a paradox: the need to maintain a firm boundary between *doctor and patient at the same time as a tight one is preserved around* their intimacy as a pair, protecting it from intrusion from outside.[4] All of this of course is part of the stock in trade of experienced doctors, taken for granted by them and mostly by all of us in our role as patients. But these paradoxical aspects of the medical role and task and of the doctor-patient relationship cannot be taken for granted if the dilemmas GPs face when responding to patients' emotional problems are to be understood.

Anxiety and defences in general practice

Although the study provided some opportunities for observation (see chapter 9), we made no systematic study of the doctors' working lives. But from their participation in the programme, we were left in no doubt about the relevance to GPs of Menzies Lyth's observations on the work of nurses. The gravity of the presenting problems in many of the cases they introduced and the bombardment by patient demand they and their practices could face have been noted. Projection into doctors by other professionals of their own conflict and anxiety about illness was also a feature of the workshop groups. Medical training may foster omnipotence, but programme members including ourselves sometimes encouraged it. Power in matters of life and death is attributed to doctors; their associated fear of 'missing something' was pointed out to us—one that is increasingly onerous as the climate grows more litigious. This adds up to a formidable burden of responsibility. The particular quality of primitive anxiety which the doctors' primary task is bound to stimulate emphasises the defensive as well as the functional aspects of the distinct boundaries within, and around, the doctor-patient relationship, which are enshrined in medical practice and tradition.

This defensive structure attempts to combat the inevitable tendency towards a lack of distinct psychological boundaries in intimate personal relationships. An intimate personal relationship aptly describes the potential and often the actual relationship between doctor and patient. The boundary between them is therefore highly functional insofar as it reinforces the psychological distinction between the 'self' and the 'other'. In the study, however, once GPs were explicitly into the area of emotional upset and marital and family stress this psychological boundary between doctor and patient was liable to be disturbed. Fresh uncertainties and anxieties could be introduced when active consideration had to be given to the impact on the doctor of the patient's way of relating and to their interaction if the difficulties were to be understood and helped. That was clear in Dr Joyce's case. And, as we have emphasised, GPs could often be at pains to deny their personal influence in engendering emotional change in patients when in fact the relationship had evidently been highly influential.

The exclusive boundary around the doctor-patient relationship is equally functional, as a protection of the patient's privacy. But this, too, can be disturbed in cases of emotional stress when it is recognised that the boundary of the patient as an individual has to be redrawn so as to make the trouble comprehensible. The patient has to be conceived of as including aspects of the personalities of the other(s) without whom he or she is incomplete in a dynamic psychological sense. Significant others are not then separate entities to whom the patient merely reacts for good or ill, but are integral to his or her psychic economy. If the person is seen as an open system and part of a larger one by virtue of close relationships with others, then these others have always to be borne in mind. They have to become part of the consultation, as it were, if their meaning and purpose in the patient's inner as well as outer world are to be understood. These others are, however, outside the conventionally closed boundary of the doctor-patient relationship (and they may be seeing another doctor in the same or another practice as was Mr Dixon in Dr Joyce's case). As workshops repeatedly protested, who then is the patient? How is the boundary of the caring system to be defined?

In the study, the implication of a systemic view of the person was not that effective help invariably required both partners or other members of the family to be seen and worked with together; the work with the Bergmans and Angela Samson showed this not to be so. Its significance lay in the challenge it presented to traditional conceptual boundaries and to the doctors' established professional defences against anxiety. The challenge and the uncertainty arising when an attempt is made to modify defences against anxiety were reflected in GPs' comments. The fear was frequently voiced that one might be over-whelmed by the patient; what might ensue if one "lifted the lid of Pandora's Box" as one doctor put it? At the same time there was uneasiness and guilt about an acknowledged tendency to 'dodge issues'; about failure to explore informed 'hunches' on matters other than strictly medical ones which were part of the patient's presentation; about the defensive 'medicalising' of consultations. There were misgivings about seeking refuge in the belief that, because of the continuing relationship with patients, one could 'wait and see'.

For any practitioner, defences against anxiety are an amalgam of personal characteristics and those that have been built into common professional practice over time as a way of dealing with task-induced anxiety. For doctors, unconscious as well as conscious personal defences are required to manage the tension inherent in their paradoxical situation. The way such psychological mechanisms evolve and are reflected in behaviour is a highly personal matter, part of the personality of the practitioner and therefore an aspect of his or her technique. At this personal level there are few practitioners as idiosyncratic as doctors; but it is also true that in no profession are socially structured *collective* defences more firmly established than in medicine.

Within this discipline, with its highly developed sense of professional authority, GPs have chosen to function in small, largely autonomous units in primary care. The work GPs brought into the study showed that these units differ widely, each group—each practitioner—articulating the common theme of their profession's socially structured defences in distinctive ways. Dr Browne's and Dr Joyce's cases reflected such differences (see also Dr Sanders' case in chapters 2 and 9). The doctor-patient encounter is thus not to be understood solely in terms of the interaction of the two parties but also in terms of the part played by professional culture. While this can facilitate task performance it can also powerfully inhibit it.

INTER-DISCIPLINARY COLLABORATION

The significant point about inter-professional collaboration in the cases contributed by doctors is that hardly any was reported, even by way of referral —the most characteristic medical relationship with another practitioner. It is certainly open to GPs to try and resolve the personal and professional dilemmas that can arise for them in dealing with psycho-social problems by referral, either within the agency—to a counsellor or social worker if one is attached to the practice—or to a visiting specialist or a therapeutic organisation outside. These were predominantly not the solutions sought by GPs in their study cases, however.[5] None of the practices involved had an attached social worker as far as we know. First one and later a second practice had marriage guidance counsellors working in them during the study, but they were not involved with the cases doctors presented. The Bergmans had a short spell of psychotherapeutic work in another medical setting but this was alongside the GP's marital work and, in general, referral 'out' was a question rarely raised by doctors as a means of getting the emotional trouble looked after elsewhere. When it did come up in the workshops the proposal was generally open to question, as in the discussion of Dr Joyce's and Dr Ward's work with the Dixons, for example.

Three doctors presented cases in which their practice health visitors (also members of the study programme) were involved. The amount of contact between the two varied from the close to the minimal, and as in Dr Sanders' case it was the health visitor who liaised with other non-medical agencies with or without reference to the doctor (see also chapter 6).

In only one reported instance was a doctor invoked by a non-medical professional from outside the primary care team, and there were only five other cases in the GP series where workers in other agencies were known by the doctors to be in current contact with the patients or their families (four probation officers and one social worker). There was no significant communication with any of them, the work of the respective practitioners being independent of each other. The study series as a whole confirms the impression given by the doctors' cases taken alone, namely that if GPs seldom communicated with outside non-medicals, non-medicals outside seldom communicated or engaged with them.

This reciprocal lack of interaction between practitioners in the interests of clients and patients for whom responsibility was shared lies at the heart of the problems we are concerned with. The defensive patterns of non-medical practitioners and agencies, discussed elsewhere, are equally involved in the triangular relationship arising when collaboration is attempted (or avoided). Here, however, interest centres on the part played by primary care doctors in what amounts to a collusion. It was clear that for most doctors the main object of participating in the study was to explore the implications for their own practice of direct work with marital and related family stress—rather than issues about referral to specialised agencies, for example, or problems of collaborating with non-medical practitioners concerned with related difficulties which affected their patients or their families. These were clearly not considerations which led the majority of our doctors to bring cases into the study even though problems of collaboration were part of its brief. For the GPs, inter-disciplinary collaboration was mainly by association in the work of the mixed discipline workshops and other events in the study programme.

How is the dearth of transactions between doctors and those in other disciplines outside their practices to be understood? What can be concluded from the fact that so little was heard about the subject from medical members?

Boundary issues are sharply raised by collaboration, and the tight boundary doctors maintain around their relationship with patients is bound to militate against effective working relationships with other professionals. As we noted above, the medical preoccupation with confidentiality, though a manifestation of the 'closed system' view of the doctor-patient relationship, also expresses an ethical principle. This principle may be thought to gain further justification in practice when there is ignorance about third-party practitioners, perhaps uncertainty about their professional integrity or about the implications for them or their agencies of information revealed, even if incidentally, in the course of a working relationship. These and other aspects of the problems collaboration raises for doctors emerged anecdotally during the study. Doubts were widespread about the practicality of closer working links with those from other disciplines outside their practices. Several doctors spoke of difficulty in mobilising resources or help for patients from social services and were impatient and exasperated at the "bureaucratic" responses of some agencies; some said they were reluctant to involve practitioners they did not know, people who in any case might move from their area without warning before a piece of work was completed. But others went beyond practical difficulties and were sceptical—even openly hostile—about the idea of joint work. One GP described such collaboration with other professionals as "a recipe for the dilution of responsibility" (we were unaware at the time that this phrase was a quote from Balint's work which we refer to below).

We should note here that although some of the doctors' comments about other agencies were clearly based on experience they also reflected underlying anxiety and untested assumptions. It is telling that, having developed respect and trust in the course of the study programme, a number of GPs expressed the intention of working with their now familiar non-medical workshop colleagues from those same agencies when a suitable opportunity arose. We learned of several instances where this was happening well after the fieldwork was completed.

In his study of the doctor-patient relationship and his extended training-cum-research with GPs, Michael Balint (1964) became aware of the defensive processes at work because the burden of responsibility where illness is concerned can be 'much too great . . . everyone including the patient naturally tries to lighten it' (p. 93). Medicine has created mechanisms and institutions to facilitate *dilution of that responsibility* through referral in order to deal with the anxiety of a 'crisis of confidence' when GPs (or their patients) feel they are not knowledgeable or skilled enough at a particular juncture (ibid., p. 69). Dr Browne's urgent referral of Mr Bergman's migraine had this quality, as she very candidly made clear; even though she did not let go responsibility she was 'enormously grateful' to be able to spread it. This followed the established pattern, noted by Balint, for the crisis to be contained and the dilution of responsibility to be effected through collaboration *within the boundary of medicine*.

The work Balint reported was undertaken a quarter of a century ago. There have been many changes since then; for example, technological advances have been dramatic in medicine as elsewhere and have brought their own 'side effects' as witness the transformation of Mrs Dixon's life with its unpredicted repercussions on her marriage. The status of general practice vis-a-vis hospital medicine has improved, as has GP training. Meanwhile, the holistic movement in medicine has become substantial enough to support a professional journal, and Balint's general practice work has been developed nationally and internationally. The GPs in the study showed the influence of all these developments; in particular, their participation represented the continuing quest for what Michael and Enid Balint have called 'a deeper level of diagnosis' (see, for example, Balint, 1967; Balint and Norell, 1973).

Change, however, has in no way diminished the anxiety and uncertainty associated with the GP's task of treating illness. Overall, the task is more complex rather than less, responsibility heavier rather than lighter as more factors have been found relevant to effective diagnosis and treatment. Developments in the last two decades, including the proliferation of specialisms, have not reduced the importance for GPs of the medical profession as an entity. It is this which constitutes the doctor's 'sentient group', the term used by Miller and Rice (1967) to denote the source of emotional as well as professional support and belonging.

The dilution our GP referred to critically was that of sharing responsibility for treatment with non-medicals. With this went doubt and uncertainty not just about working with someone with a different professional bias or about the potential pressure from patients to keep practitioners divided, but also, by implication, about managing the 'not knowing' inevitable in such a medical/ non-medical relationship. The only exceptions, for a few doctors, were their 'own' health visitors, who were located within the boundary of the practice and understood (if they did not always share) the medical culture.

By contrast, practitioners from an outside non-medical agency are members of and have allegiance to a different social defence system and organisational culture from the GP. As outsiders they are liable to pose a threat to the defence embodied in the exclusive boundary around the relationship between GP and patient. Although the threesome of GP/consultant/patient is vulnerable to conflict, as Balint found, at least the dilution of responsibility remains within the familiar medical field. The threesome of GP/non-medical/patient, on the other hand, takes the doctor into unknown territory and threatens a much more radical loss of sovereignty. It is not surprising, therefore, that communication and collaboration with outside practitioners tended to be avoided by GPs; nor, since there was clearly a collusive element at work, is it plausible that medicine was alone in creating institutional mechanisms embodying the defensive use of professional boundaries.

We suggested earlier that the GPs who participated in this inter-disciplinary study were probably exceptional. Their interests and their view of their task had taken them into the area of stress in inter-personal relationships so far as their work with patients was concerned. Yet this interest did not seem to extend to professional relationships, and they had the same problems as doctors generally when it came to collaborating with other practitioners. Thus, although they adopted a wide definition of their clinical role, they remained members of an ancient and powerful profession, having a highly developed sense of autonomy; they shared its culture of independence. Within that culture, GPs have chosen to be independent contractors to the National Health Service. For them, the context and climate of their day-to-day practice militates against a conception of themselves as part of a multi-disciplinary network with the mutual exposure that effective collaboration entails. Their situation is also one in which they can easily be isolated from other doctors as well as from non-medical colleagues; there are formidable practical obstacles to inter-professional communication and collaboration, not least because the patterns of work in different institutions rarely harmonise. Real as these problems are, the overall picture from the study reflects their exploitation by GPs as part of an established social defence against anxiety, one that has its roots in the nature of patient care.

SUMMARY

An exploration of boundary relationships and their defensive use is central to an understanding of the problems faced by primary care doctors in work with the relationship difficulties presented by patients, and in their own working relationships with other practitioners.

Unconscious as well as conscious anxiety is inevitably induced by the GP's task of treating illness. Personal and institutional defences are mobilised against the anxiety which is accentuated by doctors' peculiar responsibilities in matters of life and death. As a result of this burden, they can be a prey to omnipotence as well as a prime object for the projections of those outside the profession—whether in the role of patient or fellow professional.

As with practitioners and clients in the caring professions generally, the preferred working distance between doctor and patient is a product of and varies with the 'chemistry' set up by the interplay of the personalities involved. For doctors, however, there is special imperative for firm control of the boundary between them and their patients. Behind the formulated ethical code governing the doctor-patient relationship lies the doctor's need for emotional distance as a defence against anxiety arising from identification and entanglement with the ill patient—to protect the doctor from invasion by the patient as well as the patient from trespass by the doctor.

When doctors elect to involve themselves explicitly with patients' expressed emotional problems a further element of uncertainty and therefore of anxiety is introduced. The open systems nature of the interplay between them becomes overt. The mutual influence of doctor and patient as well as the practitioner's subjective experience, i.e. the 'feedback' processes at work in open systems, themselves require scrutiny and understanding in the interests of diagnosis and treatment. To recognise interpenetration at the personal level in this way is at odds with closed system thinking and tends to threaten customary professional defences against anxiety.

Alongside the maintenance of a firm boundary between doctor and patient, the medical code of practice also supports the notion of the doctor-patient relationship as exclusive. This, too, is protective of both doctor and patient with the aim of creating conditions necessary for effective treatment, but the boundary can also be used defensively. A shift from a closed to an open systems approach calls into question deeply entrenched modes of thought and behaviour, especially for doctors. Important others in the patient's life have metaphorically to be included in the consultation—sometimes actually so. Redefinition of the boundary of the person is, in itself, apt to engender conflict, uncertainty and anxiety. Doctors have ready recourse to a powerful defence against these feelings in the guise of established medical practice and tradition.

Faced with the heavy burden of treating illness and of coping with patients' projected anxiety, GPs accept that responsibility may be diluted by referral within the practice or to specialist medical services. But while there can be interdependence within the wider medical system, the boundary between it and other professional systems tends to be impermeable and the medical system itself more a closed than an open one. In practical terms, open systems thinking at the very least requires 'mental space' for other practitioners outside the medical system to be held in the mind.

The presence of GPs in this inter-disciplinary study can be seen as a move on the part of participating doctors to explore what is involved in re-drawing the boundaries of their work. But change in patterns of relationship within and between social systems is notoriously slow and fitful. This can be better understood 'if it is seen as the resistance of groups of people unconsciously clinging to social institutions because change threatens existing social defences against deep and intense anxiety' (Menzies Lyth, 1970 p. 62).

Notes

1   Our attention was drawn to an interesting and telling distinction between GPs by Dr Peter Pritchard whose writings on training and management in general practice led us to consult him when setting up the study. There were, he said, "patients' doctors and doctors' doctors"; he felt sure only the former would respond to our invitation to participate.

2   A joke is often made of the fact that medical students tend to believe they suffer from every new disease they study. Early in his career one of us (DW) was puzzled by the contrast between different groups of medical students on attachment to a department of social and industrial medicine. Those whose next placement was to be in the maternity unit were interested and open to learning—whereas the alternating groups, due to move to morbid anatomy were invariably disengaged and impossible to teach. It was some time before it was realised that apprehension about their first experience of cadavers had closed their minds. A GP approaching retirement (not one of the study doctors) told us he had become increasingly preoccupied about his own health when treating his older patients.

3   'Opposed to the psychodynamic approach (i.e. one that takes into account the powerful role of unconscious motives) are various positions held by psychiatrists, psychologists and social scientists. These usually start from what is asserted as a scientific approach, one which assumes that theories about the origin and nature of the essential forces determining our attitudes to ourselves and others must be founded upon what is *real*—by which is usually implied some physical process in the nervous system. No-one can doubt that the mind is an activity of the brain, but the assumptions that are seldom questioned are that the highly complex factors operating at the personal level can be reduced to these "simpler processes". Modern biology has long moved from such reductionism . . .' J D Sutherland, personal communication.

4   This includes intrusion from other medicals. Doctors may not poach their colleagues' patients or interfere in their treatment. Specialists may be invited by GPs to give opinions or advice or undertake treatment, but it is the GP who has continuing responsibility for patient care.

5   The many issues raised by these solutions which aim to invoke specialist skills are therefore largely outside the scope of this chapter. Some were addressed in chapter 4 from the reverse point of view, i.e. of marriage guidance counsellors attached, as specialists, to primary care practices. Readers interested in this mode of interdisciplinary collaboration can refer to a considerable literature mainly concerned with general practice and social work. See, for example, Clayton (1963-65); Foreman and Fairbairn (1968); Ratoff and Pearson (1970); Harwin *et al.* (1970); Cooper (1971); Goldberg and Neil (1972); Ratoff (1973); Ratoff, Rose and Smith (1974); Brook and Temperley (1976); Graham and Sher (1976); Parsloe and Stevenson (1978); Gilchrist *et al.* (1978); Meacher (1979); Huntington (1981); Corney and Clare (1982); Heisler and de Groot (1984); Wilson and Wilson (1985); Sheppard (1986).

6

Health visiting

Health visitors comprised the largest contingent of practitioners in the study. All sixteen of them were based in primary care practices; between them, they contributed thirty-two cases, just under a quarter of the total series. Two-thirds of these preoccupying cases arose directly out of the routine home visits health visitors made following the notification of a birth to any patient of their primary care practices. Most cases had not been active for long, though some families were known from the time of a previous birth and there were long-standing relationships with some half-dozen 'problem families'. A few arose either from the geriatric side of the health visitor's work or as a result of her practice's involvement with chronic illness or other difficulty with which she had been asked to help.

We begin by discussing in some detail cases which particularly illustrated interactive processes in the health visitors' work and the problems of addressing them. Miss Inskip's case, the beginning of which was referred to in chapter 2, was one such; it repays further examination, especially because early clues were so insistently given.

To recapitulate, this health visitor started visiting a mother in her early thirties whose first baby had been born prematurely and was remaining in hospital for the time being. The summary in chapter 2 emphasised Mrs Batchelor's anxiety—in Miss Inskip's view, abnormally high even allowing for the circumstances of Jenny's birth. Her client's anxiety communicated itself to her in a way which seemed to blinker her to the couple's marriage and its possible relevance to Mrs Batchelor's obvious dilemma about her baby—even though she had implicated her husband in her first meeting with a completely strange health visitor.

Miss Inskip's subjective experience of her early interviews with Mrs Batchelor was that she ought to be doing something more or different—if only she knew what. She felt at a loss. She consulted the couple's GP and her own health visitor colleagues but found their responses out of touch with her own sense of uneasiness. The parallel between Miss Inskip's experience and that so anxiously expressed by her client, i.e. uncertainty and lack of support, was striking.

Looking again at the early material we notice its ambiguity. For example, there was the fact that although the Batchelors had planned the pregnancy, they had also intentionally delayed it for a long time. We do not know why, but we put forward the hypothesis that the arrangement whereby both worked and led relatively separate and independent lives must have suited them both, emotionally as well as practically. It is reasonable to suppose that they had mixed feelings about becoming parents, an event which, as we put it, involved Mrs Batchelor '... exchanging her independence in a dual-career marriage for a more dependent role with a totally dependent baby'. She may have experienced and expressed it more directly than her husband, but Frank Batchelor's traditional attitude that children were 'women's work' doubtless masked his own anxiety that becoming a father could involve him as well in having to cope with dependency. Although on this view his anxiety sprang from the same source as hers, his attitude could only serve to confirm her fears that he would not support her—in spite of the belief she also expressed that he was committed to her and the baby.

Again, though the pregnancy was a planned one, Mrs Batchelor protested that both she and her husband were singularly ill-equipped to cope: 'neither of us has had any experience with children'. Alongside this feeling of being ill-prepared to have a baby, the abrupt loss of her full-time job made her aware of how isolated she felt from friends and neighbours, i.e. her sense of dependency was awakened. We also recall that the decision to have a child followed the deaths of both Mrs Batchelor's parents, which had upset her greatly. Besides her sadness (as we later learned) that they would not see their grandchild, it would not be surprising if there were also an element of protest in this, at the loss of their support.

It will be remembered that Mrs Batchelor voiced a powerful fantasy in the first interview: that the succession of haemorrhages she experienced during the pregnancy were a sign that she was not meant to have the baby. It was indeed as though not destiny but her own body had come down on the rejecting side of her mixed feelings. Her anxious indecision about collecting the baby from hospital and her change of plan about breast-feeding suggest parallel conflicts of feeling which she could not resolve but instead demonstrated in discrepancies between intention and action.

Those were the early clues conveyed to Miss Inskip. They point to the roots of indecision about starting a family in the ambivalence of *both partners* about close, intimate relationships with their connotations of dependency and interpenetration. It was therefore not surprising to hear Miss Inskip say she felt that to 'probe' Mrs Batchelor's anxieties would only heighten them. Yet she was at the same time aware of an invitation to become involved, for Helen Batchelor could also be very open. So Miss Inskip experienced contradictory cues:

invitations to question and seek understanding—to get closer to her client—and warnings that to do so would be harmful and intrusive.

Miss Inskip first presented the case just over a year after Jenny's birth. The beginnings of the work which we have been reviewing were only the preamble to more serious later developments and working problems for the health visitor which we now consider.

Open and closed: the couple with the spastic child

After Jenny's home-coming Miss Inskip continued to visit regularly; sometimes Mrs Batchelor and Jenny were seen, sometimes the whole family, depending on Mr Batchelor's duty roster.

Miss Inskip described Helen Batchelor as "tall, attractive, slim and quietly spoken"; Frank Batchelor was simply "the opposite". But though they seemed to Miss Inskip to have lived fairly separate lives and occupied very different worlds, she got no hint of there ever having been serious problems in their relationship.

Mrs Batchelor did not handle Jenny much during the interviews. However, she was quiet and gentle with her, responding to the baby's happy disposition. In contrast, her husband was rough, but "in a playful way". Just as the house was spotless, so Mrs Batchelor impressed herself as a perfectionist and the visits were largely taken up with her doubts about her ability to mother the baby. Her physical care of Jenny gave Miss Inskip no particular concern; she coped quite well in spite of being depressed and anxious. She did however seem to need constant reassurance and Miss Inskip was regularly and reliably there to give it. Quite early on Mrs Batchelor talked about returning to work and Miss Inskip wondered if a part-time job might indeed be the answer for her.

As her visits went on, Miss Inskip began to be concerned about Jenny. She noticed that the baby's motor development was impaired and a squint had begun to develop. Her initial response was to ask Mrs Batchelor how she thought Jenny was progressing. The reply: "she's fine".

For a while, and with increasing misgivings, Miss Inskip went along with the mother's denial that anything was amiss. She knew how uncertain and anxious she felt about the baby and was loath to alarm her further. It soon became clear however that she must discuss her worry with the practice GP, and this led to a referral to the local paediatric unit.

Now Miss Inskip felt her relationship with her client began to deteriorate. Mrs Batchelor's denial that anything was wrong with Jenny gave way to demands either for reassurance that the baby was normal or else that she be given a firm diagnosis. But Miss Inskip was clear that it was the former she really longed for and that she "was not able to provide the answer Helen wanted".

No firm medical conclusion was reached until Jenny was twelve months old, when cerebral palsy was established. Miss Inskip was present when the Batchelors were eventually told that they had a spastic baby, and she conveyed the consultant's sensitive handling of the interview; but although the couple were prepared for the verdict at one level the diagnosis nonetheless seemed a shock to them when it actually came. Miss Inskip herself had been sure that her misgivings would be confirmed, but in the event she too was moved.

The paediatrician proposed they bring Jenny back in three months' time to be comprehensively assessed, psychologically as well as physically, by an interdisciplinary team over a period of a week.

After this Miss Inskip learned that the baby was now seldom taken out. Mrs Batchelor hated the idea of meeting other mothers with normal children who could walk properly and run about as she thought Jenny never would. She said she could not bear to have a physically handicapped child; she would like her adopted. Mr Batchelor however seemed less distressed by the progressively obvious handicap and Miss Inskip believed that he was more accepting of it. She thought he probably did not wish to have Jenny adopted but would acquiesce because with his work schedules and no parental support he felt Helen would not be able to cope. It all seemed "down to her" as far as he was concerned. For her part, Miss Inskip told the workshop she would support her client in whatever she ultimately decided to do.

It is relevant at this point to introduce the workshop's response to Miss Inskip and her presentation, which she made in low, even tones. It was a small, mainly female group on this occasion, three male practitioners (including both doctors) being absent. The climate was subdued.

The other health visitor in the group spoke with feeling about the dilemma for health visitors when they had doubts about a baby's progress: "it's very difficult ... can't say anything definite because no-one on the medical side will say anything definite. If [you do] and you are wrong, you are putting your foot right in it."

This led members to consider the problem of responding to clients' anxiety, and the corresponding anxiety for the practitioner about "getting it right". When it was observed that Miss Inskip's working relationship with Helen Batchelor might well be weakened by being "too cagey", she agreed: "I think I *was* too cagey." She often felt her client "didn't face up to her feelings" even though at other times she expressed them openly. She was both 'open' and 'shut'. But Miss Inskip also connected her working problem with the fact that she identified with her client "quite closely on some things ... on occasion she would clam up and put on a brave face ... I could see she wanted to cry, but she wouldn't". She thought she would have felt the same if it had been her and acknowledged serious doubts about whether she would be able to help. Again, there was a striking parallel with Helen Batchelor's feelings of inadequacy. No-one was unaffected by the painful material; the workshop logbook noted that those present "knew about pain and depression and the value of sticking with it".

Meanwhile Mr Batchelor was regarded (by the group as well as Miss Inskip) more as an additional liability in the work than as an integral part of this hesitantly established three-person family system. With such manifest anxiety vested in Mrs Batchelor, it proved difficult to see Jenny's parents as a couple who must be struggling with a shared emotional problem, now exacerbated by their baby's condition.

An important point now becomes clear. Although Mr Batchelor's words seemed to confirm his wife's belief that she would not get his support, the focus on mother and baby was precluding any reflection on the contrary signals in his actual behaviour. For example, he had accompanied his wife when Jenny was brought back from hospital; the couple had received the diagnosis together and, when at home, he did not make a point of keeping himself out of the interview as many fathers seemed to do in other health-visiting cases.

> At a home visit two days after the diagnostic consultation Mrs Batchelor was "very, very angry and bitter". In a cold and controlled way, she attacked both Miss Inskip and the GP for not picking up Jenny's condition earlier. She talked about a barrier between them preventing Miss Inskip from being any use to her. She would certainly want Jenny adopted if it proved that the child was

mentally as well as physically handicapped. She set great store by the further extensive investigation because it would decide things for her. She would never have another child—she "couldn't go through all this again". It also emerged that Jenny was being taken out even more rarely; Miss Inskip left, concerned that Jenny was now being more generally rejected by her mother.

Helen Batchelor's attack on her professional competence shook Miss Inskip's own belief in it. Until now she had held onto the reality that others in the primary care practice had also found it difficult to relate to Mrs Batchelor. Now her underlying doubts were confirmed. "It was very difficult ... I felt very vulnerable." The way Mrs Batchelor expressed her anger made discussion impossible; it would have been much easier if she had been openly in a rage and told her "to get out". On the other hand, looking back on the meeting, Miss Inskip was not really sure her client believed all she had been saying, "she was *so* angry ... had to get at someone". Nevertheless the impact at the time was such that she actually sought out her health visitor colleagues to discuss transferring the case to one of them. Their response, however, was to counsel and support her in continuing with it.

Visiting again a few days later, she met both parents and at once sensed "an atmosphere". Mrs Batchelor engaged her in conversation while Mr Batchelor, having acknowledged her, sat detached, looking out of the window. Then Jenny was abruptly passed to him and he at once began to show Miss Inskip what the baby could do. This was more, he said, than the paediatrician had been able to observe; and he thought the physiotherapy was helping Jenny. Helen Batchelor disagreed despondently; Jenny was "just as bad as she's ever been". Miss Inskip believed he was over-optimistic and supported his wife's need to express her feelings in something akin to "a bereavement situation". To a question from a workshop member which implied that both parents had suffered the loss of the anticipated normal, healthy baby, she said emphatically that there had never been the slightest hint that either blamed the other for what had happened.

When they were next seen together, things were easier. Helen Batchelor was more encouraged, especially by the regular physiotherapy and the purposeful intervention it represented. She had been out with Jenny and had visited another mother with a handicapped child. At this point Miss Inskip thought she was beginning "to work through the physical handicap".

In this less anxious and defensive situation, Frank Batchelor told her there had been constant disagreement between them on how to bring up Jenny ever since she was born, i.e. before the handicap was apparent. He wanted them to discuss their differences with Miss Inskip, but his effort to do so failed in the face of his wife's resistance; again she "clammed up". Miss Inskip felt she should end the interview; their relationship "seemed altered", so she left, encouraging them to talk together.

This first report of the work ended with a further brief meeting with mother and baby at the health centre. Mrs Batchelor had greeted Miss Inskip warmly and was open and cheerful. She said she and her husband were sitting down to talk, and through Jenny she had linked up with yet other mothers with handicapped children, some of whom were clearly worse than hers. It also seemed as if she might be reconsidering having a second baby; she had got herself an appointment with an obstetrician to try to discover whether the difficulties during her pregnancy were likely to be repeated.

The workshop was perplexed about the couple's interaction and there were conflicting views about it. Mr Batchelor had shown another side of himself, had not in fact opted out and had made an effort to get differences in their attitudes to Jenny and the future explored with Miss Inskip. True, he had not been able to persist, but did not subsequent events suggest that his attempts to have things out between them had improved their relationship and contributed to Mrs Batchelor's freer and more positive attitude to the baby? Some members were sceptical, however. Could the couple's long-established pattern have altered? The pregnancy, the haemorrhages, the premature birth and the belatedly confirmed handicap—all must have so spoken to their worst fears as to "drive a wedge between them". The couple still seemed separate and divided to these members and Mrs Batchelor's anxiety and ambivalence remained dominant for them. But these differing ideas were not developed or examined. The group became preoccupied with Miss Inskip's predicament and this centred round the difficulties in her relationship with Helen Batchelor.

In working with her, members expressed the view that Miss Inskip must have conveyed important messages to Mrs Batchelor (to both clients, in fact, but this was not noted). For example, she had considered getting her client 'adopted'—taken on by a colleague—but had managed to continue in the work; Mrs Batchelor would surely have picked up her capacity to "stick with it" in spite of uncertainty. Thereby she was likely to have been helped to do the same for Jenny. She could not have failed to register the health visitor's empathy and that she had not reacted directively, for example, by opposing talk of adoption, but had indicated that she would support her in whatever she decided. With these points made, it was suggested that the practitioner underestimated the quality of her relationship with her client. She was urged to "take courage ... your relationship could stand the weight of more directness and plain speaking".

Comment

The way Miss Inskip's subjective experience paralleled that of her client, as she seemed to be taken over by Mrs Batchelor's anxiety, exemplifies the struggle practitioners can have in finding an effective working distance from clients or patients; a position in which they are neither so close as to be immobilised, nor so distant as to be out of touch and therefore without insight and influence. Her work also strikingly showed the propensity of the work-task to evoke personal, often deep-seated anxiety in practitioners.

The workshop's behaviour had the same characteristics. The largely female group of practitioners was progressively captured by Miss Inskip's dilemma. Even at one remove, Mrs Batchelor's anxiety was powerful enough to be conveyed into the group by the practitioner, especially because it spoke directly to her own. The collective response to her was very similar to her response to her client. As the workshop logbook recorded, plain speaking was inhibited to an unusual degree for this group; and this was clearly for fear of upsetting Miss Inskip. There were numerous enquiries about how she felt discussing this case, and whether it was being helpful to her. Thus, just as Mrs Batchelor's feelings dominated the relationship with Miss Inskip, and got in the way of recognising the maturational struggle within the couple's marriage occasioned by the birth of their baby, so it proved difficult for the group to attend *both* to the practitioner and to the couple's interaction. This even though members were aware of its crucial effect on the baby's care, upbringing and future welfare.

Miss Inskip reported the case again five months later when all members of the workshop were present.

> Jenny was taken for the week-long multi-disciplinary assessment which both parents attended. Mrs Batchelor raised the issue of adoption right from the start and

throughout the week with various members of the assessment team, not least the social worker, an older woman whom Miss Inskip thought she "probably uses to communicate with as a mother figure ... she finds it very easy to talk to her". At the end of the assessment Miss Inskip was invited to join a case conference of all the professionals who had taken part. "We were very much on tenterhooks as to what was going to happen" because of all that had gone before; "the mother was wobbly, too".

The team concluded that, though physically handi-capped and likely to need treatment for her eyes, Jenny was not mentally impaired. The clinical assessment pre-sented little difficulty; it was Mrs Batchelor's preoccupa-tion with adoption that dominated the discussion. "What came over was that all the people who had been involved during the week had found it extremely difficult to understand how Helen could want Jenny adopted." Meanwhile, Miss Inskip was to visit less often in future and the social worker would be seeing more of Mrs Batchelor than she.

Miss Inskip also joined the paediatrician and the physiotherapist when the results of the assessment were discussed with the parents. Such meetings usually lasted a quarter of an hour; this one went on for an hour and a half, "trying to get her to see that she had a perfectly normal girl mentally and that it was just her physical problem. I think it did sink in a little bit that their daughter is going to be perfectly all right mentally—but they obviously have quite a long way to go." Miss Inskip said she could see and sympathise with what Mrs Batchelor was saying, but could also appreciate that, "because [the staff] met so many children with severe handicap whose parents apparently came to terms with it, they found it difficult to understand why she was unable to accept Jenny's condition".

For their part, the Batchelors had been very much at one during the week. They now made it clear that they wished to be left alone for a month or so to think things over. Shortly before this second and last presentation, Miss Inskip heard from the GP that they had asked for further consultations; she thought they were looking for someone who would contradict the assessment team's diagnosis.

Miss Inskip had begun by reiterating the anxiety and ambivalence shown by Mrs Batchelor from the start and the difficulty she had in working with her. But this time the group paid scant attention to these antecedent events and Miss Inskip's technical problems. If members tended to be taken over by the practitioner's experience and got too close on the first occasion, they were very distant from her on the second.

The situation described by Miss Inskip had subdued and depressed the earlier, largely female group, though they had tried to grapple with its complexity. Now there was a climate in which people took issue, to the point of over-simplifying. Those previously present were silenced for most of the session. The opening protest by a woman practitioner exemplified the kind of feelings evoked: "no-one accepts the adoption thing ... everyone seems to be saying they have an ordinary, normal child. Why doesn't someone say, 'look at the responsibility of taking this child on'?" It will be clear that this member had distorted Miss Inskip's account (for example she had not said the clients were told they had 'an ordinary, normal child'), but the fact went unremarked. The doctors took up positions, too. They rejected the idea of ambivalence; Mrs Batchelor simply wanted to be rid of Jenny. They were also critical of the assessment team and by implication of Miss Inskip who was treated condescendingly. The view was that the professionals involved would inevitably look on adoption as a failure and had therefore been deaf to Mrs Batchelor's feelings of rejection towards Jenny—this in spite of Miss Inskip's quiet assertion to the contrary on her own and the team's behalf.

It took most of this second session for members to extricate themselves from the very powerful dynamic and for those present on the previous occasion to become vocal; then, for example, the other health visitor did challenge the over-simplification and spoke forcefully about the complex emotions stirred up "when you have a child, especially one like this". Only at the end of the session could there be interaction and mutual influence between those with different experiences—and attention paid to Miss Inskip's working problems.

Comment

The point here is not the validity or otherwise of the criticisms of the assessment team's reported behaviour but the dogmatic, all or nothing nature of the general response. People tended to become caricatures of themselves. The first and second presentations did indeed have a different focus, but we believe the phenomena observed in the two workshops represented opposite defensive reactions to the high level of anxiety and despair aroused in these experienced professionals by the account of the Batchelors and their handicapped child.

Frank and Helen Batchelor had presented a united front during the assessment process. This suggests that a familiar unconscious psychological manouevre was being employed, in which one side of a conflict of feelings within and between the partners is projected outside the marital system as a defence against anxiety about mutual destructiveness within it (Sutherland, 1962). So instead of difference about Jenny being articulated between husband and wife contention was now between the Batchelors, apparently at one in favouring adoption, and the assessment team, apparently unanimous against it.

The second workshop discussion reflected this. Whereas in the first Frank Batchelor was separated off as a liability, in the second he was subsumed under his wife's identity. The Batchelors were quite undifferentiated by members. 'Them' and 'they' were synonymous with 'Mrs Batchelor'. Her husband, Jenny's father, was neither acknowledged nor referred to as a separate person. References to him in Miss Inskip's introductory summary were quite lost. So neither workshop was able to sustain a focus on the interaction of the two marriage partners, or to go beyond the salient anxiety surrounding mother and baby.

The uncertainty and anxiety, personal and professional, which this case raised for Miss Inskip were evident in the first presentation, and members responded to them. For most of the second discussion, both aspects were virtually ignored; and as already noted, she was treated kindly but condescendingly by the doctors, albeit without awareness. It was as if her work was secondary to that of the other professionals involved. Only belatedly was her commitment recognised; that she would have a continuing responsibility in view of her statutory duty to monitor the development of children under five, and that the work would therefore be shared between her and members of other disciplines located in another institution. Miss Inskip responded to the mention of collaboration with a rare show of asperity: she did not expect to have "much of a working relationship" with her social work colleague. Only if she took the initiative would she find out from her what was happening in the hospital-based work. In the closing stages of the workshop discussion it was recognised that, as well as having practical implications, this could serve to reinforce the pattern of Mr and Mrs Batchelor's difficulty in reconciling positive and negative feelings in relationships; these could be kept separate as between the 'good maternal' social worker and the 'bad unrewarding' health visitor.

Follow-up

Informal follow-up when Jenny was nearly five revealed that the idea of adoption had been abandoned. She could still not walk unaided though there was every hope that she would do so eventually. Her eye problem persisted, but with glasses this bright child was not disadvantaged and was doing well in nursery school.

She was, however, felt to suffer from a surfeit of parental attention, especially from her mother whose life now revolved around her care and treatment. The assessment centre staff had been concerned enough about this and its effect on Jenny to suggest to Mrs Batchelor that she should have another child, but she was now set against it. The care of Jenny was of common concern to both her parents but otherwise they seemed to go their own way as before, and there was no visible conflict in their relationship.

Problems of collaboration between Miss Inskip and the centre social worker had not in fact materialised. The latter had left shortly after the last presentation and had not been replaced. Miss Inskip's own contact with the family was now infrequent and coming to an end.

Comment

It is of particular interest that Mrs Batchelor's shame and impulse to reject Jenny were apparently converted into the opposite—anxious attachment and over-protection; both were defensive against conflicting feelings. As before, apparently, the professionals were mainly concerned with the relationship between mother and child. Perhaps the Batchelor's old pattern of interaction had indeed reasserted itself, only slightly modified, with Jenny becoming Helen Batchelor's full-time job. Perhaps that was how the practitioners once again perceived them.

The relationship system created by Frank and Helen Batchelor was one in which fear of conflict and change made it difficult for them to mediate extremes of feeling in their relationship—for example, between closeness and distance; dependence and independence; perfection and imperfection; optimism and pessimism; love and hate. Potentially creative differences between the couple had been briefly glimpsed in the parents' respective reactions to Jenny's birth and disability; but they were not sustained. The evidence suggests that their fear of conflict and uncertainty was communicated to the health visitor and other professional helpers, inhibiting them from addressing marital issues relevant to the future well-being of the child.

This case has a significance wider than the particular characteristics of the Batchelors or of Miss Inskip herself. Some of the prevailing anxieties, particularly those concerning conflict between dependence and independence, perfection and imperfection, are constantly and inherently present in health-visiting work; we came to see that some of the defences activated in Miss Inskip were characteristic of health visitors and built into their professional culture.

If Miss Inskip's case was notable for the early clues to what the work was likely to be about, it was often much more difficult for health visitors to know what they were in for when clients crossed the threshold into their caseloads. Such was Mrs Hunt's experience in the next case. She expressed the dilemma as follows: "we go into what we hope will be a normal family; then problems gradually appear (being our clients does not *in itself* imply problems, as it does in probation, for instance). I could ignore them, or try to take hold of them; if I do so, it will be difficult to work with the client and [I will] maybe have them for years."

Abstinence and greed—the sleepless baby

John and Elaine Gray were in their early thirties when their first child, Laura, was born. They had just moved house; Mr Gray became unemployed soon afterwards and was still out of work when the case was presented six months later.

Mrs Hunt had found Elaine Gray accepting of her, warm and articulate, anxious to do everything right regarding the baby and her welfare. This had included two-hourly breast-feeding day and night for the first five months. She was devoted to the idea of feeding on demand and had been part of a group of women with similar views. She was exhausted, however, not least by spending two or three hours every night trying to soothe Laura to sleep. The baby's difficulty in sleeping had become so entrenched that Mrs Hunt had got her client into a behaviour modification programme to try to rectify the problem.

Laura was well physically, plump and a voracious feeder; in fact Mrs Hunt had advised Elaine Gray that she was over-feeding her. She was a cautious, nervous child, uneasy with people generally, but had begun to trust and respond to Mrs Hunt.

Mrs Hunt found John Gray very different from his wife. A simple, slow speaking and thinking man and inarticulate—very "laid back". He was giving her far too little money out of his benefit, was out a lot with his mates and drank too much, especially given their slender income. The couple were therefore in dire financial straits. He took small part in looking after the baby; but he too was worried about Laura's problem in sleeping, though he never allowed his own nights to be disturbed.

Just how fraught things were only became fully apparent when Mrs Hunt met both parents for her six-month health check on the baby. It was a tense, uncomfortable visit and she made a further appointment to talk about the situation which was so obviously bearing heavily on Mrs Gray and, through her, on Laura. John Gray was out when Mrs Hunt kept the planned appointment; she thought he was avoiding her, and looking back she felt she had been ambiguous about her wish to talk to both parents, or at any rate not firm enough to "capture John". Alone with the health visitor, Mrs Gray gave vent to her feelings about her life and her four-year marriage.

She had been the only child in a restrictive "Victorian family". Her parents, who she said had never liked her husband, were kept unaware of the marital difficulties; Elaine felt her mother would say "I told you so", just as she was sure to be disapproving of her approach to Laura's care.

Elaine had been attracted to and married a man not only slower and less articulate than herself but someone whom she knew had never had limits set nor his impulses restricted by his parents. He too was an only child and she gave examples of his mother's indulgence of him. Mrs Hunt thought them an ill-assorted couple, but Elaine was obviously fond of John's parents and they seemed to be of her and their grandchild.

Before her pregnancy both partners had mostly been employed, she especially, but changing jobs quite often. Although they had never before been in such deep financial difficulty as now, Mrs Gray had had an injunction served on her husband about a year before Laura's birth because of his neglect over money. According to her this had a salutary effect—until she stopped work when they moved and he lost his job soon after she delivered the baby. Paradoxically, it had been Mr Gray's idea that she should become pregnant when she did, because they were "getting on".

Now they were having more rows about money, and the way he restricted her through his indulgence of himself. She, articulate in their exchanges, became frantic at his muted reaction and his sulks. Mrs Hunt felt the situation was "explosive".

Her suggestion that they seek help from marriage guidance was turned down by Mrs Gray because "he wouldn't go". However, shortly before her report to the workshop, she was able to involve a social worker to help the Grays sort out the financial tangle and avert the loss of their telephone and possibly their tenancy.

On first consideration the workshop answered the question, 'what is the matter?' on the lines: the mother, an only child, living a long way from home and with few friends, is exhausted with her first baby but has landed herself with a less bright, self-centred husband who fails to support her financially, practically or emotionally. When she protests, he withdraws; she gives up and things go from bad to worse as the tension builds up. The presenting problem of the child's sleeplessness was seen to be the product of Mrs Gray's spiralling tension and weariness.

An alternative view was then developed. Starting from the Grays' apparently incongruous choice of each other, the hypothesis was considered that each had been attracted by aspects of the other's personality that were missing from their own because of their early experience. For Elaine this could be expressed as 'latitude', for John 'restriction'—opposite poles of a shared basic problem about setting limits and having limits set. It was unconscious conflict in these areas within each of them that was now being externalised and acted out in their relationship. Currently, abstinence and privation appeared to be mainly located in Mrs Gray, greed and indulgence in her husband, i.e. they were back where they started as children.

All the indications were that the transition from two to three had compounded their respective difficulties. The move to extend the boundaries of the relationship system—to create a family—was potentially developmental but inevitably gave rise to stress, now fast becoming unmanageable. Elaine Gray's 'no limit' approach to the baby seemed to reflect a compulsion to make good in her what she felt she had not experienced herself. For John Gray, himself an over-indulged only child, his wife's responses to Laura would be sure to resonate with deeply anxious feelings, for example, about having to share and the setting of limits. The extreme differences Mrs Hunt described, now triangulated through the child, would be likely to engender the explosive atmosphere she had sensed.

None of this minimised the importance of the practical and material problems the couple faced, but Mrs Hunt said these ideas helped to make sense of her experience—especially the mother's apparent difficulty in acting on advice she had repeatedly offered about feeding and about managing the sleep problem.

Presenting the case two months later, however, she reported that although the previous discussion had seemed enlightening it had been overtaken by events occurring shortly afterwards. The eruption she had foreseen had occurred.

During Mrs Hunt's absence on a course, the Grays had a particularly acrimonious row when John Gray had been drinking. In the course of it he fired a gun (which, it turned out, had been under their sofa for months) and Mrs Gray called the police to whom she made a statement. Her husband was arrested and remanded in custody, charged with attempted manslaughter. Before long, however, Mrs Gray withdrew her statement and the charge was then reduced to illegal fire-arm possession. Mr Gray was released on bail but required to reside with his parents and observe a curfew. Neither Mrs Hunt nor her social work colleague had seen him since.

Salient points from the second report were:

After the shooting, Mrs Gray was confused and showed contradictory feelings about her husband. The social worker helped her to get everything in her own name and organise herself as a single parent; on that basis she was better off in practical terms, managing more competently without her husband. She did not want him back; Laura needed a father "but not the one she's got". However, Mrs Gray veered between anger at her husband and excusing him. She said on one occasion he "wouldn't hurt a lamb". It was the row that provoked him. He had never been violent. Mrs Hunt was pretty sure they were meeting and she had the strong impression that it was hard for her to be without him, not least sexually.

While often returning to the idea that her husband was provoked (i.e. by her protests), Mrs Gray was adamant that she had no part in what had happened, nor in their preceding difficulties.

There were marked changes in Mrs Gray. Now anxious and hypochondriacal, she was also demanding and exploitive—of others besides Mrs Hunt; she never acknowledged the considerable help and support she received, for example from her in-laws and one particularly kind and reliable neighbour. Mrs Hunt commented, "it was take, take, take".

There were changes too in the relationship between Laura and her mother. The child was more clinging and fretful, tearful, quite unadventurous and now wary even of Mrs Hunt who felt increasingly concerned. Though Mrs Gray expressed anxiety about her, she actually treated her roughly sometimes as they vied for attention on Mrs Hunt's visits. She had not been able to use the behaviour modification programme, nor to establish feeding and sleeping routines. It was more and more clear how ambivalent she felt about responding to Laura 'on demand'.

Mr Gray's parents saw their daughter-in-law and granddaughter every day. Generous and supportive to a fault, they had taken them out, including a visit to John when he was in prison. Elaine had not wished to see him there but Laura had spent time with her father. Meanwhile Mrs Gray kept the episode from her own parents for several weeks. Only after a series of frantic 'phone calls to Mrs Hunt, full of trepidation, did she make one visit to them.

Mrs Hunt felt "drained" by her client. Health visitor and social worker kept in close touch—"we're our own little support group". Their overt tasks had been clearly differentiated (HV, health checks and advice on Laura; SW, financial management), but both continued to take up opportunities to talk about Mrs Gray's feelings and reactions towards her husband. They adhered strenuously to an agreed policy: to be reliable and "not be rejected whatever she does". However, after Mrs Gray withdrew her statement the social worker was increasingly "frozen out". Elaine told Mrs Hunt, "I've withdrawn the statement so there's no point in her coming". But her attachment to Mrs Hunt was preserved; "she seems to regard my visits as normal".

It took some time for the workshop to assimilate Mrs Hunt's second report. Eventually it was seen that the unexpected turn of events was consistent with the earlier formulation. What had been under-estimated then was the violence with which the Grays rejected in each other what could not be tolerated in themselves. A male social worker in the group noted that, on the face of it, it was out of character for the 'laid back' Mr Gray to react as he did; he asked the metaphorical question: "who, in effect, pulled the trigger?"

Comment

In psychodynamic terms, it was the *rigidity* of the defence of splitting in both partners (and the degree of anxiety this indicated) which had been overlooked in the first discussion—in spite of Mrs Hunt's foreboding. The ultimate explosion was one the couple had literally been sitting on for a long time. In its aftermath they emerged just as rigidly differentiated as before, but now the opposite way round. In the absence of her husband, Mrs Gray exhibited the greed and exploitiveness she had so bitterly complained of in him. Although Mr Gray had not been seen, it seemed clear that by his potentially lethal outburst he had ensured that firm limits were put round him, first in prison, then by a curfew and a condition of residence which, ironically, now obliged his indulgent parents to contain him.

Mrs Gray's conflicts of feelings were very obvious. Her psychological defences, among them denial that she had any part in what had happened, were not effective in avoiding the emotional tension. It also affected the practitioners, who both experienced a great deal of anxiety and stress. They clung together for mutual support; together they could admit to each other how angry and resentful the demanding Mrs Gray made them feel—though they suppressed these feelings when they were with her. Their quest for a firm footing through adherence to their separate statutory roles was not an effective defence against the anxiety that working with Mrs Gray embroiled them in; since they both felt free to engage with her personal relationship problems, sameness predominated over difference. But Mrs Gray seemed to make rivals of them in her mind; and it was she who separated them out. The social worker who had helped her become financially independent, as if a single parent, was inevitably associated with her initial impulse to get rid of her husband (i.e. what he stood for in her inner world as well as his impact on her outer world). Once her accusing and rejecting statement to the police had been withdrawn, she progressively limited this worker's access. Meanwhile her attachment to Mrs Hunt was sustained. The health visitor, who had the longer relationship, had also taken care not to go along with the assumption that Mrs Gray would permanently reject her husband. But more than this, she was the one practitioner who carried no stigma, whose visits were 'normal', as Mrs Gray seemed to feel—the corollary of Mrs Hunt's comment that 'being our clients does not in itself imply problems'. This made the health visitor a more welcome embodiment of maternal care for Mrs Gray than the social worker who, like her own mother, was made to stand for disapproval of her marriage and for thrift.

In this way the two practitioners came to represent the split in Mrs Gray's internal world between the giving mother she longed for and the depriving mother she hated and feared; the same split as she maintained between her mother-in-law and her own mother. The next phase showed Mrs Gray's capacity to carry this split into her relationship with one practitioner only, the health visitor whom on the face of it she had preferred.

> The main feature of Mrs Hunt's final report, eight months later, was the marked change in her relationship with Mrs Gray, and the working difficulties that had arisen in consequence.
>
> Soon after the previous presentation, the social worker had ceased to visit, though she kept the case open. Around the same time it was openly confirmed that Mr Gray was seeing his wife and baby regularly at weekends and that these visits had become more and more extended.
>
> In contrast to the welcome she had previously received, Mrs Hunt began to feel she was seen on sufferance. The difficult relationship between Laura and her mother preoccupied her but she felt unable to address it; "from a health-visiting point of view, it's very unsatisfactory ... every time I leave, I come out with the feeling that whatever I've said or done has been smudged". She felt intrusive when she tried to open things up; "it's as if she sees me as checking up on her".
>
> While Laura's feeding and sleeping difficulties caused her concern, she felt they were not *the* problem, "just a way of expressing what is happening in [Elaine's] life with John. She couldn't say no to John ... always contradictory messages to him as there are to Laura. But it is difficult to work on anything when Elaine is so resistant and there is no practical crisis to force her to." At the same time Mrs Hunt did not want "to be inquisitive ... she'll tell me about her relationship with [John] if and when she wants to".

All the other members of the workshop also had experience of resistant clients or patients, but as they tried to bring this experience to bear on Mrs Hunt's working problem they and she became increasingly frustrated and fractious. To them it seemed that Mrs Hunt was "digging in her toes"; to her that they were being inappropriately prescriptive. She protested, "I feel none of you are willing to accept that this is it!" The impasse persisted for a long time and seemed as difficult to budge as the one Mrs Hunt felt herself to be in with Elaine Gray.

It began to dawn on members that they were acting out a clear reflection of a powerful process in the interaction between health visitor and client. One commented, "we are now being with you as you feel you would be with her if you tried to break the deadlock ... you experience us as if we were scrutinising, not understanding and not listening; trying to take away your sovereignty"; but, protested another, "we are only trying to make connections".

Once the reflection process was recognised, there was greater understanding —and greater freedom to consider what approach might be possible and practical. Members could now use their experience, not to be prescriptive, but to appreciate the difficulty of overcoming the kind of stalemate Mrs Hunt described, even with consistent work which it was now hard for her to undertake. Meanwhile, they were free enough to notice that she did not know the outcome of John Gray's court appearance; whether a probation officer had been involved and indeed whether work was going on with the other half of the marital system, but independently. A further question was therefore posed: would it be helpful and in role for a health visitor to take the initiative and get in touch with the probation service—did it matter? Mrs Hunt was forthright: "it does matter. We should communicate and we haven't." Another health visitor ended the session by recalling a case of hers in which she shared responsibility for clients with a practitioner from a different agency. Originally she had felt, "they haven't got onto me so why should I contact them? It was only after presenting the case here that I felt I should make the effort and do it."

Follow-up

We heard about subsequent developments in this case up to the time Laura was two years old. Although Mrs Hunt normally cut down the frequency of house calls once a child was eighteen months old, she continued to visit every six weeks or so out of concern for Laura's emotional state. But she encountered overt rejection from Mrs Gray who knew the period for regular visiting was at an end. Mrs Hunt did however help to arrange child-minding when her client found employment.

Mr Gray was not on probation. With the offence finally reduced to being without a licence for a firearm, he had been fined. He moved back into the home briefly but soon returned to his parents, ejected by Elaine when she took up with a much younger man she had met at work.

Laura's sleep problem persisted and she could only settle if she was in her mother's bed; her separation anxiety was increasingly obvious in response to her mother's hostile feelings towards her—even more explicit in the context of the new sexual relationship. Then, with divorce proceedings in train, Laura in turn was ejected—handed over to Mr Gray who had shown an unlooked-for capacity to take responsibility for his daughter's care.

Mrs Hunt and her social work colleague had remained in touch, and at this point exchanged roles. Mrs Hunt withdrew and it was the social worker who took on the task of safeguarding Laura's welfare. John Gray was ultimately awarded custody, the child to be brought up by himself and his parents.

Comment

The ambivalence of Mrs Gray's attachments was evident as was her limited sense of autonomy in close personal relationships; though we have encountered her husband mostly through her descriptions and his known actions, we can assume the same to have been true of him.[1] As Mrs Hunt observed, Elaine Gray "defends herself, puts distance between herself and others"; specifically, those others whom she had once been close to but now experienced as hostile and persecutory. This happened with her mother, her husband and her child, as well as with the social worker and eventually the health visitor.

The conflict evidently got inside Mrs Hunt herself, as she was drawn into the family's problems by events and her growing awareness that Laura's sleeping and feeding were affected by stress in the parents' marriage. On the one hand she felt she should not be inquisitive and intrude into the privacy of Mrs Gray's relationship with her husband. On the other hand she was firmly convinced that this was the source of Laura's difficulties which it was her job as a health visitor to try to relieve.

Her dilemma about her own role also affected her thinking about the roles of other agencies. It would have been a relief if the marital trouble could have been looked after by marriage guidance, but this was resisted by Mrs Gray (citing her husband's presumed reluctance). Mrs Hunt then invoked the social worker to tackle the financial plight—another manifestation of marital stress though it could not be treated explicitly as such. The two practitioners' original collaborative plan was itself radically affected by the Grays' continuing marital vicissitudes. It was also affected by the way each practitioner participated in the collective dynamics of her own discipline and agency, and we shall return to this case in chapter 9 to discuss that inter-institutional dimension.

For the moment we are concerned with health visitors' practice and how the interplay between them and their clients can highlight tensions in their accustomed definitions of their role and task. By the remarks with which she introduced her work with the Grays, Mrs Hunt implied a belief that as a health visitor she was free to choose whether or not to 'take hold' of problems emerging in the course of routine interviews with clients following the birth of a baby. However, she also emphasised the anxiety of doing so, and the way it transgressed the principle—valued by clients and practitioners alike—that health visitors' clients are 'normal'. This case shows that the matter can be less clear-cut in practice.

The case examples so far have been extensive so as to convey process and the complexity health visitors can face in the kind of difficult cases they introduced into the study. The briefer illustration which follows casts further light on transactions between the client system and the health visitor system. Once again, in the case of the Driscolls, the client system embodied the defences against anxiety evolved by individual, couple and family—their characteristic way of interacting with and relating to others, to events and the world around them. For Mrs Quiller, the health visitor system embodied the interplay of her personal defences and those developed and maintained collectively in her service and clinical setting.

The writhing lady and her family   Throughout Mrs Driscoll's childhood and adolescence her mother had nursed her father at home during his progressive, fatal illness. The diagnosis of familial cerebellar ataxia had only been revealed on his death when Mrs Driscoll was already married and had just had her own first and only child. Learning that the disease had a fifty per cent chance of transmission via either sex, she had begun to suspect that she herself was affected soon after her daughter, Yana, was born. There had been a delay in her diagnosis too, and because of her emotional state she was initially treated by anti-depressants; she was sterilised soon after the illness was confirmed.

Now in middle age, as was her husband, she was severely handicapped by constant involuntary writhing movements, and dependent on him and her teenage daughter for all but simple washing and dressing. With the co-operation of the local authority, the house had been adapted to meet Mrs Driscoll's needs. She was no longer safe in the kitchen, but the family managed very well practically. Being self-employed, Mr Driscoll could come home often during the day. Yana also devoted much time to her mother and came home to help at lunch time. Mr Driscoll's parents lived nearby and were very supportive; Mrs Driscoll's arthritic mother could not do as much as she would have liked, but neighbours were actively helpful.

Emotionally, however, the situation was very different. Mrs Driscoll was usually depressed and lethargic but was also liable to mood swings. Occupational therapy was available at a local centre, but she refused to go because of her embarrassment about eating in public and problems of toileting in a strange place. She reluctantly agreed to make more effort to go on social outings with the family, principally to relieve the pressure on them; she was deeply ashamed of her condition. She could also be very garrulous, and at times husband and daughter would scream at her and each other in exasperation.

She had complained of tension between herself and her husband in the past, but Mr Driscoll made it clear that he was unwilling to discuss their private affairs with outsiders (and she could not go anywhere without him and their car) so counselling help had not been sought. Meanwhile, at surgery, Mr Driscoll apparently contrived never to leave his wife alone with their GP who, it seemed, had never insisted that he should. Mr Driscoll himself was known to have hypertension and tension headaches, and whilst he did so much at home he also escaped from the house when he could. Yana was also irritable and tense at times; and it was not surprising that the adolescent girl should have conflicts of feeling about her mother and her own situation. She devoted much time and attention to her mother, indeed her life revolved around her needs to a worrying extent. On leaving school, for example, she chose between the jobs available on the basis of the freedom to get home if needed rather than the career prospects offered.

Introducing the case to the workshop, Mrs Quiller stressed the fact that she was the only practitioner whose role it was to visit routinely to assess the medical and social situation without some precipitating crisis. It was part of her job to call regularly on the handicapped patients of her primary care practice and to encourage them to lead as full a life as possible. But in fact much of her advice had been ignored by the Driscolls and she had not been able to visit them very often because of competing demands on her time (principally her mandatory work with mothers and young children).

With this background Mrs Quiller's first presentation focused on her recent experience. During a home visit made after a lengthy interval Mrs Driscoll had dropped a bombshell. She had unexpectedly talked about marital and sexual problems with much pressure and in lurid detail. Mrs Quiller was all the more taken aback because she was accompanied by a student health visitor, and neighbours were also in and out during the interview. When the same thing happened again a week later she asked the GP to visit with her. He, an older doctor, gave his patient factual advice in an avuncular way and expressed his opinion about differences in sexual needs as between men and women. This seemed to Mrs Quiller to have brought an astonishing transformation; after a few days Mrs Driscoll was off anti-depressants, was brighter and able to talk more coherently and reflectively.

During the presentation it emerged that almost a year previously Yana had 'blown up' while Mrs Quiller was away. The locum health visitor had arranged for her to see a male counsellor attached to the practice. A short series of interviews had centred on the girl's anxieties about the implication of her mother's illness for her own sexual and maternal future.

Noting what a beautiful girl Yana was, as her mother had clearly been, and how this made the situation all the more poignant, Mrs Quiller was very open about the disturbing impact the case had on her and about the guilt she felt at not having done more previously.

She discussed her work with the Driscolls again in the workshop seven months later, during which time she had been rather more active, paying bi-monthly visits to Mrs Driscoll and also meeting with Yana, at home and outside. There had also been a family interview.

Mrs Driscoll continued to be less depressed and took more care of herself. But the pressure with which she talked still made it difficult to be with her; it was her intrusiveness that prompted Mrs Quiller to arrange office interviews with Yana. At times she thought the mother was dementing (a known effect of her condition as it progressed) but at others Mrs Driscoll talked purposefully about herself and the illness.

A major theme of the sessions with Yana was the break-up of her relationship with her boyfriend—connected, Mrs Quiller thought, with her fear of contracting her mother's illness. She resisted Mrs Quiller's suggestion that she go back to the practice counsellor and also refused to see the family doctor, though she consulted a part-time woman GP about menstrual pain. Mrs Quiller then proferred the idea of genetic counselling, available at a nearby hospital. Yana took this up, though anxiously, and her father took her to the interview. The facts and probabilities were put before her at what proved to be a one-off session; they were also provided in written form to take away with her. It had been agreed that Mrs Quiller should meet the whole family following the hospital appointment.

Hitherto she had had virtually no direct contact with Mr Driscoll. Now she gave a vivid vignette of him in what had been an intense and stressful experience for all concerned (not least for her). He sat near to his wife, stroking and comforting her, and then doing this for Yana when she came close in her own distress (as a member of the workshop observed, it was as if his own feelings were suppressed and his anguish was related to through caring for the women).

During the family meeting Yana made her attachment to the health visitor clear; it was her she wanted to talk to. This left Mrs Quiller fearing that she "would not be adequate to help". She had in fact been hoping that the genetic counselling session at the hospital would have led to continuing work there. But in spite of her doubts about being able to help (and the fact that she had found the practice counsellor uncommunicative and unsupportive) she felt she should respond to Yana's request. She did not envisage further counselling work with the parents in view of Mrs Driscoll's condition and the inhibiting effect of her husband's embargo on discussing their relationship.

Comment

Marital and family stress precipitated by and rooted in incurable illness is at the other end of the spectrum from that occasioned by the psychological and social transition surrounding the birth of a baby. The latter, however problematic and uncertain, contains the seeds of hope with the beginning of a new life. For Mrs Driscoll and her husband and teenage daughter, the situation to be accommodated and the quality of uncertainty that went with it were profoundly different — as was the impact on the practitioner involved. A probation officer in the workshop caught something of this when he commented on "the ghastly prospect of working with someone who can't get better".

The case showed how anxiety raised by incurable illness and its inevitable outcome can constrain thinking and feeling and make it more difficult to consider the designated patient as part of an interacting system of relationships. In the workshop, practitioners of all disciplines were affected in this way. An experienced GP member commented on "the enormity of the problem and the sense in which intervention is somehow doomed to failure". He acknowledged later that he had "colluded with the group in keeping the focus on the disabled patient . . . while wishing for a formulation that would take in the wider family". During Mrs Quiller's second presentation, he was still advocating "specific aims [in the work] because it is too much to take on all three, the whole family". Meanwhile the earlier attempts of one or two members to consider the implications of Mrs Driscoll's illness for her husband and for their relationship had failed in the face of a preoccupation with Yana's plight and her need for help in her own right.

The workshop's reactions had much in common with those of the medical services involved. These were also focused on the patient and corresponded with the health visitor's initial description of her own task: a continuing assessment of the medical and social situation of the handicapped patient— along with offering encouragement and advice.

When Yana had drawn attention to herself during Mrs Quiller's absence in the preceding year, that event had apparently been encapsulated as well. She did indeed need help for herself then, but presumably her parents too were worried about the implications for her of the hereditary illness. She was treated as if in isolation from them. At the same time, in terms of her own developmental needs Yana was approaching adulthood still enmeshed in a highly anxious family system. It was unlikely that she could become freer to pursue her own life —short of a destructive breakaway—without some work with the whole family that would help her and her parents to release their anxious grip on each other. The workshop encountered a similar difficulty in holding the individual members of the family in mind *as well as* their mutual influence and interaction.

This difficulty mainly arose from members' need to defend against anxiety. Also essentially defensive were the criticism and competitiveness in the group. As one member put it, "we all seem to feel we could have done better". Some were incensed that the "enormity of the problem" seemed to have been quite unfairly lodged with Mrs Quiller; the GP should have been an active leader of the primary care team. Others were irritated with the health visitor for passively accepting the situation, pointing out that when she did take the initiative the GP readily made a domiciliary visit with her. Yet, bearing in mind the discussion in chapter 5 of doctors' unconscious as well as conscious problems in managing the boundary between themselves and their patients because of the nature of their interface with illness, it is not surprising to find that the primary care practice operated well-organised defences against the anxiety, conflict and uncertainty inherent in such a case. One defence was to try and keep the issues —and family members—in separate compartments. This was a defence Mrs Quiller shared, as witness her hope that Yana's problem would be securely lodged with the genetic counsellor.

As we have seen before, however, such institutionalised defensive splitting does not succeed in relieving the anxiety felt especially by the practitioner in the front line, like Mrs Quiller. Without benefit of a support system where the anxiety could be safely expressed and its source in the family system understood, it was difficult for her to free herself from enmeshment in the powerful, unconscious family dynamics—given that she could not stand apart like her more remote practice colleagues. For example, it proved impossible for her to question Mr Driscoll's embargo on discussing the inevitable stress in the marriage. Yet, while the fact that he never left his wife alone with the GP could indicate his fear of what she might reveal and where it would lead, it could also suggest their *shared* embarrassment and shame about the effects of his wife's illness on their lives and his need for them to look at this together—if someone would risk it with them. For Mrs Quiller to have done so, however, would have meant exercising an autonomy she did not feel, just as Mrs Driscoll felt none in the face of her illness and her dependence on her husband and daughter. A conflict between helplessness and the professional competence she felt was needed and expected of her was something Mrs Quiller evidently experienced often in this case. Beyond any individual idiosyncracy, the theme of struggle between dependency and autonomy again emerges as a familiar one in health visitors' work generally.

Then there was the related difficulty in this family about 'being heard'. The doctors in the workshop pointed out that the illness probably accounted for the pressure and inappropriateness of Mrs Driscoll's lurid revelation of sexual and marital difficulties as well as her dramatic response to her GP's intervention. The illness may well have loosened the bonds of conventional reticence, but her behaviour also indicated her desperation to get her feelings out and listened to. Meanwhile, the content and didactic nature of the GP's advice were probably less important in bringing about the observed change in her than the fact that, through Mrs Quiller, she had gained her doctor's ear.

On the face of it, the first workshop discussion had not done much to elucidate Mrs Quiller's problem. But the change in the pattern of her work and of her engagement with the family thereafter was as dramatic in its way as the change in Mrs Driscoll after the doctor had been invoked. Like her client Mrs Quiller had been listened to and heard, and her dilemma taken seriously. This proved more important that what was said.

Thereafter we see the health visitor finding a way of relating to the family. She did so via Yana in spite of worry about her competence and mixed feelings about working with her. It was both courageous and insightful to have initiated the family session following Yana's genetic counselling appointment. Painful as it was, this was the first time the girl and her parents had been given such an opportunity to express their feelings and distress together. The family had been recognised and treated as a relationship system. In a situation in which no specific medical remedy was available—the sense in which intervention was doomed to failure, as the workshop GP put it—she now began to offer what Winnicott (1986) called 'care-cure'.

HEALTH VISITORS AND THEIR SETTING

The health visitors taking part in the study were based in urban and rural primary care practices, large and small, but organisationally they were part of the community nursing service of a district health authority. A few joined with doctors from the practices in which they worked, but most came into the study on the initiative of their director of nursing services.

They were predominantly an experienced group of practitioners, including several fieldwork teachers responsible for students on practice placements. All had trained as nurses, most had attained seniority and some were also qualified midwives. As health visitors their career-path had taken them from the physically intimate task of caring for sick people in hospital, under the direction of doctors, into work more concerned with the promotion of health than the treatment of illness, preventive and educational rather than remedial in orientation, with home visiting as the predominant medium for practice. It was their distinctive role with mothers and newly born and pre-school children, more than their separate administrative and management structure, that supported the health visitors' claim to autonomy within the primary care team. Their independence, particularly of medical colleagues, was sometimes vigorously asserted during the study, but this status was not a secure one. Although only a few of the cases they contributed were directly concerned with their working relationship with doctors (Mrs Quiller's was an example) yet, especially when medical issues obtruded, the work could produce echoes of their erstwhile hospital days.[2]

The largest category of cases, young children and their mothers, reflected their major work-load. As a client-group this was distinguishable from all the others considered in the study: it was not a problematic one by definition (as Mrs Hunt pointed out). The fact that health visitors were geared to work with a predominantly well population was underlined by a senior administrator who told us that about eighty-five per cent of their work was with 'normal' families; they should refer the remaining 'abnormal' fifteen per cent or seek to share them with other practitioners. A fieldwork teacher commented in the same vein when she said, "we are really a referring agency".

However, 'normal' and 'abnormal' responses to change are in fact often difficult to distinguish in practice and few families stay permanently in one category or the other (Rapoport, 1965). This is particularly so when mothers, couples and families are experiencing the psycho-social transition occasioned by the birth of a baby (even more so with an ill one). Here it is normal to feel stress. Even though the change is essentially natural, the period of disequilibrium may well be considerable, and the related uncertainty for the practitioner—even an experienced and professionally secure one—equally prolonged.

Inevitably questions then arise about what response to make; for example, whether to adopt a stance of 'wait and see', demand-response (familiar in general practice); whether to engage and attempt to exploit the possibilities for personal growth often present at such times—work which can enhance the quality of the child's emotional environment and is therefore prophylactic (Clulow, 1982); whether to invoke a colleague in the same or another agency. Health visitors were beset with uncertainty and conflict about their equivocal sanction for a treatment as opposed to a preventive role with the marital and family stress they actually encountered. The normal/abnormal dichotomy, often invoked as their touchstone, in fact accentuated health visitors' uncertainty about 'grasping the nettle' as one of them put it. They often expressed concern about the large number of unseen clients who they felt were at risk of neglect if the potential demands of problem cases were accepted.

Health visiting, with its deeply-rooted if ambivalent connection with medicine, has undergone many changes since its inception in the 1860s. The accelerating pace of change in recent years has made for uncertainty, and our study reflected further aspects of the change process. Whilst historically the definition of the health visitor's role had broadened to the point of becoming a formidable burden (Hicks, 1976), our colleagues were now faced with cuts in resources which made their problems about priorities even more acute. But their central role, as always, was still to preserve infant life and improve its quality (Jeffrys and Sachs, 1983). Work in the service of the young remains the core of health visitors' practice and, as the cases brought into the study testify, the main source of their working problems.

BOUNDARY DEFINITION AND INTERACTIVE PROCESSES

The vulnerability of infants and young children, their reliance on what Winnicott (1949) so tellingly called 'good-enough mothering', the far-reaching ramifications of the bonding process between mother and child as a basis for the child's development and fruitful later relationships (Bowlby, 1979), all compel attention and fire the imagination. The symbol 'mother-child' is one of the most powerful in the emotional life of all of us. It is a relationship that tends to stir strong feelings, both conscious and unconscious, because of its archetypal quality. The associated conflicts of primitive feeling about dependence and independence in close attachments, alive in the inner world of every individual, are highlighted incessantly in the main strand of health visitors' work. The tasks which have dominated their professional history as well as their day-to-day work—and may well have influenced their occupational choice—must therefore have considerable subjective importance to practitioners in this field.

Of all those who joined the study programme, health visitors were among the most insistent that the frequency of marital problems made them want to explore the implications of marital and family dynamics for their practice. In most of the cases they contributed, marital stress and sometimes overt conflict had become significant early on in the work. In the rest, including the small number concerning elderly clients, the loss or disablement of a spouse was an important feature. But in such an exploration they faced major changes, personal and professional, in their approach to their work, particularly in surmounting their diffidence about intruding on intimate heterosexual relationships, and the conceptual difficulty of turning to a systemic frame of reference. These shifts in perspective were faced by all participants who were not marital specialists but posed problems peculiar to health visitors by virtue of their role and tasks.

Thus, although health visitors were very well aware that marital stress could adversely affect children and their care, yet their task, with its focus on mother and child, induced them to draw a tight conceptual and experiential boundary round that dyad—and to see husbands and fathers relative to it, as we saw in the work with the Batchelors and the Grays. In many cases the men were seen as opting out. For example, one couple had been thrown into disarray following a difficult birth and the diagnosis of a blood disorder in their child. The health visitor recognised that an anxious preoccupation with success and failure was a central feature of their marriage. She reported that, once married, the husband had applied himself to his career with increasing urgency. His pursuit of success at work had distanced him from his wife who said she felt let down by him during the recent crisis—which had left her to bear the failure since the condition was found to be hereditary in her family. But she also told the health visitor that she was sure he was as anxious as she was. They were different, though: "he keeps control of his feelings, I'm emotional". The presenter and another health visitor in the workshop agreed that "poor communication" was a very common problem for couples but that this husband's reactions were "typical of most of the men we meet in our work".[3]

However, when the mother-child dyad is regarded not as a closed but as an open system, itself part of a larger one, the father/husband has perforce to be seen not merely as a facilitator—good, bad or indifferent—of the maternal unit but as an integral part of the interacting couple at the heart of the family relationship system. Their sexuality created it and their respective fears and anxieties, as well as their hopes, are inevitably heightened by the birth of a child. The kind and quality of their anxieties and the defences mustered against them depend on the meaning of the event for each partner. Of particular relevance therefore are the unconscious phantasies and conscious feelings which childbirth, dependency in the infant and dependency in the adult evoke for the parents respectively—*and* for the health visitor as she engages with them.

For the health visitor's practice to take account of interactive processes in marriage and the family thus asks more of her than the development of an extended array of applied techniques. It calls for an extension of conceptual boundaries and a modification of feelings, conscious and unconscious, about the mother-child relationship and about herself and her role in relation to it. Health visitors' mixed feelings about such a shift of boundary in their work were especially evident early in the study. To pay attention to the couple was often felt to be a diversion from their proper role in child health, while to address the marital relationship directly was to be intrusive.

Just how anxious it could feel to involve both partners was illustrated by a very experienced and insightful health visitor. She found herself quite unable to suggest to a mother that it might be a help to talk with her and her husband together about a troublesome issue affecting their child which it seemed her client could not raise with him. However, she achieved a helpful joint interview in which their differences were got into the open for the first time—by leaving her gloves behind and going back to collect them when she knew the man would be home!

It is, of course, the case that health visitors do not always get the chance to meet fathers, but in fact they did in almost half of the study cases. Miss Inskip's work with the Batchelors, however, exemplified the difficulty of putting into practice what health visitors understand theoretically—that the parental couple and the interplay between them are the context for the child's emotional and physical development. As we saw, the working culture, the practitioner's subjective experience and the couple's collusive pattern of interaction combined to restrict her perceptions of the problem and her repertoire of possible responses to it.

CHARACTERISTIC ANXIETIES AND DEFENCES IN HEALTH VISITING

This study is not the first to reveal conflict and uncertainty in the health visitor's professional role. Clulow (1982) noted that:

> conflicting pressures centre on the health visitor as mediator between different worlds, generating tensions which need either to be contained or defended

against. The positioning of the health visitor between the worlds of infant and adult, the medical world of the health visitor's past professional experience and the social world of her families, and a world which sanctions prevention as opposed to one which expects treatment, creates particular opportunities. It also creates problems of identity and needs for containment which are in some ways analogous to those of parents who, in a different sense, are between worlds and having to cope with change (ibid., p. 99).

The parallel drawn by Clulow between the health visitor's experience and that of her clients was also evident in the present study. A crucial link between the two seemed to lie in the anxiety inherent in a conflict between dependency on the one hand and autonomy on the other. Health visitors have to reckon with the tendency for dependency and autonomy to move around in close family relationship systems, often in bewildering ways, or else for vigorous attempts to be made to keep them distinct—out of fear that the one must forever preclude the other. The objective features of the work are bound to stimulate in health visitors themselves similar primitive emotional processes, some of which may be conscious, others repressed and unconscious.

With their 'normal' families health visitors can be 'good-enough mothers' to the mothers and, through them, support the family's capacity to manage the uncertainty engendered by change and the dependency the system has to accommodate during pregnancy, birth and children's early years. In so doing they are enabled to occupy a sanctioned role as community nurses and to keep that degree of distance between themselves and their clients they feel to be appropriate to it.

Such a working structure serves to avoid anxiety and to sustain professional competence and autonomy. It therefore operates as a defence (a socially organised, institutional one) in support of task performance in the health visitors' traditional role with ordinary families. Efforts in the workshops to understand the dynamic processes giving rise to evident distress and complex working problems were frequently experienced by health visitors as threatening this defence, i.e. as attempts to turn ordinary 'normal' clients into extraordinary 'abnormal' ones. Thus, in the case involving the baby with a blood disorder the health visitor stood firmly by her initial assessment that this was "an average family with normal conflicts but with the extra anxiety about their baby", and her view that her work with them was routine.

Even when realistic concern about burdensome case-loads and increasing pressure on resources was allowed for, the health visitors' belief that involvement with 'problem cases' must inevitably be detrimental to their main (i.e. 'normal') client group, their feeling that to pay attention to the parental couple was diversionary, and their associated reluctance to 'grasp the nettle' could all be seen as expressions of a similar defence against anxiety. That health visitors should react ambivalently to a change in perspective is in no way remarkable. Analagous feelings were common to almost all practitioners throughout the disciplines. It was the emphasis on the normal/abnormal dichotomy as the form and content of the defence that was characteristic of the health visitors as a group.

As we have seen, this distinction seldom reflected the reality of practice and did little to advance it. Once relationship problems obtruded and the anxiety-provoking influence of the client system was unavoidably felt by the practitioner, personal and institutional defences could become more rigid; occasionally they could be overwhelmed. Strenuous attempts to 'keep things normal' reflected the former process. What it could be like to feel overwhelmed was movingly expressed by one health visitor who said (of her involvement with a family through the birth of their first child and a subsequent cot death), "I felt I had been caught up in a dangerous game where there were no rules, where anything could happen and where I was alone". She conveyed a crippling sense of helplessness; of being too close to and invaded by the clients. Her feeling of being alone also revealed the need for an effective sentient group within which to externalise and understand the anxiety and thus recover personal boundaries and competence in the work.

HEALTH VISITORS AND INTER-PROFESSIONAL COLLABORATION

Health visitors' characteristic defences against the anxiety arising from conflict between dependency and autonomy also influenced their relationships with other practitioners.

Shared responsibility cases

Unlike the GPs and marriage guidance counsellors, health visitors contributed many cases which could have involved them in working relationships with practitioners outside their own profession. The wives, husbands or children in two-thirds of the families discussed were known to be seeing their doctors during the work reported. A slightly larger number of families, not always the same ones, were known to be in touch with other practitioners. There were very few where no other professional appeared to be involved.

Having clients in common by no means implied that there was communication between the practitioners concerned. Like those in other disciplines, health visitors were liable to be affected by the anxiety and related defences in the client system, particularly when denial and the splitting off and projection of feelings were salient. Thus, while Mrs Hunt readily agreed that it would have been appropriate and useful to get in touch with the probation service, she was influenced at the time by Mrs Gray's denial of any connection between her own behaviour and events, or the reactions of others. Her client's defences, powerfully employed, were reflected in the health visitor's own conflict about making connections. Connecting up with her colleagues in probation would also have meant keeping the absent Mr Gray in mind. We have seen, however, that the health-visiting service's tendency to focus exclusively on the mother-child dyad helps health visitors avoid uncomfortable feelings that can be evoked when directly addressing troubled relationships between husband and wife.

In chapter 5 we described as collusive the failure of doctors and non-medicals outside primary care to work together across their respective agency boundaries. Generalised assumptions about each other were seldom tested against reality and misperceptions were therefore preserved. Although health visitors were more often in contact with other agencies they too could become involved in similar collusive processes, as in the following example.

A crisis following an extra-marital affair showed one of the younger health visitors to be trusted and valued by a mother who sought her out in much distress. The possibility of marital counselling was raised by the health visitor and the client promptly contacted the marriage guidance council on her own initiative asking for an interview for herself. She was then advised to involve rather than exclude her husband and they both attended. However, the health visitor was astonished at the suggestion made in the workshop that by liaising with the counsellor she could make a creative contribution to work with this couple. She felt that the "intensive, internal work" of the counsellor was of greater merit than the "peripheral, external work" of the health visitor. It was difficult for her to accept that the two could be complementary. Discussion in the workshop revealed a widespread belief that communication by community professionals with counsellors was not encouraged by marriage guidance. An experienced marriage guidance counsellor present made it clear, however, that for their part counsellors often feared the reaction of other professionals to approaches by themselves.[4] The issue of confidentiality, often cited as the stumbling-block to communication, turned out to be a very secondary issue (see chapter 4).

In the earlier extensive case examples, we saw how influence was exerted on practitioners by clients whose sense of autonomy was threatened or fragile. Such influence is inescapable. It is a way of communicating what cannot be put into words. Mrs Batchelor's attack undermined Miss Inskip's confidence just as her own belief in her ability to manage independently had been threatened by her pregnancy and her premature delivery of a damaged baby. The health visitor, who identified with her client in some respects, was made to know what it was like to feel dependent and without the assurance of support when vulnerable. Such a sense of loss of autonomy commonly induces hostility and resentment (often unconscious).[5]

Miss Inskip bore the brunt of Mrs Batchelor's anger and blame both of which were assiduously kept out of the couple's marriage; these split-off and displaced feelings were then reflected in her anticipated relationship with the hospital social worker (just as they were so dramatically in the workshop). The process served to reinforce the boundary between the two workers in Miss Inskip's mind, limiting the chances of their exploring their different perspectives, the essence of collaboration.

Another health visitor's comment at the end of Mrs Hunt's case may also be recalled: 'they haven't got onto me so why should I contact them? It was only after presenting the case that I felt I should make the effort and do it.' A different case with a different dynamic impinging on a different health visitor, but a similar theme. Whereas Miss Inskip had no opportunity to try and change the pattern of interaction with her colleague in the light of increased awareness— because the social worker left and was not replaced—the workshop experience had enabled this senior practitioner to free herself from a defensive stance, recover professional autonomy and use it in the service of communication. Lengthy, time-consuming exchanges were not involved, but through her initiative the service network became a reality for both practitioners in the interests of a client for whom they shared responsibility.

Referral and joint work

Referral was a major issue for health visitors, who were concerned with the topic more often than any other discipline in the study. The health visitor series included a few cases in which it was mandatory to invoke other practitioners [6] and some, like Mrs Hunt's, where the outcome of referral was joint work— which, incidentally, did not reduce the health visitor's input.

Workshop discussion of cases where referral was being considered or had actually taken place revealed a juxtaposition of two contrasting reactions by health visitors. There were cases where referral was clearly stimulated by a wish to shed or share the burden of problematic clients; and, less frequently, those where the health visitor was determined *not* to refer—to avoid intrusion into her often 'maternal' relationship with her client.

Like the lack of communication over 'shared responsibility' cases, an anxious impulse to refer was often associated with unfounded attributions of superior, more valuable skill to others along with under-valuation of the health visitor's own distinctive competence. Such a projection of competence into others not only left the individual with the experience of being denuded of it, but could also give rise to hostility and envy.

Among the disciplines, health visitors were notably open and provided vivid examples of the way such processes could impede inter-professional collaboration. One complained of the lack of response by the social services department to her referral of a depressed, waif-like young mother in financial difficulty while her husband was in prison. She was angry at the way she and her client had been ignored—in spite of her hand-delivered letter of referral. On the face of it her feelings seemed justified, but as the discussion developed she commented, "I see I must be more positive . . . not assume that 'them out there' are the experts in every case . . . I must stand and fight, not run away and justify my action *post mortem*". Another practitioner referred a case to a child and family guidance clinic and this led to a plan for joint interviews with the psychiatric social worker. The plan broke down after the first session because the two practitioners had not explored and clarified their different perspectives and roles. Neither felt they should repeat the experience and instead agreed to liaise while seeing the client separately. This did not work either and prompted the health visitor to say, "I felt kept on the outside of [her] 'heavy' interviews", adding that she wished she had never made the referral in the first place.

The last example illustrates not only the hope that referral would ease the health visitor's burden, but also the conflicting sense of it as an intrusion that threatened a hitherto exclusive relationship; third parties could be difficult to admit. One mother was greatly helped following a post-natal depression by the health visitor's perceptive responses to her unrealistic anxiety about her child. Marital problems since before the birth were revealed, as well as difficulties with an intrusive mother and a long series of traumatic previous relationships with men. The question of referral, whether for specialised marital or individual help (the husband had not been seen), was speculated on in the workshop, at which the health visitor protested violently that members wanted to take the case off her. It then emerged that the client family had moved to an adjoining district some months earlier, and she had been putting off the necessity, not of referral, but of transfer to another health visitor—with the sad and angry feelings of loss that this would entail.

Like practitioners of all disciplines, health visitors found it difficult to acknowledge the reality of attachment between clients and themselves, whether the attachment was positive, negative or ambivalent. The threat such feelings could pose was highlighted when health visitors moved and had therefore to terminate their work and effect a transfer, often at short notice. The most telling instance arose on the ending of two years' intensive work with a very deprived young divorced woman whose mother had rejected her in very basic ways. Not only had the health visitor given painstaking attention to the physical problems of a sickly child, she had very effectively 'mothered' her client—which at times had called for real toughness and the survival of vicious verbal attacks and acting out—to the point where the young woman became much more able and effective in the care of her children. The health visitor was severely shaken by her client's reaction when told of her imminent departure—including angry complaints to the GP that "no-one has ever looked after me". Workshop discussion again centred on separation and loss and the anxieties to which this client was particularly vulnerable on the breaking of a valued attachment. The fact that such feelings had not been anticipated and acknowledged with the client was bound to make the parting and transfer to another practitioner more difficult. The health visitor then movingly exclaimed, "it doesn't seem right that you should get to matter so much to them".

To seek to refer or involve another practitioner in joint work is often a creative and sometimes a required course of action. But, as we have seen, decisions about obtaining appropriate help for clients or patients are commonly neither straightforward nor rationally determined. They can represent attempts to export anxiety or dilute it. Meanwhile, health visitors inevitably carry with them into their work in the community the powerful influences of their formative training in hospital nursing. Failure to acknowledge feelings arising from attachments between client and practitioner, idealisation of more 'expert' or resourceful agencies (with a corresponding diminution of the health visitor's sense of personal competence and authority), as well as a tendency to deal with the fear of being judged 'irresponsible' by projection and blaming, can all be seen as transformed versions of defensive themes observed by Menzies Lyth (1970) in the hospital nursing service.[7] However, instead of the defences being operated within the social system of the hospital, health visitors were employing them whilst working in the community, and this inevitably influenced the interplay between them and practitioners in other social systems in which different defences were employed, defences which might be incompatible with theirs or lead to collusion between them.

SUMMARY

The cases health visitors contributed to the study came from the problematic sector of their practice. Their work with this minority group revealed a characteristic experience of anxiety arising from tension and conflict between dependency and autonomy. Health visitors' practice is dominated by the compelling primacy of the mother-child relationship which (like their secondary roles with the chronically ill, disabled and elderly) is bound to activate practitioners' defences against this universal anxiety about dependency, with its roots in infancy. Similar conflictful themes in their clients' lives and in their own professional status speak to this anxiety constantly.

The dilemma does not obtrude in work with most of their clients (though there is always uncertainty about whether these 'normal' clients will cross a threshold and become 'abnormal', i.e. problem ones). Here the health visitor's personal defences against the underlying anxiety inherent in her professional tasks are supported by the socially organised defences of the health-visiting service. Its procedures, administrative structure, rituals and values—its culture—help to sustain personal and professional autonomy.

However, as health visitors in this study showed clearly, their ubiquitous role with mothers, babies and young children, as well as that with their other clients, *unavoidably* exposes them to some situations in which the characteristic anxiety is bound to become more acute. Faced with a sick, disabled or disturbed child, a distraught and non-functioning mother or related marital and family stress, health visitors inevitably experience a heightened tension between dependency and autonomy in the work. Established defences, personal and institutional, may then become more rigid or even be overwhelmed. In either event, the inescapable anxiety is difficult if not impossible to confront and master, and practitioners can lose both their capacity to make flexible and imaginative responses and their realistic sense of personal and professional autonomy.

Where inter-professional collaboration is concerned, rigid defences militate against conducting relationships with other practitioners inter-dependently. When personal and institutional defences are felt to be under threat, health visitors are prone to exaggerate their dependency and to deny their distinctive competence and authority in a process primarily aimed at 'exporting' anxiety.

Health visitors who took part in this study, like other participants, hoped thereby to improve the quality and range of their practice. In their case, this hope was related particularly to the work with 'problem' clients for which they had equivocal sanction and little support. In spite of evident uncertainty, they were however drawn into it by the clients, by their assigned responsibility and (on the evidence of our experience) by their determination to continue engaging with their service's characteristic developmental struggle—to reconcile and mediate between dependency and autonomy.

Notes

1   The system of splitting behaviour exhibited in the Gray's marriage corresponded with what Mattinson and Sinclair (1979) described as the 'net and sword' pattern of interaction, where conscious rejection and unconscious yearning alternate within the relationship.

2   The report of the Community Nursing Review (1986) recommended the establishment of discrete neighbourhood nursing services. Aiming to remedy what were seen as weaknesses in community nursing and primary care, this would bring district nurses,

health visitors and school nurses together into a separately managed service. One of the main arguments was the need to strengthen the independence of these practitioners *vis-à-vis* GPs and affirm the health visitor's professional identity as a nurse in the community.

3   Anecdotal evidence from this study, especially from the health visitors and doctors, supported findings by other researchers (for example Brannan and Collard, 1982) that, though there are changes afoot in society, dependency and the feelings associated with it can still pose special problems for many men. Meanwhile investigation of the effects of unemployment on marriage has offered a reminder of the importance of work in confirming masculine identity and as a vehicle through which to express the capacity to care and succour; and the close association of love and work (Mattinson, 1988).

4   The belief that difficult relations between health visitors and marriage guidance counsellors are mainly due to the latter, rather than reciprocal, was obvious in the evidence of the Council for Education and Training of Health Visitors and the Health Visitors Association recorded in *Marriage matters* (Home Office/DHSS, 1979).

5   See Mattinson (1988, Part III), for a discussion of dependency and loss of competence and personal autonomy in the unemployed.

6   Part of the procedure established to protect children thought to be at risk of non-accidental injury.

7   Avoidance of feelings and not acknowledging attachment is comparable to the defence Menzies Lyth (1970, p. 50 *et seq.*) described as 'detachment and denial of feelings'; exporting anxiety by involving experts, to 'the reduction of the impact of responsibility by delegation to superiors'; the tendency to blame and project irresponsibility, to 'collusive social redistribution of responsibility and irresponsibility'.

7

Probation

Seventeen cases were contributed by the five probation officers and three senior probation officers who took part in the study. Our focus in this chapter will be on those cases (the majority) which concerned criminal offenders. A few others arose from the probation officer's role as welfare officer in civil court actions over child custody and access, which is outside our scope to examine here.[1]

Since most offences are committed by young males, much of the work of probation officers is concerned with this group; their clients are often single, at a stage when close family attachments are not the predominant relationships in their lives nor (on the face of it) immediately relevant to their offending behaviour. But there is a significant proportion of probation service clients who are embedded in family relationships either as married adults or as adolescents living with their parents, and whose delinquency can be seen to be related to those active attachments. As might be expected, all the preoccupying criminal cases contributed to the study were of this kind and the family dimension made it more likely that other agencies were involved. The number of women offenders was disproportionately high. In our two case examples both husband and wife were clients.

In the early 'in-house' phase of the study programme, Mr Webster presented to the probation workshop "the most complex and difficult case I've had for a long time and the one where I'm most closely involved with marital stress as an acute problem here and now". He was also involved in inter-agency tensions, but his first presentation was almost entirely taken up with details of the family and his own three-year involvement with them. He kept meticulously to the headings and sub-headings of the form we were using for research purposes,[2] and gave a clue to the possibly defensive function of this way of proceeding when he broke off to repeat, "as I'm telling you this it sounds the most complex and awful case". Even our abbreviated opening summary gives an idea of how true this was.

The baby-sitter Chris and Carol Weekes' relationship had begun when she used to baby-sit for him and his first wife. Mr Weekes, then thirty-three, had intercourse with fifteen year-old

Carol, and went to prison for it. His relationship with his wife was already deteriorating, with Chris unemployed and drinking heavily (after their fourth child had died in infancy), and she divorced him after this incident. Within two years, Chris and Carol were married; the older two of his three children had run away from their mother's custody to join them in the squat where they had set up home; even though the oldest was only a year younger than Carol, the divorce court had endorsed this arrangement (after investigation by Mr Webster) but made supervision orders on the two boys; Carol had become pregnant; the family had been re-housed; Chris, still unemployed, had committed more offences, including shoplifting jointly with Carol; and both were on probation—Chris' order including a requirement to receive treatment for alcoholism. The limited information about their respective family backgrounds showed that both had been middle children in large working-class families. Chris' mother had died when he was fourteen, and he had been bitterly hostile to his step-mother; he had married first at nineteen.

For a year or so, the couple had two probation officers, Mr Webster for the boys' supervision orders and a colleague for the couple's probation orders. Some months after the latter orders expired Chris Weekes committed two further offences—breaking into a slot-meter in their house and obtaining bicycles for the two boys by deception (a false declaration for hire purchase). The other probation officer having left, it was Mr Webster who prepared the social inquiry report for the crown court; in it he was doubtful whether a further probation order could be effective. Mr Weekes was still subject to a suspended prison sentence for one of his previous offences, and this was activated together with a sentence for the new offences: nine months' imprisonment in all.

Amongst the information Mr Webster was giving the workshop were two events in the months leading up to these new offences: Chris Weekes' father had died and Carol had become pregnant with their second son (born between Chris' arrest and sentence). So split up between the various headings on the form were these events that no-one in the workshop made the chronological connections or considered their possible significance in Mr Weekes' re-offending. Mr Webster was in any case chiefly concerned with a more recent episode, in which Carol Weekes committed a further offence.

Her husband's imprisonment had left Mrs Weekes with a new baby and a two year-old to look after; her two stepsons (now nineteen and sixteen) soon returned to their own mother. Still only twenty herself, she could look for little support from her parents who were both chronically ill and had younger children still at home. She became an almost daily visitor to the probation office where as a prisoner's wife she was offered support not only by Mr Webster but by the whole staff team, through their call-in facilities and the mothers and babies group for which transport was provided from her outlying council estate. Mr Webster felt she was becoming "dependent on myself and the team". All the provision outside her home, however, did not prevent her from despairing inside it. She complained that rising damp defeated her efforts at redecoration, ruined the family's clothes and was responsible for her children's recurrent chest infections. As Mr Webster put it, "all the stress became irrationally focused on the house". One day (after calling out her GP for the children yet again) she set fire to it. The house was rendered uninhabitable, and she was charged with arson.

Even before Carol Weekes precipitated this crisis, the various practitioners involved with the family had become concerned about whether she was coping as a single parent, and had held an inter-agency case conference. Now the picture became more ominous. Mr Webster enlisted the help of a woman colleague in preparing the social inquiry report; their interviews with Mrs Weekes focused on what had led up to her extreme act of fire-raising. She confirmed rumours that she had become involved with another man, who had moved in with her; the relationship was stormy and violent and she had eventually got him to leave two days before she set fire to the house. She also spoke of her violent feelings towards the children. Though she insisted she had made sure they were safe from the fire, it was clear that the responsibility of caring for them on her own had been a major factor in

bringing her to the limit of her endurance. She acknowledged losing her temper frequently with the two year-old
and fearing that she would "lose control" altogether.

At a further case conference it was decided that both
children should be placed on the 'at risk' register, and that
Mr Webster should be the key worker in relation to this;
there was no local authority social worker involved with
the family. Mrs Weekes and the children were perforce
staying with her parents, but no-one found this satisfactory. Mr Webster set about getting them re-housed and
they were soon allocated a mobile home by way of
temporary 'homeless families' accommodation. Meanwhile, Mrs Weekes was put on probation for two years for
the offence of arson.

The last heading on the form was 'other salient factors'.
Under this catch-all rubric Mr Webster noted that there
had been "relationship problems between Carol and Chris"
during his prison sentence; with normal remission, this
had two months to run at the time of Carol's offence. Mr
Webster commented that the news of the fire had aggravated Chris Weekes' feelings to the point of declaring,
"I'm never going back". This was still his attitude so far as
staff at the prison knew, but to Mr Webster it was not so
clear cut. He knew from Carol Weekes that she wanted her
husband back, and he "suspected that Chris would in fact
return". Faced with this uncertainty his policy had been to
wait and see. Chris Weekes had been released two days
before he presented the case in the workshop.

In the short time available for discussion on this first occasion the present
position was only briefly glimpsed. Mr Webster had offered an appointment at
his office the previous day for the Weekes together, in case Mr Weekes should
have returned to his wife; they had not turned up, but Mr Webster was
intending to visit Mrs Weekes' mobile home (for the first time) immediately
after the workshop, when "I expect he'll be there". The workshop discussion,
however, did not dwell on the current situation and the working problems—or
opportunities—this might present for Mr Webster. Members seemed so
"overwhelmed by the amount of information" (as Mr Webster later noted)—to
say nothing of its disturbing nature—that they tried to make it more
manageable by getting every legal and procedural aspect straight, and
establishing which category of work applied to husband and wife respectively.

They became especially preoccupied with the responsibilities Mr Webster had taken on in accepting the role of key worker in respect of the children being at risk. It was exceptional for a probation officer to do this, as Mr Webster acknowledged; he had sought approval, in discussions with both his senior and the assistant chief probation officer, before agreeing. But his service colleagues in the workshop (who included two senior probation officers) felt he had allowed himself to be pushed by the other practitioners at the case conference into accepting tasks and responsibilities that were not properly his as a probation officer. His job, they told him, was to focus on Carol Weekes and the offending behaviour for which she had been put on probation; his involvement with the family had been complex enough before, but now it was being further complicated. A strong view developed in the workshop that Mr Webster had "taken on too much".

Comment

The all-probation workshop seemed as meticulous about legal and procedural categories as Mr Webster had been about the headings on the form. Now members were taking this concern a stage further by exhorting Mr Webster to cut down his involvement, resist pressure from other agencies and concentrate on his most basic task. In chapter 2 we suggested that an individual practitioner who goes back to basics in this way may be defending against anxiety. Here it was his colleagues who urged the practitioner to narrow his focus. Was this defensive on their part?

Practitioners sometimes do take on too much and get their objectives muddled, and it can be salutary to call for clarity by reference to primary task. But there were anomalies in the workshop members' approach which belied this common-sense view. In the first place, although Mr Webster's acceptance of the key worker role was indeed open to question and debate, since it was so unusual, his colleagues dismissed it out of hand. Improper pressure from other agencies was assumed without further ado, although in fact Mr Webster had given no details of the case conference discussion and had made it clear that he had the authority of his probation service superiors for his decision.

A second anomaly was the other members' insistence that he should focus on Carol Weekes alone. This overlooked the fact that Chris Weekes, as a released prisoner, was potentially his client as well, albeit a voluntary one. Even in the static terms of categories of work, therefore, a proper responsibility of Mr Webster's was being denied. More dynamically, Mr Webster's presentation of the case at the moment of Mr Weekes' release suggests that this event might well have been the source of an immediate working problem which was troubling him, but which he and the workshop were failing to address.

Both the authors were present at this workshop and were part of its failure. Indeed, we unwittingly made a specific contribution. As in all the other workshops at this early stage of the programme, we had taken some of the session to clarify with members the purpose and use of the various forms we had prepared for recording the work. This emphasis on form and structure is likely to have aided and abetted the defence used by Mr Webster and the other members here. As the study programme went on, however, we came to see a defensive invoking of rules as widely characteristic of the probation officers' culture.

If there was defensiveness, what was the anxiety? The evidence lies as much in what was not said as in what was said. The two main tasks of the workshop were both neglected. Just as there was no exploration of what had actually taken place between the practitioners at the case conference so there was no attention given to the meaning of Mr and Mrs Weekes' offending in the context of their marriage relationship. Yet they had committed some offences together, and their most recent crimes were domestic—Chris breaking into their own meter, and Carol setting fire to their own home. We have already noted that the timing of Chris' last offences, following the death of his father and the start of Carol's second pregnancy, went unremarked; likewise the timing of Mr Webster's presentation, two days after Chris' release from prison amidst uncertainty as to whether he would return to Carol.

Despite all these links which were there to be made, the workshop insisted that only offending, and only Carol's offending, should be the probation officer's concern. Yet the extraordinary offence she had committed was not explored either. If anxiety was signalled by what was avoided, then we could surmise that what Mr Webster felt was 'awful', and his colleagues felt was 'too much', was some combination of the alarming nature of the offence; the extremes of violent and dependent feelings in the Weekes' marriage and other relationships; and his own complex involvement with them. Some further light was cast on this when Mr Webster presented the case a second time at the next fortnightly meeting.

> Prefacing his account with another reference to pro-gramme guidelines, about the need to avoid being "swamped with material", Mr Webster added, "I've been at the case conference all morning so it's fresh in my mind".
>
> Chris Weekes did return to Carol on his release from prison, and when Mr Webster visited (after the previous workshop meeting) he found "a pretty awful situation". At the door, a startled Carol hastily urged him not to reveal that he knew about yet another lover she had taken between the fire and Chris's release. Inside, Chris greeted him with: "I'm leaving anyway—just heard she's been carrying on with this other fellow—I'm not an idiot". It transpired that the man had called round and been

welcomed affectionately by the two year-old. Chris spoke scornfully of the mobile home (which was in Carol's name) as a "pigeon house"; he went on insulting her, calling her "a cow—it runs in the family".

Faced with "not an easy situation for me to handle", Mr Webster explained "what would happen if they separated, what he would have to do if he left, what kind of help I could give him, and what my contact would be with Carol —she'd continue to see me under the probation order. That was that."

A week later, the couple called at the probation office.

Chris had indeed left, but after a few days had come back "for a trial period, to see how things go". Now they had run out of money; Carol had spent some of her benefit on tools for Chris to apply for jobs (so far without success), and all his release grant had gone. Mr Webster knew from experience that it would take all day for them to negotiate successfully with the DHSS for extra money; he explained the procedure and encouraged them to keep at it. This entailed several cross-town journeys, with the couple arranging to rendezvous at Mr Webster's office; but they kept missing each other so that Mr Webster saw them more separately than together during the day. In the course of this he impressed on Carol that he expected to see her the following week at the first meeting of an induction group for new probationers. As well as being her probation officer he was co-leader of this group, where the aim was to encourage members to think about why they had committed offences and how they could stay out of trouble in future.

Mrs Weekes did not turn up at the group. She was not at the (voluntary) mothers and babies group earlier the same afternoon—for some reason the usual transport had not called for her—so the expectation that she would stay on from one group to the next did not materialise. Mr Webster wrote her "a stiff letter" saying he wanted to see her to discuss this "serious situation in view of the probation order".

The following day (just before the workshop) the case conference re-convened to consider the Weekes' situation now that Chris was out of prison. Mr Webster, mindful of the previous workshop discussion, decided to re-open the issue of who should be the key worker and this took up much of the meeting. It was agreed that responsibility would instead be shared between the health visitor as 'prime worker', and the senior social worker (whose department was still not directly involved with the family) as "case co-ordinator". Mr Webster's role would be to "work the probation order" with Carol, focusing on "helping her to increase her understanding of her offending behaviour". He was "very happy about that decision, which gives me a much more limited and clearly focused role".

That completed Mr Webster's presentation, but he contributed more information as the workshop discussion ranged back over these events:

A prison-based colleague had reported that at one stage during his sentence Chris Weekes had said he did not wish to see Mr Webster who had "helped Carol but had never been any help to him". Mr Webster had visited him in prison nonetheless but the issue seemed not to have been fully resolved. There were more details of Mr Weekes' very strong reaction in prison to the news of his wife's fire-raising. Like many prisoners, he had already been nursing the dread that she was being unfaithful, and now veered between those intensely jealous feelings and angrier assertions that she was mad and he wanted nothing more to do with her. He got into fights with other prisoners who referred to what Carol had done.

On the day when Mr Webster saw husband and wife variously at the office, he heard of another comment by Chris, this time relayed by Carol: "he thought my job was to keep marriages together, not break them up—the mothers and babies group on her own, the induction group on her own—it would break up the marriage".

During Mr Webster's home visit Carol "just sat very quiet, cowed under the barrage of insults". Mr Webster felt Chris was "totally dominant" and "lays down the rules" in their marriage, but he knew of no physical violence.

The case conference was concerned that since Chris's release Carol seemed to have "withdrawn" her previously frequent contact with the probation office and the health visitor; the conference members felt "certain that it's him stopping the contact".

In contrast with the first workshop discussion, members now pursued the issue of Mr Weekes' status as a client in his own right, questioning whether Mr Webster had offered him help unequivocally and suggesting that joint work with the couple might be more effective than insisting on Carol's attendance at the induction group. A workshop member observed that to Chris Weekes, powerless in prison, Mr Webster must have seemed a rival, detracting from Carol's attachment to him and even sympathising with her offence and her unfaithfulness.

The *volte-face* by workshop members was striking. In the first presentation Mr Webster had given them 'too much' to cope with and they had responded by insisting on adherence to basic task. By the second meeting Mr Webster appeared to have accepted their strictures and carried them out to the letter; now that he was so firmly on that side, his colleagues found themselves more in touch with the other side, could readily imagine what Chris Weekes must be feeling, and came nearer to recognising Mr Webster's dilemma.

The workshop did not however manage to hold both sides together and come to an integrated view. Instead, the discussion became bogged down in yet another legalistic issue—whether Mr Webster was correct in defining Carol Weekes' failure to attend the induction group as a breach of the terms of her probation order. The issue was not unimportant (a point arises from it which we discuss later in the chapter) but the undue time devoted to it confirms that it was serving as another defence against confronting anxiety.

Comment

It was clear that Mr Weekes, despite his ostensible 'dominance', felt humiliated by his wife's behaviour and excluded from her relationship with Mr Webster whilst he was in prison. Mr Webster's focus of attention had indeed shifted radically towards Mrs Weekes. Originally concerned with the older children's welfare under the aegis of the divorce court, he had dealt mainly with Chris Weekes as their custodial parent, with Carol entering the picture only as his teenaged partner—scarcely older than the children. Recently, however, with Chris once more in prison and his children gone, it was the obvious neediness of Carol Weekes and *her* two children that came to the fore, together with anxiety about these children's safety. Carol's offence and her new status as a statutory client confirmed her claim on Mr Webster's attention. The case conference practitioners (as reported) seemed to echo this focus on Carol by regarding Chris' return mainly as an obstacle to their work with her.

The immediate anxiety, for both Mr Webster and his workshop colleagues, no doubt arose from the sexual misbehaviour of the clients and the way a practitioner could become implicated in this. Throughout his long involvement with the couple Mr Webster had, correctly, maintained a non-judgemental attitude towards their personal life. Chris Weekes had had intercourse with his under-age baby-sitter; in spite of being unlawful and duly punished, this event had paradoxically become the foundation of their marriage, which Mr Webster then accepted. When her husband was in prison Carol Weekes broke the sexual rules in her turn, but Mr Webster did not withdraw his support; inevitably that laid him open to accusations of complicity—most acutely at the time of Mr Weekes' release from prison. On his visit to the mobile home Mrs Weekes indeed implicated him as she opened the door. It was not surprising that he managed only a stilted (and highly procedural) response to the angry distress of Mr Weekes; as his workshop colleague pointed out, he was in Chris Weekes' eyes a rival—yet in his own eyes he had been responding to Carol's manifest dependency, and he must also have felt betrayed just as her husband did.

This was the dilemma that Mr Webster had in effect brought to the workshop, not naming it in so many words but *conveying* it to his colleagues as he told the story. It resembles the 'third party' dilemmas in marriage guidance counselling discussed in chapter 4, where we pointed out links with the early oedipal conflicts of the clients. Here such links can only be suggested—but vividly nonetheless—by Carol's marriage in adolescence to a man old enough to be her father, a man who for his part had lost his mother when *he* was an adolescent and rejected her replacement.

These 'incestuous' connotations of the Weekes' marriage, compounded by Carol's unfaithfulness and Mr Webster's involuntary implication in a triangle with the couple, make it understandable that he and his colleagues sought to defend themselves against facing the sexual anxiety that was bound to be stirred up. This, however, powerfully constrained their capacity to reflect on the meaning of the couple's offending behaviour—and thus to address the service's primary task of reducing it.

For the second presentation made it clear that Chris and Carol Weekes were struggling with a shared problem essentially about attachment, in which sexual and criminal misbehaviour alike were the means rather than the end. Each wanting but at the same time mistrustful of the other as an attachment figure on whom they could rely, confirming each other's mistrust by their actions and their destructive retaliations, they separated only to come together again—but their coming together seemed epitomised by the way they kept missing each other the day Mr Webster was helping them with the DHSS. They resembled the couples whom Mattinson and Sinclair (1979) described as caught in a pattern of ambivalent attachment.

The more fundamental anxiety here, both for the Weekes and for their probation officer, arose from their extreme fluctuations of feeling between helpless dependency on the one hand and violent jealousy and rage on the other. This pattern was not explored or understood in the workshop, though it was well documented in Mr Webster's reports of Chris and Carol Weekes' behaviour. Chris' offences seem to portray a helpless sense of inadequacy; his more furious feelings were submerged in this way of behaving (perhaps also in his drinking) but emerged in his violent reactions to Carol's behaviour when he was confined in prison and immediately after his release. Carol too portrayed extreme dependency as a prisoner's wife, but having evicted her violent lover she became only too aware of violent feelings in herself. Helpless to control them, she let them loose on the house—and her claim that in so doing she was protecting her children seems entirely believable in a psychological sense.

The couple's own struggle was echoed in their triangular relationship with Mr Webster. Each had known him for several years, each in turn had claimed priority in his attention, and each had risked losing his support by their behaviour. As a probation officer he personified the lawful and resourceful world by which they felt deprived and against which they retaliated. Yet he had managed, within the constraints of his task, to stick with them and show concern for both. He was in fact someone to whom each of them could, and did, form an attachment—albeit ambivalent and increasingly rivalrous as between them.

Mr Webster was inevitably affected by the dynamic fluctuations of feeling in the Weekes' interaction both with each other and with himself. This was reflected in fluctuations on his part—albeit less extreme than theirs—in the responses they evoked in him. As divorce court welfare officer he was for a long time prepared to be very supportive, but at the point when he took on the different role of assessing Chris Weekes as an offender he witheld a recommendation for probation, i.e. he could not envisage further supportive care being effective to prevent the unresponsive Mr Weekes offending again. Instead, with the husband imprisoned, he mobilised all the probation office's resources to offer support and care to the wife.

Though alarmed by Mrs Weekes' subsequent offence and her acknowledgement of violent feelings towards her children, he stuck with her and invited the court to take the risky but merciful option of probation for a serious crime. But at the point when Mr Weekes' fury was released from the confines of prison it seemed impossible for him to offer care to either of them. It was not long before they turned to him again for help with their finances, which he gave; but meanwhile he was falling back on more controlling measures—explaining procedure, getting tough with Carol Weekes over the induction group and pulling out of the key worker role on the inter-agency front.

Mr and Mrs Weekes' dependency and deprivation called forth a caring and at times indulgent response from their probation officer; their violence and destructiveness, a controlling and at times rejecting one. Over the course of his work with the couple Mr Webster fluctuated between these responses—and during Mr Weekes' imprisonment he perhaps divided them between wife and husband. The clients' splitting of the neediness from the anger constrained the worker from exercising care and control *simultaneously*, the one tempering the other, so as to offer them a way of containing these conflicting impulses—i.e. their primitive splitting defence was replicated in him. Thus the Weekes conveyed to Mr Webster their own dilemma, just as he in turn conveyed it to the workshop members, whose *volte-face* from one meeting to the next in their interaction with him reflected the same pattern of fluctuating responses.

Both the dilemma and the constraints against resolving it came primarily from the couple. But the dynamic tension between care and control is a characteristic source of anxiety for probation officers and gives rise to characteristic defences.

Follow-up

The Weekes were still together, with a third child (following a miscarriage), when Carol's probation order ended two years later. She had made good use of the induction group; when Chris was put on probation again, for an old offence held over from before his imprisonment, he was excused attendance at the group because it now included one of Carol's ex-lovers. Mr Webster, however, felt he "never really re-engaged" with Chris, who by the end of his one-year order was still drinking heavily and in danger of prison for unpaid fines. By that time the social services department was directly involved; as the social worker took more responsibility concerning the family, Mr Webster felt more rejected by them and his contact "tailed off". When last heard of, they had just been re-housed by the local authority; their garden backed onto that of Chris's first wife.

Comment

An uncomfortable triangle and the anxiety of how to manage it lay at the heart of Mr Webster's working dilemma. The follow-up material confirms the earlier picture of the couple's struggle with their own shared dilemma concerning reliable attachments, with constant reference to third parties, and the replication of this three-way dynamic in their relationship with Mr Webster. Even the original triangle between Chris, Carol and the first Mrs Weekes was potentially still active.

We can see comparable triangular dilemmas affecting the professionals throughout the case narrative. In the first workshop discussion, for example, members protested at the interference of a third party—the case conference—in the probation officer's proper relationship with his client. According to the second presentation, the case conference itself later cast Mr Weekes in the role of a third party interfering with the united efforts of the assembled practitioners to help his wife. In the follow-up period, Mr Webster's 'rejection' by the couple in favour of the social worker (recalling Mrs Hunt's case in chapter 6) exemplifies the 'triangle of collaboration' which is ever present in inter-agency work.

Triangular themes were again evident in the next case, though the working issues were quite different and inter-agency tensions were aroused in the workshop rather than in the case itself. Perhaps because the study programme was by now well established Mr Chambers, a senior probation officer, was much less guarded in his presentation to the interdisciplinary workshop than Mr Webster had been with his own colleagues back in the early stages. He readily included his own thoughts and feelings as he brought the case as an urgent problem 'off the cuff'.

Separate or together   Mr Timpson, halfway through a three-year probation order for stealing parcels from doorsteps, had been transferred to Mr Chambers from a woman colleague who was leaving the service; now, six months later, Mrs Timpson too committed an offence of theft and came under his supervision. She had been shopping and finished up having a few drinks. "She can't remember anything else till she woke up in a police station dishevelled and in a mess with the police saying that she'd lifted a bottle of spirits from a shop. Though she didn't remember, she pleaded guilty." He had heard a lot about her from her husband but so far had only seen her three times—two meetings on which he based his social inquiry report, and one since her two-year probation order was made. Mr Chambers himself was due to move in three months' time to head up a new community service unit elsewhere in the county.

Like her husband, Daphne Timpson was in her mid-thirties. She had been on probation once some years earlier; more recently, after several further convictions, she had served a short prison sentence. Mr Chambers had tried to see her then, and at other times since taking over her husband's supervision, but she had always refused. This time, to his surprise, she was co-operative and thoughtful at interview, seemed to trust him and wanted to be on probation—so long as she was seen by him and on her own. Her husband had apparently reminded her of Mr Chambers' past efforts to help and had been an advocate of probation. But he had assumed they would be seen together and was put out and anxious about her being seen for weekly sessions without him. However, Mr Chambers felt he had no option but to accept Daphne's stipulation if he was to engage with her. He thought, too, that she was probably right. She would be best seen without her husband; she had more potential for change than he.

Daphne told Mr Chambers that she and most of her numerous siblings "could not be cared for" by their parents and were brought up in orphanages in Wales. She seemed to have been reasonably happy there, and later in a hostel, though rather solitary and self-contained. She went into the army at seventeen, accumulated six 'O' levels and married her first husband, a soldier; she left the army soon after the marriage but continued to work in the same unit as a civilian.

Her first pregnancy resulted in a still-birth, and she was discovered to be diabetic. A second pregnancy was successful and she gave birth to a daughter, but within a short time this marriage broke up; she "fled" with her daughter to one of her relations in another part of the country and then took up council accommodation back near where she had spent her time in the army, in the area covered by Mr Chambers' office. Here her health and her situation started to deteriorate. She had a minor heart attack, became depressed and began drinking heavily. Not surprisingly, there were diabetic complications and the condition became unstable. She began offending (by now she was twenty-eight), and shop-lifting led to her first period of probation. "There was an eruption of some sort every few months." Meanwhile, Daphne's care of her young daughter had begun to cause concern.

At this point the social worker members of the workshop contributed to Mr Chambers' presentation. They recalled that Daphne's previous probation officer had called in social services, leading to the little girl being taken into care, fostered and eventually adopted by the foster parents. And they endorsed what Mr Chambers had gathered from Daphne—that none of this happened against her will; quite the reverse. She felt she "could not care for" her child and indeed the adoption had been at her instigation. The social workers also confirmed that she kept regular contact ("she's become 'auntie' to the child in an unusual and helpful way") and seemed determined that her own chaotic life should not impinge on her daughter. "With her she's very sane and sensible".

Nick Timpson was also Welsh and previously married, but appeared to have no contact with his ex-wife or children. Mr Chambers knew less of his history than of Daphne's, but the record showed that he too came from a large family. He had also been in the army but unlike Daphne (who had got on well) he could not cope with it; his service was brief. Unable to control violent tempers and impulsive behaviour, "he has been described as having a disturbed personality though not suffering from any specific mental illness; he occasionally seeks medical help and is usually now treated by 'Modecate' injections".

During his long history of frequent, mainly minor, offences "the court has lost patience with him on a number of occasions and he has served several prison sentences". His family had disowned him at one stage and it was Daphne who ended the estrangement.

Daphne had met Nick a year or two after her daughter went into care. They were in similar circumstances: in trouble with the law and drinking heavily. They lived together for a while and then married in spite of opposition from Nick's previous probation officer. Now two years old, the marriage had been marked by violent rows from the beginning. "Nick is less intelligent, more impulsive and irrational, yet Daphne describes a feeling of care for him as if she needs to look after him—in spite of the fact that one could say he's quite a nasty person.

There's something about him like a wayward child whom she's looking after ... they've stuck together for a long time and everyone is quite amazed ... the marriage survives for some obscure reason."

One of the social workers interjected what a relief it had been from their point of view when Nick was in prison and "off the scene for a bit", but Mr Chambers quoted Daphne's own judgement that she was "not much better than him" and that on her own she "goes to pieces". And there was another side to it. "Nick also sees himself as looking after Daphne. He's said to me, 'whatever would happen to her if I wasn't there?' He tries to arrange everything about her life, her medical treatment, her foster home visits which he tries to gate-crash—everything." Daphne however resisted any interference by him in her daughter's life.

He also came with her to the probation office. "Every quarter of an hour during our interviews Nick would knock, stick his head round my door to say something or other ... he invades the space Daphne now says she wants for herself." His preoccupation with Daphne's health was again confirmed by the social workers; they knew, for example, that he had made strenuous though unsuccessful efforts to get a grant to buy a refrigerator so that she could store her insulin safely.

The Timpsons had taken "waifs and strays" into their home from time to time, and felt good that they were helping someone. But "it always blows up and they chuck them out, with Nick coming into the office to moan about how awful these people are".

The presentation, embellished as it was by the social workers from their earlier knowledge, ended with Mr Chambers' comment that the couple's manifest problems (their parlous financial state, their drinking, her bouts of depression, his wild behaviour) were obviously inter-linked with their offences and in some way related to the way they felt about each other. But he was not clear how this applied to the offence which got Daphne on proba-tion.

Mr Chambers opened the discussion with a clear statement of his dilemma and the confused feelings the couple had engendered in him: "I don't know where it will go; having made the initial contract to see Daphne on her own, how and at what level can I work with the marriage? I need to, but don't honestly know how. And there is the very significant change in my relationship with Nick. I think he's very fearful of all I might learn about him from Daphne." Nick in fact suspected that the probation service was still opposed to the marriage, and Mr Chambers admitted that he certainly had very different feelings about the two of them. "I've struggled with Nick, but can't get through to him. You can to Daphne. She's a better bet." He wondered how to handle these feelings, some of which derived from other people's views, some from within himself and his own experience of the Timpsons. Taking sides like this made him feel "somewhat guilty" and induced uncertainty.

To begin with the social workers also took sides, concentrating attention on Daphne and her positive potential; the way she had managed the fostering and adoption, and her successful efforts to reconcile Nick and his family. One said, "she's quite a remarkable person really", and another, "from what I've picked up, your brief is to work with her to build on her self-esteem, but *not* to touch on the actual dynamics of the marriage". Mr Chambers was not so sure: "if that's my brief, it's very difficult to keep to", especially as Nick and Daphne both filled their interviews with talk about each other; there were complaints in plenty but also concern.

Mr Chambers' struggle to be fair enabled the group to entertain the idea that each partner might unconsciously embody a dynamically important aspect of the other's personality; that their ambivalent attachment to each other and the shared defences of splitting and projection could therefore be seen as attempts, however abortive, to become more integrated.

One of the social workers was then able to draw on her child-care experience and relate it to Daphne. It would be characteristic of a child in an impersonal long-term care institution to be torn between a longing for personal and individualised love and a self-destructive anger and despair at not achieving it; Daphne's marriage to Nick would re-create that conflict in her. The group gave some credence to the idea that through her concern for the 'quite nasty' Nick she was perhaps caring for the (projected) bad aspect of herself. Though the origins of Nick's corresponding conflict were obscure, he seemed to have been left with an anxious need to find and repeatedly test a relationship which could contain him and his destructive impulses (as presumably his parents, the army and his first marriage had not done) and which also offered him the opportunity to be reparative.

These efforts to understand the dynamic underlying the couple's interaction led members to see the significance for these two clients of Mr Chambers' attempts to relate to them both and mediate between them—separately *and* together. From this the group went on to consider some of the implications of his impending departure, and the clients' transfer. Mr Chambers had clearly become important to them both; they might well act-out because of an inability to express and manage their feelings about his leaving them; "they could go on the booze, commit offences or she'll misuse the insulin".

Comment

The workshop had reached a useful understanding of the dynamics of the Timpsons' marriage. In the process, however, Mr Chambers and the other members (only social workers and a health visitor on this occasion) had to contend with the influence of those dynamics upon themselves. In particular, Mr and Mrs Timpson's different ways of defending against anxiety about their destructive impulses seemed to get reflected in some of the interactions between the social workers and Mr Chambers.

Mrs Timpson, the solitary orphanage child, hoped to segregate the good side of herself (for example her care for her daughter) away from the bad which she tended to split off and project into her husband. Periodically the bad would erupt in her own delinquent behaviour—of which, however, she could remain literally unconscious through drink. Mr Timpson, whose behaviour was reminiscent of a neglected child enviously trying to muscle in on mother's relationship with father (or the other children), hoped to repair the damage he feared causing by becoming solicitous and clinging. Thus under the pressure of anxiety she resorted to separateness, he to togetherness.

This conflict of theirs had given Mr Chambers the working dilemma he could not resolve. Impressed by Daphne's greater potential for change, he had allowed her wish for segregated interviews and he acknowledged a tendency to take her side. However, when the social workers joined him in this tendency from their prior knowledge of her responsible behaviour as a mother, Mr Chambers was impelled out of fairness to remember the other side and stress the couple's togetherness.

In taking up these positions the practitioners were certainly affected by the dynamic influence of the client relationship system they were discussing—via the reflection process (Mattinson, 1975) which we have encountered in previous chapters. But they divided on very significant lines. It was the quality of parenting that seemed to sway the social workers, whilst the probation officer was motivated by fairness.

We shall be discussing the anxieties and defences arising for social workers in connection with good and bad parenting in the next chapter. Meanwhile Mr Chambers' concept of fairness bears a family likeness to the earlier emphasis on rules in Mr Webster's case. It certainly served a more constructive purpose here, keeping him (and the workshop) in touch with both sides of the dilemma, but the discussion had to go beyond mere fairness to reach an understanding of how the two sides related to each other in the couple's interaction.

On this occasion the understanding did not extend to seeing how, specifically, the Timpsons' criminal behaviour was related to this interaction; Mr Chambers had given no information about the contexts of their respective offences. It was therefore not fully established in what way working with the marriage would be relevant to the probation service's core task, even though Mr Chambers was firmly convinced that it was.

When he presented the case again three months later the issue became clearer but—just as the first discussion had predicted—it was now bound up with the fact that he was leaving.

> Mr Chambers in fact began with a reminder of his departure, now imminent. Transfer arrangements had been made; Nick would have a male officer, Daphne a woman. Members present on both occasions immediately wanted to know how this had come about. Had the clients requested it? Would there be joint meetings? Mr Chambers explained that at first Nick still wanted to have the same probation officer as Daphne, and again demanded that they be seen together. Daphne continued to hold out for separate sessions. Mr Chambers felt she was entitled to this; she had regularly kept her weekly appointments, the basis of his original contract with her.
>
> Nick reluctantly accepted defeat and then demanded a separate officer. Mr Chambers took the line of least resistance. "It all got too complex for me to work out what the best ploy actually was. In the end, I just said: 'right, if that's what you want'." It would not preclude joint meetings; "because the marriage is so integral to their lives and problems I still have at the back of my mind that progress for this couple will be marked by their being able to meet and negotiate together". He intended to pass this idea on to the officers taking over the case.
>
> Nick now seemed tense and more nervous; he appeared to have "gone downhill in terms of his drinking behaviour and his acting out". One morning he called without an appointment. He told Mr Chambers he had a terrible hangover, after being drunk and insensible the night before—"he'd spent their social security giro, sixty pounds, on the one night's spree ... it was the first time he'd ever come in and told all without being taxed about it. It nonplussed me. I just shook my head and said something like, 'that's a silly thing to do'. I felt it was like a

dog bringing a bone." Mr Chambers recalled that he
had often noted in his case record, "I wish Nick would
admit to —." Now he had done so. But he did not seem to
want to do anything about it; "he just tells me—makes a
confession".

Daphne's reaction to Nick's binge and the loss of their
social security money was to steal a bottle of spirits and
break into their electricity meter, for both of which she
was charged. And "she blamed him for starting another
cycle of depression". At this Nick "settled down to feeling
that her being in trouble again was quite a good thing".
He became increasingly involved and curious about what
Mr Chambers would say in his report for the court.
Daphne was realistically worried, knowing that with her
record she might receive a prison sentence. But, "the
probation task being to keep people out of prison", Mr
Chambers recommended community service (concurrent
with her probation order). This was duly accepted; Nick
attended court and was very pleased at the outcome.

For her community service Daphne was directed to
work in an old people's day centre; "she loves it; gets on
with the old 'uns and says, 'it's the best thing that's
happened to me'." Nick insisted on going with her to the
centre in spite of her protests, until the community service
organiser had to write to him forbidding him access; "he
got very upset about that".

Nick himself was then summoned by the court for non-
payment of an outstanding fine and was given a seven-day
prison sentence. But he had time for a 'last fling' and Daphne
was again left without money. She vowed to Mr
Chambers that she would never have him in the house
again. However, when Nick reported following his release, he was back at home. At her next interview Daphne
"sheepishly confessed to having him back but said, 'I
don't have anything to do with him. He's sleeping down-
stairs. None of his friends would put him up so he had
nowhere to go—I took him back but he's like a lodger'."

Nick now seemed increasingly resentful towards Mr
Chambers. At his latest interview he said: "I don't think
probation is helping any more." Mr Chambers reminded
him that he had wanted it, to help him "to off-load, to
avoid anxiety building up and therefore relieve the need to

act-out". Nick said he did not need that any more and asked to report fortnightly instead of weekly in future. Mr Chambers agreed. Nick was a long way into his three-year order, so "by rights and in fairness we can't insist that he comes every week".

The one social worker present this time suggested that Nick only confessed his binge to Mr Chambers to "get in first" before Daphne told him; a comment which recognised the triangle between Mr Chambers and his two clients, albeit in the side-taking mode of the first workshop. Other members saw Mr Timpson's binge and confession, followed by his resentful denial of any value in probation, as demonstrations of his conflicting feelings about Mr Chambers' departure. It was as if a child were reacting to a parent about whom he alternatively phantasised contrasting images: of strength and concern, and of weakness and untrustworthiness; as if the child feared the power of his own destructive impulses to bring about his own abandonment.

Mr Chambers endorsed this. He felt Nick had "either killed me off or he's come to the conclusion that I'm a total dead loss. He's incredibly sensitive to any slur on himself. He and people like him are very difficult to work with; it's difficult to tune in to the sense of power they feel they have when you see them as so inadequate—a difficult gap to overcome." Then the discussion brought Daphne back into the equation; in her too there was both an infantile omnipotence and an opposite "sense of being quite helpless". These were the contradictory attributes which she and Nick essentially shared but which moved around between them in such bewildering ways—as did the anxiety about destructiveness so evident in their periodic efforts to make reparation. This was recognised as a familiar pattern in many of the probation and social services clients whose cases were studied in this and other workshops.

A health visitor asked what was Daphne's reaction to Mr Chambers' departure. He replied, "she's been far more stable about it. It's been discussed quite carefully; she seems quite happy to be moved to somebody else." The social worker recalled Mr Chambers' surprise at the beginning that Daphne had engaged with him so readily; "I'm sure she's attached to you, but is it that she just needs to be attached to somebody—that anyone would do?" Mr Chambers thought Daphne was showing "the good side of herself; she's now the perfect client, saying how probation has given her a chance to talk". Then he went on, "and there's poor old Nick—drinks the money away, gets into prison. He's all that's bad."

As to his own feelings about leaving the Timpsons, Mr Chambers acknowledged he had come to like them both, even Nick; but "I don't think my going will make an enormous difference or that they're being hurt by it. I have some personal feelings but you get used to that . . . leaving people." Because of his departure, no follow-up information was available.

Comment

It was paradoxical that Mr Chambers should reveal, almost in the same breath, his grasp of the Timpsons' interactive system and his denial of the importance of their attachment to him (or his to them). In one sense he was probably right in thinking his departure would not make much difference; it repeated a familiar pattern for Nick and Daphne and their reaction was predictable. But Mr Chambers, though he stressed to the marriage guidance counsellor that probation work had to be "relevant to the clients' offending behaviour", seemed to be overlooking what was indeed a relevant connection here. The Timpsons had started acting out their shared conflict of feelings about his departure while he still had a strong working relationship with them. The three months before he left might have afforded the opportunity to try and bring their mixed feelings towards himself into consciousness, in the containment of the caring system, and see if this could illuminate for them their conflicting feelings towards each other. That would have been highly relevant to their offending behaviour; even granted the difficulty of working with them pointed out by Mr Chambers, it might have 'made a difference'.

That Mr Chambers could not focus his work in this way indicates the constraints he was under. The Timpsons put great pressure on him with their demands about transfer arrangements and their acting-out (including Daphne's new offences—which the discussion ignored). Needing some way of managing the anxiety, he fell back on the custom and practice of the probation service. It is clear from his handling of both Daphne's and Nick's demands that he found relief (but also further constraint) in customary notions of 'contract' and 'fairness'. There was actually no legal rule or procedure to determine whether or not Daphne should be seen together with her husband, or by the same officer, nor how frequent Nick's appointments should be; the rules being silent, contract and fairness became just as unalterable and served the same purpose. The real position was that most of these matters were within Mr Chambers' power to decide at his discretion, but in practice he felt powerless (another instance of the way the Timpsons' interaction with him reproduced the dynamic of their own relationship). The normally imaginative Mr Chambers seemed unable to see beyond the contract and consider whether it could be re-negotiated, or to see beyond the fairness to consider how relevant it was to the client's predicament.

Mr Chambers' own predicament can also be seen in the context of *his* contract with the probation service, which allowed for him to be posted to his next job under a policy of ensuring a fair distribution of staff resources. In such circumstances he invoked a common defence against the anxiety of breaking attachments by minimising their importance. But this was not peculiar to probation officers. The social worker who wondered if 'anyone would do' for Daphne Timpson was on the same track, and in fact the denial of attachments between clients or patients and their practitioners was widely found throughout all five disciplines.

PROBATION OFFICERS, THEIR SETTING AND THEIR CASES

The probation officers were recruited to the study programme as individual volunteers responding to an invitation circulated by the chief probation officer. Whilst they joined under the authority of their service, therefore, there was less selection by management than in any other discipline except general practice— the freest agents of all. At the outset there were five main grade probation officers (including the only two women) and two senior probation officers, all working in generalist mainstream probation teams. By the end of the programme three years later only one had left the service, but most of the others (including his replacement) had moved to specialist roles like Mr Chambers. Only two maingrade officers stayed in the same generalist posts throughout. Such moves were decided by the senior managers.

This reflected some important features of a modern probation service. Within a relatively low overall turnover there was much more internal movement of staff than in the past, with senior management deciding how officers should be deployed over an increasingly diverse range of activities. With specialisation growing, service chiefs took responsibility for managing the tension between continuity in each area of work on the one hand and, on the other, ensuring that no one specialism lost touch with the organisation as a whole and no one officer was left too long in a narrowly-focused or particularly stressful job.

Underlying this was another, older tension between the traditional autonomy of the individual officer (still visible in the free choice of joining the study programme) and the more corporate values implicit in the management structure which has been built into the service nationally during the past quarter of a century of expansion. Through the 1980s those values have become ever more explicit as the service has responded to pressure from central government to demonstrate that it can control delinquent behaviour effectively by non-custodial supervision. A key Home Office (1984) paper on national objectives and priorities for the service was promulgated during the study programme; we were therefore working with an agency in the midst of the pressure for change.

We have already seen some of the influence of this change, in Mr Collins' case in chapter 2 as well as Mr Webster's. Both officers, under pressure, fell back on the bedrock of their basic task which they conceived of as dealing with their clients' offending behaviour.[3] Nevertheless, all the officers who took part in the study saw, as one put it, "the need for a better understanding of the nature of marital difficulties and their relevance to the problems that cause or underlie criminal behaviour"; i.e. they were interested in broadening their focus in relevant ways.

This points to another fundamental tension in probation values: whether the service's purpose in working with offenders is 'care' or 'control'. The officers who took part in the study recognised official pressure towards more emphasis on control and were willing to comply, but at the same time they were unwilling to relinquish their belief in care. Much of their work embodied this conflict.

In keeping with their interest in the aims of the study programme, the cases they contributed were very 'marital'. In four instances both husband and wife were designated clients; besides the two cases already described in detail, there was another in which both spouses were on probation and one where a prisoner and his wife both sought help during and after his short prison sentence. The other clients, all of whom were on probation or the subject of a social inquiry report before sentence, were either married or living with their parents, and the probation officers had invariably included the spouse, or both parents, among those they sought to engage with in their work (in only one case was this approach defeated, by a woman who was adamant that her husband must not learn of her shoplifting offence).

The nature of the offences their clients had committed was also consistent with the idea that marital and family problems, springing from social and emotional deprivation, were relevant factors to be addressed. Some crimes actually took place within the household: besides the domestic offences of Mr and Mrs Weekes and Mrs Timpson there was a mother who had caused grievous bodily harm to her infant and an eighteen year-old boy who had assaulted his mother. All the other offences could be readily linked with emotional and relationship problems: indecent exposure by another eighteen year-old, driving whilst disqualified by two married men (both clearly reacting to intolerable tension at home), shoplifting by Mrs Timpson and two other married women, drink-related burglaries by Mr Goodband (chapter 2) and one other man, a gambling-related embezzlement and Mr Timpson's theft of parcels from doorsteps.

CHARACTERISTIC DILEMMAS AND DEFENCES IN PROBATION WORK

Individuals, relationships and the law

In practice, the links that were there for the making were often not made, as we saw in Mr Webster's case; when they were, the implications were difficult to grasp, as Mr Chambers found. Whilst officers always extended the range of their interest beyond the individual client, it was rare for them to take the further step of focusing on a marriage or family as a dynamic system in which the individual's behaviour might be understood as the expression of problems which involved *both* spouses or *all* family members within that system's boundary. Rather, spouses and parents might be seen as generally supportive to the client, in which case the officer would try and reinforce this or (like Mr Collins) leave well alone; or else as having a bad influence, when the officer's concern was to mitigate this or protect the client from it. Close relatives were certainly conceived of as important figures in the client's immediate circle, but it was a circle of which the client remained the centre.

The point was strikingly illustrated by the three cases in which both husband and wife had offended. Mr Webster, Mr Chambers and the third officer were well aware of marital difficulties and on the face of it they had a ready-made opportunity to take the dynamic interaction between the couple as their focus in working with both clients to understand and reduce their offending behaviour. But in all three cases other considerations prevented such a focus being adopted. Mr Webster allowed the different procedures for a probationer and an ex-prisoner to keep his work with Mr and Mrs Weekes in separate compartments; Mr Chambers allowed the 'good' wife to make an individual contract which kept him from addressing her interaction with the 'bad' husband; while the third couple, like the Goodbands in chapter 2, were at one in giving their probation officer only the benign half of the picture—until their child's injuries forced the malign half into view.

In these husband and wife cases, paradoxically, it looked as though the very fact that each partner was a client in their own right became a reason for not working with them as an interacting couple. Whilst practitioners of all the non-marital agencies experienced anxiety about opening up intimate areas of marital conflict, there was a more particular dilemma for probation officers: an approach which conceives of a couple as a two-person system with one boundary around the pair is in conflict with the clear boundary fixed around each individual before the law—from which is derived the probation officer's duty towards each client.

As the workshop discussion of Mr Webster's case demonstrated, in probation work the client can be very clearly and individually defined by the order or category which gives the probation officer responsibility for them. In no other discipline was there so precise a definition—not even in the exclusive doctor-patient relationship in general practice. When this was combined with a narrow definition of task (as Mr Webster's case again showed) there were important consequences for collaboration with other agencies.

Yet we cannot criticise the law for attributing criminal responsibility to individuals, nor suggest instead that it should hold accountable those wider systems of which individuals are interacting members. The nearest the law does come to recognising an interactive system is the criminal charge of conspiracy, notorious for its imprecision and the difficulty of rebutting it. The individualistic view of human behaviour which the law generally enshrines thus affords wholesome protection when it comes to pinpointing culpability.

When it comes to sentencing, probation officers are correspondingly concerned to protect the uniqueness of the individual from rule-of-thumb disposal, i.e. to let the punishment fit the person, not just the crime. The document on values and priorities drawn up by this local probation service in response to the Home Office document mentioned above asserted 'the individual worth of each person' and declared the service to be 'committed to the notion of individualised justice'. Thus, whilst acknowledging the pressure for more control, probation officers made their stand for care on the value of the individual—as recognised by law—rather than on the broader but less easily defensible ground of social and personal relationship systems.

Care and control: the probation officer as mediator

The relative values of care and control have been debated in the probation service throughout its history, but in the last twenty years or so the terms of the debate have changed. It is no longer a question of what attitude towards offenders is considered morally right by probation officers themselves; increasingly they have had to take account of the feelings of victims of crime and the demands of society at large as expressed in the public arena of the media, the courts and the political process. In the 1980s the concept of 'value' itself acquired the new connotation of 'value for money'; the criterion of cost-effectiveness and the threat of competition have been applied to the probation service as to other state undertakings. Probation is certainly cheaper than prison, but can only claim cost-effectiveness if it succeeds in curbing the criminal activities of those subject to supervision in the community. In crude terms, the service has been told to improve its credibility or face being reduced to a marginal role.[4]

But whilst the pressure for more control has been mounting, it would be a mistake to suppose that there will not also be continued public pressure for humane and caring alternatives to imprisonment in appropriate cases.

Although these opposing pressures may intensify or fluctuate with the prevailing national mood as expressed by official policy, they nonetheless represent fundamental conflicts which are always present in any social order, and it is precisely these conflicts which the probation service exists to address.

It is just such a conflict that a probation officer regularly encounters when a court calls for a social inquiry report before sentencing an offender. In preparing the report and presenting it to the court the officer stands as mediator at the boundary between society and the offender. Facing the offender, the officer stresses that society demands he should undertake to obey the law; facing the court, he stresses that there is a social context to the individual's lawbreaking and a realistic chance of reform with appropriate help. It is through this brokerage, interpreting each party's pressing concerns to the other and maintaining the confidence of both, that the bargain of a probation order may be achieved. This is the quintessential role of the probation officer, going back more than a century to the police court missionaries who first intervened in this way to offer an alternative to imprisonment.

If such an alternative is indeed to be effective, a strong enough form of containment for delinquent impulses is required, within which focused work with offenders outside the literal containment of prison can be pursued. The probation order has traditionally supplied this; it holds together the officer and the client—no-one else—within a structure set by the court which lays down the terms and the time-span of the order. As our study showed, however, the very strength and clarity of such structures make them a ready defence for probation officers to fall back on when they themselves experience anxiety under conflicting pressure—from their exposure to the dynamics of clients' relationship systems on the one hand, and from government, senior management, courts or other agencies on the other.[5]

In a field where the raw material, so to speak, is criminal behaviour, it should not be surprising that a characteristic defence against anxiety is to hold fast to order and structure. Dishonest and violent impulses are without doubt present in every citizen; actual criminal behaviour occurs when these impulses are acted upon rather than restrained or repressed. Professional criminals may act consciously and with calculation, but for the most part they do not come the probation service's way. In our study, those who did were more likely to be caught up in unconscious conflicts, originating in their early life experience but intolerable for them to manage inside themselves; instead, conflict was played out between members of a relationship system (marriage, family or peer group), and when that could not contain the anxiety individuals acted out the conflict by breaking the law.

Offences of personal or sexual violence, of fire-raising or of breaking into private homes, as well as crimes related to drunkenness or drug-taking, can be deeply alarming and disturbing to those whose task it is to deal with the offenders, not least because they too may know more or less consciously of such impulses in themselves—to say nothing of the 'ordinary' dishonesty of theft or embezzlement. The anxiety thus aroused can readily call forth the wish for structure and control. As we saw in both case examples, however, this response can blind practitioners to the fundamental dilemmas which underlie their clients' criminal behaviour, and therefore to the opportunity to make a different response which could often be more effective.

Such a response would have been consistent with the mediating role; to help offenders, and their spouses and families, develop for themselves the capacity to contain and mediate conflict instead of acting it out against the law.

In exercising the profession they have chosen, probation officers occupy a privileged and crucial position. Standing in the midst of the conflict between the criminal court and the defendant, their task is to gain the confidence of both sides and mediate between them. In order to do this well it is an advantage—perhaps a prerequisite—to be able to identify with both sides sufficiently to understand their concerns: the social order *and* the disorderly individual, the need for control *and* care. If this sometimes evokes for officers residual dilemmas of their own, their job gives them constant opportunities to put that experience to work in helping others in conflict. But to be aware of conflict to the extent of identifying with both sides is not a comfortable condition. Mediation may be the preferred way of managing it but the defence of splitting is also likely to be resorted to, in the unconscious process set in motion by threatening anxiety. Instead of confronting the conflict and helping clients do the same, officers may then hold on to only one side and lose the other.[6]

Boundary management in the probation service

On the face of it probation officers have no control over the amount of criminal work that comes to them, which is almost entirely the consequence of decisions taken by the courts. But this is too simplistic a view. The social inquiry report is not only the probation officer's instrument of mediation between court and offender; it has also functioned as a regulator of the inward flow of work to the service, though this function has been less well acknowledged and understood (cf. the cases of Mr Webster above and Mr Roberts in chapter 9). To assist the court in deciding how to sentence an offender, the report usually includes the officer's opinion on the suitability or otherwise of the defendant for probation, community service, or any other kind of order which would place him or her under the probation service's supervision. Whilst the decision remains that of the court alone, the probation officer's report naturally carries weight and both sides expect it to do so.

At the time of our study, however, the service nationally had for some years been concerned that its influence with courts was decreasing, as more offenders were being sentenced to imprisonment and the use of probation orders was showing a gradual decline. It was consequently being forced to recognise that magistrates and judges—reflecting the changing mood and philosophy in society generally—were questioning the effectiveness of rehabilitative measures—i.e. care—in curbing crime and calling for more control. This was part of the pressure which gave rise to the Home Office document and the responses it called for from all local probation areas.

One specific response of this local service was to initiate discussions with the local magistrates on what probation officers actually did with offenders once they were put on probation. It was in these discussions (as we later learned) that the service undertook to set up the induction group for all new probationers which Carol Weekes failed to attend. Mr Webster's anxiety about this was therefore heightened by knowing that the group had been instituted to satisfy the courts that offending behaviour was taken seriously by the service. He had followed service guidelines by specifying in his social inquiry report that the induction group would be part of the regime if Mrs Weekes were put on probation. Hence the confusion about whether attendance was in itself a requirement of her probation order. In strict legal terms it was not, but Mr Webster had cogent reasons for treating it as if it were.

On the 'output' boundary, the probation officers seldom referred clients to other agencies, but here too they could regulate their work-load by the procedure of applying for early discharge of probation order. Again, the decision was the court's, but we heard of no application being refused. 'Good progress' was invariably cited, but in several cases it was clearly the news that a social worker had become involved with the family which prompted the probation officer to apply for early discharge and so 'leave the field clear' for the other worker. There were further examples in some of the social workers' cases of probation officers having done this, and it threw some light on their approach to collaboration, which we now consider.

PROBATION OFFICERS AND COLLABORATION

If the probation service is under pressure to protect its standing within the criminal justice system, officers may be constrained in their capacity to work flexibly and imaginatively with other agencies as well as with their clients. The pattern that emerged from the probation series of cases is particularly interesting. In a programme aiming to study inter-agency work, the proportion of their cases in which another agency was known to be involved was among the lowest—about two thirds, on a par with marriage guidance counsellors and GPs. On the other hand, the proportion of these cases in which they were actively collaborating with the other practitioners was higher than in any other discipline. This group of actively collaborative cases, however, had a clearly defined character. It comprised all the cases where children were on the official 'at risk' register; one (Mr Collins' in chapter 2) in which there was an inescapable duty to inform the other agency; one in which the other practitioner's involvement was specified in the probation order; and one where the officer herself had referred the case to a child and family guidance clinic (the only instance of a referral for more specialised treatment in the whole probation series).

It appeared, then, that probation officers duly collaborated with other practitioners whenever this was enjoined by a legal or procedural requirement, but not otherwise. We were told about collaboration at the managerial or policy-making level without such constraints, but this was the pattern we saw at the level of practice.

Collaboration was not an easy matter for probation officers. In three cases officers were stimulated by the programme to get together with other practitioners and offer conjoint marital or family interviews with the aim of addressing relationship difficulties that were clearly relevant to the offending behaviour of the probation client (as well as to the other practitioner's concerns). These were in fact the only instances of probation officers attempting to shift their focus of work from the individual to the interactive relationship system of which the individual was a member; it was as if officers felt they could better address this focus by linking *themselves* up in relationship with a colleague. In the event, however, all three of these initiatives ran into difficulties and were interrupted. We shall be discussing one of them in detail in chapter 9, but here it is worth noting a particular moment of tension that occurred in it. At a case conference the probation officer encountered disapproval from the other practitioners (including the social worker with whom he set up the marital interviews); their remarks implied that as the representative of law and order he ought to have made sure that the father, who had injured his child, was put in prison. The other agencies' proper concern at this point was for the safety of a child at risk; the probation officer's equally proper—but unpopular—concern was to offer the court an effective alternative to imprisonment for an offender. There were echoes of this conflict in both the cases described in this chapter—at the case conference in Mr Webster's case and in the workshop in Mr Chambers'.

There was indeed a structural dilemma for probation officers inherent in the position their agency occupied in the network of services. In the context of the criminal justice system their statutory function was to provide alternatives to imprisonment in appropriate cases. Their caring role was thus highlighted. Even though there were times when the courts themselves wanted an alternative or could see it was appropriate, probation officers were liable to a general suspicion of being 'soft' from that quarter. On the other hand, in the eyes of other helping professions they were often scarcely differentiated from the rest of the criminal justice system, which was stereotyped as punitive. Here their perceived role was controlling. Even though (as we have seen) there were times when other practitioners themselves wanted an offender put in prison, probation officers were liable from this quarter to a general suspicion of being 'hard'. When they engaged with others across the boundaries of their own profession, therefore, probation officers experienced contradictory pressures according to which direction they were facing. They tended to feel accused by the law of being unwilling to control; by their colleagues in other helping professions, of being unwilling to care. They were thus in the middle of a conflicting triangular dynamic (see chapter 9).

Their reaction to these pressures varied with the circumstances and the individual officer's personality. Sometimes they seemed anxious to appease, like Mr Webster over the matter of Mrs Weekes' attendance at the induction group (the follow-up material showed that in different circumstances he could be more flexible with Mr Weekes over the same issue). At other times they were sufficiently autonomous—or bloody-minded—to withstand the accusations and do what they thought right.

In any event they ran the risk of entering into a splitting and projective interaction in which one party represented care and the other control, but these two imperatives were not held together by either party, nor by a constructive partnership. In one case a particularly ferocious judge, who (as reported) regarded social services as even 'softer' than probation, put a child-abusing mother on probation and set the probation officer to be a watchdog over the social worker. Once out of the courtroom the officer reacted against this by defining his task as 'offering the client something for herself', i.e. care, and worked with her sympathetically on her feelings about her childhood and her present predicament. He assured his social services colleague that so far as he was concerned the judge's instructions were *ultra vires* and he had no intention of interfering with her work. His refusal to accept the controlling function enjoined on him by the judge left it, paradoxically, to be picked up by the social worker who indeed took seriously her monitoring and surveillance role with the children. But the caring and controlling functions seemed to remain split between the two workers, with confusing results for the client who had not only expected care as well as watchfulness from her social worker but had certainly looked to her probation officer to help her confront her bad feelings —her violent impulses and her guilt at injuring her child. Although the two workers conscientiously kept in touch and exchanged information, they did not resolve this confusion of role for some months. In Mr Chambers' case the interaction between himself and the social workers in the workshop had a similar quality.

SUMMARY

Our study showed that whilst probation officers were subject to similar anxieties to those experienced by other professionals when they engaged with personal and relationship problems, there were also distinctive anxieties peculiar to them. These arose from the disturbing nature of crime as a disorderly means of acting out internal and external conflict; from the struggle (inherent in their public mandate) to reconcile what could appear irreconcilable opponents—the offender and society, care and control; and from the current pressure on their service to deliver effective supervision of offenders in the community. A related tension between autonomy and conformity was reflected in their own relationship with their employing agency and senior managers.

Like other practitioners, they defended against anxiety by denial of the attachments they and their clients formed, by reducing their perspective from the holistic to the compartmental, and by falling back on a narrow definition of their task. Characteristically they had not one but two such definitions, which were never mentioned together: to keep offenders out of prison, *and* to work with them to reduce their offending behaviour. These constituted another duality which could often seem impossible to reconcile, though officers never gave up the struggle to do so. It was a particular feature of their work that in their characteristic role as mediator their characteristic defence—under an overload of anxiety—was splitting.

Above all, probation officers made defensive use of the many rules, categories and procedures of their setting, together with concepts of mandate, contract and fairness, against the anxieties inherent in their job. In collaborative situations it was this that sometimes gave their colleagues in other services the impression that (as one put it) "probation officers are a law unto themselves".

Notes

1   For an investigation of probation officers' divorce court work see the recent study by our colleagues Clulow and Vincent (1987).

2   This form, giving factual details about the case, was meant to be distributed to workshop members as background material for the presenter's freer verbal account of his or her assessment, current work and problems. At this stage, however, the workshop procedure was very new; Mr Webster had omitted to bring copies of the form for members and instead read it out, with amplifying comments. The form thus became the presentation.

3   In the past, as one of us (PP) recalls, probation officers sometimes had to be reminded that their clients had committed crimes, and few would have described their basic task in this focused way. In 1989, Home Office minister John Patten was still complaining, 'Many probation officers would prefer to die rather than say "What I am doing is applying the punishment of the courts". You have to drag it out of them and hang them up by their thumbs' (Interview in *Social Work Today*, 9 March 1989).

4   Mr Patten again: 'I think that many sentencers in magistrates and crown courts do not have confidence in present non-custodial sentences being tough and demanding enough and in the level of supervision being high enough ... If the probation service itself or individual officers don't want to take part in this, then we shall have to look elsewhere' (ibid.).

5   Clearly the same defensive use can be made of the rules governing the various statutory licences on which prisoners may be released under probation officers' supervision, though there were no examples in the study; these licences have a tight structure of accountability upwards through each level of management to the parole authorities or the Home Office itself.

6   Mr Patten ended his interview by recognising something of this: 'It is a difficult and demanding job having to supervise what are punishments and at the same time to befriend and help; but that is their skill. There shouldn't be a clash between supervision and caring ... This is an acutely difficult job but retreating into a shell and saying we are only actually doing one of those things is ludicrous' (ibid.).

8

Social services

This chapter must stand unsupported by narrative case examples. We under-took not to include detailed case material without full discussion with the practitioners concerned, and the social workers who took part in the study programme were not available to do this. The decision had been taken at a meeting between the social workers and the assistant director who had succeeded to the senior management liaison role partway through the programme. The main reasons given were that working with us on a book had not been part of their original undertaking in joining the programme, and could not be a priority at a time when the department was 'inundated' with a surge of new child abuse referrals.

Whilst we regret the omission, these circumstances are not without illustrative value in a chapter on the agency which was both the most hierarchically managed and the most beset by 'siege mentality' of all those we worked with. In our estimation the social workers had included some of the most thoughtful and committed individual participants of any discipline in the programme even though some freely expressed their doubts about aspects of it. Their collective non-participation in the writing of the book indicated not only something of the nature of their own agency but perhaps also how it was liable to carry negative feelings—'do the dirty work'—on behalf of others in the service network. If so, what impoverishes the chapter turns out also to epitomise its main themes.

THE SOCIAL WORKERS AND THEIR SETTING

More than any other agency, the social services department's senior manage-ment originally set out to plan its participation in the study programme in a corporate way. At first, social workers from only two area teams were to take part; a sizeable contingent from each team would help maximise the impact of the programme's training component which could then be evaluated and spread to other teams. Because of some (unrelated) industrial action in the two teams concerned, however, a second plan was eventually implemented—with the active encouragement of other participating agencies—whereby more area teams were represented, if possible by two or three practitioners. In this way fourteen social workers altogether, including five senior social workers in team leader posts, were drawn from city, small town and rural areas to take part. During the programme three of the basic grade social workers left the department (a higher proportion than in any other agency). The social workers' series of cases was the highest total contributed by any discipline.

A summary of how these preoccupying cases came to the social services department shows at once that social work can hardly be considered apart from an inter-agency context; it also shows what social workers meant by the remark we often heard them make (only half in jest) that they were the dustbin for everyone else's problems. Half the cases they contributed had been referred to them by a total of eleven other agencies. The referrals came most frequently from health visitors, but also from the whole range of judicial, social, medical, psychiatric and educational services. The other half of the total arose from direct requests for help by members of the public either on their own behalf or on their children's.

It is clear from this how wide and how exposed is the intake boundary which a social services department has to manage. The siege mentality which often prevails now is far removed from the original vision of the Seebohm (1968) Committee whose report led to the setting up of these departments. Central to Seebohm's philosophy was the concept of a universally available social service to seek out and meet the needs of the whole person, the whole family, the whole community. Even though the concept was never fully embodied in legislation, the expectations of other agencies and the general public were raised and social workers themselves embraced this aspiration as local authority services expanded in the 1970s. Some still hold it, but they find themselves left with the 'dustbin' feeling which is its absolute antithesis; and increasingly, like the dustbin, they have been despised and kicked when things go wrong. This highly contradictory experience has grown more acute in the 1980s, but it began for social services departments almost from the beginning of their short history. They were first set up in 1971-2, and the first three official reports on notorious cases of child deaths were published within three years,[1] all pointing to 'failures' by social workers—a theme regularly repeated since by a succession of further reports as well as judges, politicians and media commentators. Meanwhile the concept of universal availability to meet all social needs has been widely criticised. In most local authorities it has in practice been abandoned, some reluctantly accepting that cuts in resources make it impracticable, others seeing it as too idealistic and global in the first place.

Whether the major changes in prospect for the 1990s will do anything to raise morale remains to be seen, but there is no doubt that the contentious climate of the first two decades of social services departments has been debilitating. Social workers have been liable to find themselves at odds with their managers, their political employers, the general public and each other about the entire philosophy, theory and practice of social work. Thus the stress inherent in what social workers do has been exacerbated by the lack of a professional identity that could be agreed and valued both inside and outside the profession. The boundaries of social work—within which social workers should be sure of their distinctive role and competence, and across which they receive a public mandate and are in turn publicly accountable—have resembled a war zone more than a workable frontier.

THE CASES AND THE DILEMMAS

In the county where our study took place the department was already affected by the general pressures of public criticism, anxiety about child abuse and financial stringency. The intake of new cases was increasingly regulated by set criteria reflecting its priorities and available resources. There could be local variations according to the philosophy and circumstances of the different area teams and their managers, but the highest priority was given to duties specifically laid down by statute. Virtually all the cases contributed to the study were of this kind. Although all the area teams were generalist, most of the cases involved child protection,[2] establishing this as the social workers' overwhelming preoccupation. The largest group of cases concerned children registered as being at risk of harm at their parents' hands; in some cases abuse was confirmed, but most of the children were on the register because it was suspected or feared. The very low proportion of cases involving sexual abuse reflected the fact that our fieldwork was completed by the mid 1980s before the eruption of public concern which made this a new major preoccupation (see chapter 10 and Appendix).

Another group of cases involved older children who had put themselves at risk by running away from home or truanting from school; whilst these children needed help in their own right they also attracted attention to failures on the part of their parents to care for them effectively. Concern for the well-being of children even without immediate risk to their safety had also led to intervention with families deserted without warning by the husband and father and consequently in financial as well as emotional crisis. The same concern was activated when a recent client telephoned again to say she wanted a separation from her husband and was expecting twins; and when (in the only example of long-term residential or foster care) a child of eleven, whose mother had virtually dumped him on the department as an infant, asked his social worker to let him go and live with her and her new husband.

Thus in most of their reported cases the social workers were concerned with the interests of children whose parenting was, or was feared to be, deficient. Their most characteristic dilemmas stemmed from the expectation that they would be able not only to protect the children but somehow to make up the deficit.

Accusations of failure

This expectation is not only implicit in the duties laid on social workers, it also accords with the concern and conviction which motivates people to join the profession. But on the showing of these cases it was an onerous and confusing responsibility that social workers were outwardly and inwardly directed to shoulder. By intervening to supplement or provide a substitute for unsatisfactory parenting they were by implication passing judgement on the parents and assuming a quasi-parental role themselves—whether or not it was formalised by a care order. This inevitably left them open to the accusation, sooner or later, that they too were 'unsatisfactory'.

The accusation might come in many guises: the mother who behaved as recalcitrantly as her child, making the social worker feel as impotent as in reality the mother was; the parental couple who had treated their child harshly but whose united denial put the social worker in the position of seeming to be the punitive one; the adolescents who sabotaged their social workers' plans by absconding or making a suicide gesture; or the workers from other agencies whose anxieties made them intolerant of the social worker's caution about removing a child from home.

There was no instance of official or judicial criticism of social workers in the cases they contributed, and the department had never had to face a child-death inquiry. Nevertheless, we heard through one of the probation cases of a local judge who so mistrusted social services that he tried to take away their power to allow an abused child (in care) to return home, by purporting to make it a requirement of the abusing mother's probation order that she should not have the care of him and instructing the probation officer to act as a watchdog (see chapter 7).

The social workers and the department were indeed still committed to a preventive approach of not removing children from home if there were realistic prospects of improving and supplementing the care given by their natural parents.[3] Sometimes there was little difficulty in following this policy, but inevitably there were many instances when the issue of whether a child should or should not live with its parents became acute and a decision had to be made and justified. This was regularly a point of maximum anxiety for social workers, and of maximum tension between them and other professionals involved with the family. The issue might concern either a child's removal or its return home, and might have been raised by parents, by children, by other agencies or by urgent necessity; but invariably the prospect of a child being transhipped across this threshold aroused strong feelings in everyone concerned. The same was true in the few cases where residential care was being considered for dependent adults.

For many of the social workers the insistent anxiety was whether the last state might be worse than the first. Especially when harmful parenting was suspected but the available facts remained confused and inconclusive, social workers were often quite explicit that they feared doing more harm than good themselves. They could envisage that they would probably have to intervene, but saw the intervention itself as potentially heavy-handed and persecutory rather than helpful; even a miscarriage of justice.

Thus, in the containment of the programme workshops, we discovered that social workers needed no external accusers. They were the first to blame themselves, often in anticipation. Their professional self-esteem was undermined not only from outside but from within, by anxiety that they might be perpetrating the very failures of parenting which they were committed to making good.

As if to underline the point, one fifth of the social workers' cases concerned actual or would-be care-givers in their own field. Some couples and one divorced woman who applied for approval as (much-needed) adoptive or foster parents gave the assessing social workers doubts which they found it hard to articulate, let alone resolve. Though ostensibly offering to care for children, these volunteers' way of life and behaviour so resembled that of clients (as one of them had in fact been) that the social workers inwardly questioned their motivation and capacity for the work; yet outwardly they found it hard to confront them with this. In the workshop discussions feelings ran unexpectedly high as the social workers and other members struggled to locate these applicants firmly one side or the other of the boundary between 'clients' and 'colleagues'. Even more disturbing was the case of an established and valued foster-parent couple whose marriage erupted in acrimony, each spouse appealing to the disconcerted senior social worker for support against the other as their foster-children's needs went unconsidered. Closest to home of all, nearly half this group of cases concerned social workers or care staff employed by the department who became clients, either in their own right or as parents of referred children. The statistical points are not of course made in relation to total workload, but as an indicator of prevailing anxiety for practitioners who were asked to select cases that preoccupied them. In this group of cases the social workers revealed how inescapable was the spectre, seen through the looking-glass, of themselves as bad care-givers.

Parents, spouses, children: the splitting of the family system

When a child's well-being or safety is endangered, anxiety is natural and the parents are normally mobilised to act protectively. When the danger is felt to come from the parents themselves, however, a conflict of feelings is set up in those who must take responsibility. When professionals are already beset with external and internal accusations of their own failure, it can be seen how powerful are the constraints of the child-protection task.

This was illustrated in a striking way by the social workers' difficulty in carrying out their own stated wish, in joining the programme, to develop the use of a marital focus in their work. In the handful of cases in which some of them did consistently address the clients' relationship as a couple, children were non-existent or were causing no concern. Amongst this group, in fact, were the only cases in the series which involved no statutory responsibility, and since these came from one rural area team they cannot be regarded as typical. But they were notable for the openness to new learning displayed by social workers who for once could lift their eyes above child-protection concerns.

The paradox here was that most of the social workers had believed when they joined the programme that couple relationships were relevant to the whole range of their work, and above all to child-protection cases; the department's resources were committed only because they and their senior managers saw the development of marital work skills as beneficial precisely in the statutory workload. This expectation at first looked capable of fulfilment when the social workers proved to be working with both parents in more than half their child-protection cases; although much of the work was with the mothers, fathers were also engaged with, and some couples were regularly seen together over long periods. On examination, however, it became clear that these clients were consistently treated as *parental*, not marital, partners. Problems in their own relationships tended to be avoided by clients and workers alike. If they surfaced at all, the social workers usually felt unable to open them up with their clients for fear of being seen as intrusive. This, they felt, might jeopardise the clients' acceptance of them and thus make it more difficult to monitor the vital child-protection issues to which they had to remain alert at all times. Beneath this the fear of doing more harm than good was once again clear.

Nevertheless, even in these burdensome child-protection cases a few attempts were made by social workers, encouraged by the workshops, to work on a marital focus with the agreement of the parent couples. The explicit aim was to help safeguard the children's well-being (i.e. the agency's primary task) through addressing relevant problems which the parents themselves had identified in their own relationships. One case in which this kind of work was attempted jointly with a probation officer is described in chapter 9. However, all these attempts were interrupted after a very short time, in contrast with the marital work undertaken when child-protection was not the primary task. They were overtaken by resurgent anxieties about the children's immediate safety, which caused the social workers to switch their focus back to the parenting and become preoccupied with their monitoring and protective role.

In switching focus in this way they felt they had no alternative, since protection of the children was their paramount responsibility. It was impossible to say they were wrong, but this regular diverting of social workers' attention was fully consistent with the view of these families developed in the workshops, i.e. that in their relationship systems the problems suffered or acted out by the children were often dynamically displaced versions of the parents' problems which the latter could not confront with each other in their own relationship. Their wish to accept marital help was genuine but inevitably ambivalent; as soon as the inherent anxiety of this work began to be felt, the old system of displacement onto children and parenting issues reasserted itself. This challenged the social workers' capacity to hold to their alliance with the clients' genuine wish to work, and to their own belief in joining the programme. Even though the workshops afforded reflective space that might have helped them sustain these capacities, they were clearly constrained from doing so by overwhelming task-related anxiety.

As we suggested in chapter 2, such anxiety fuels an unconscious process in which practitioners' defences become aligned with those of their clients, so as to disconnect the presenting problem from other issues, lose sight of a more holistic view and fall back on the narrowest bedrock of primary task definition. As we have been discovering in this and the other chapters in Part II, however, this bedrock turns out to afford no security from anxiety. For the social workers, as soon as they locked onto the exclusive focus of protecting children from bad parents they became a prey to further anxiety, i.e. that they themselves would be bad care-givers. This was the pattern classically described by Menzies Lyth (1970). The basic task-related anxiety—here aroused by apprehending that a child was in danger from its parents—was not well enough contained, but instead was met with defensive reaction—here a reductionist narrowing of focus. This not only impaired effective task performance, because the problem could no longer be thought about and worked with as a whole, but also meant that the basic anxiety was never fully mastered and in turn gave rise to an aggravated anxiety of failure, of doing more harm than good.

This aggravated anxiety appeared so ingrained and pervasive in the social worker's experience, as we noted earlier, that in each new instance the above process was compressed and instantaneous. Basic and aggravated anxieties were felt simultaneously and the reductionist defence was rigidly and automatically employed in the attempt to ward off both kinds of anxiety. We are not of course suggesting that social workers should hesitate in an emergency when it really is the case that nothing else matters except the child's urgent removal from harm. But the cases we heard contained very few emergencies of this sort. What preoccupied the social workers was typically a situation which was worrying but in which firm evidence was hard to come by and precipitate action was not appropriate; it was in these situations that anxiety was so difficult to master and constrained their capacity to think. Even in the occasional case which did require, and receive, prompt protective action, the same pattern appeared once the emergency was over. As one social worker put it, "I've done the right thing, but what do I do now? I feel exhausted and muddled".

Love and hate in social work

Because the level of anxiety was often so high and the basic and aggravated anxieties so compacted together, it was difficult to trace specifically how the first, when uncontained, generated the second. Whilst there were powerful external pressures, we were impressed by the way these seemed to find a ready echo in the social workers' self-accusations, which spoke of equally powerful internal pressures. We came to the conclusion that in large measure these derived from the fear of unacceptable and unmanageable ambivalence towards their clients. On the one hand, the social workers' concern and commitment was unmistakeable; on the other hand, evidence accumulated (though it could hardly ever be acknowledged) that they also experienced hatred and contempt, especially towards parents who put their own children at risk and who resisted efforts to help them. In a rare moment of complete frankness a social worker who felt defeated by resistant parents said:

> I almost feel bugger them, let them go, but they have three small children and what are they going to do to them? It makes me feel angry that they can mess children's lives up like that, and they might have two or three more. Those are just instinctive reactions.

The last sentence indicates something of this honest worker's anxiety at what she had just said, as if it could not be permissible and normal for a professional carer to have bad as well as good feelings. Bad feelings therefore had to be discounted as 'just instinctive' if her professional self-esteem was to be sustained. Others of her colleagues, though seldom as candid, indicated a similar conflict by their way of referring to their clients in weary tones as "these people" and by their frequent expressions of cynical mistrust which appeared alongside—but could never be reconciled with—their wish to help and the devoted work they put into it. This kind of irreconcilable conflict of ambivalent feelings was in our view the prime source of internal pressure generating the aggravated anxiety and defensive reactions to it.

As well as the almost universal resort to reductionism, another apparent defensive reaction was to overcompensate for bad feelings towards bad parents by treating them as wayward children. This enabled the social worker to maintain the role of a benign parent-figure, and indeed many of the client parents were immature and did make a powerful appeal for parenting. Whilst some work of a nurturing kind was often appropriate and useful as a component of an overall social work strategy, it sometimes led to a collusive denial of the real adult responsibility of the parents. This was not in the interests of the real children, but when events obliged the social workers to focus again on the latter they were once more plunged into bad feelings towards the neglectful or endangering parents, and into the resultant internal conflict and anxiety.

INTER-AGENCY ISSUES

The high rate of referral from other parts of the service network—which, like Mattinson and Sinclair (1979), we often heard described as the 'bombardment rate'—coupled with the requirement that social workers should bear the main responsibility for child protection but continue to collaborate with other professionals, meant that inter-agency relations too were imbued with defensive behaviour. In this arena the social workers found another way of dealing with their unacceptable conflict of feelings towards bad parents by turning the bad feelings and the blame onto the other practitioners. At one level there was some justice in this; it was apparent not only from the social workers' cases but also from several contributed by other disciplines that in making a referral other practitioners were indeed seeking to offload their own intolerable anxiety into the 'dustbin' of the social services department.

Case conferences

This exporting and re-exporting of anxiety and blame was not conducive to constructive collaboration by either party. Although in nearly all the social workers' cases they knew that other practitioners were actively involved, it was only in half the series that they described attempts at collaborative work. Often this was in the unavoidable formal setting of a child-abuse case conference, or a family meeting at assessment centre or child and family guidance clinic. Here the social worker often felt on the defensive, usually against pressure from other professionals to adopt the panacea of removing the child from home into care. One social worker noted that she was "rendered speechless" by such pressure from a practitioner who pleaded "for the child's sake". The implied accusation of heartlessness was so immobilising that the social worker literally could not articulate her firm conviction that it was more in this 'problem' child's interests to be contained within the family where the problem was rooted. Thus, when the blaming started, the holistic view could not be held onto.

In another example, the case conference itself appeared to get caught up in a process of reflection (Mattinson 1975) or re-enactment (Britton 1981) of the abusing family's dynamics. Both the social worker and the health visitor were accompanied to the meeting by senior managers of unusually high rank, each of whom issued accusations and warnings to the other's front line subordinate whilst giving strict orders to their own. In the family under discussion, the two immature young parents were each under the thumb of their own powerful parents who seemed unable to relinquish control and hand over responsibility to the young couple for running their marriage and their new family. The parallel was only noticed when the case was discussed in the workshop. No effective working plan could be thought about and negotiated in the case conference, which was caught up in an unconscious process whereby (in Britton's words) 'the basic situation remains unrealised and unchanged whilst new versions of it proliferate' (p. 49).

In the face of accusations implied or openly stated by other professionals, it was not surprising that social workers harboured counter-accusations which they revealed in the workshop discussions. There was, for example, the probation officer who offered the court an alternative to imprisonment for a father who had admitted injuring his child. Even though the man had been convicted of a quite different offence, the social worker (and other professionals involved) felt strongly that the probation officer should have seized the opportunity to make sure he was removed from the family. In this case other workshop members too sided against the probation officer—who was also a member and defended himself vigorously (see chapter 9). There was also the GP who raised the alarm about a child's safety, on inconclusive evidence, and then failed to turn up at the next case conference. These and other practitioners were felt to be irresponsible, able to come and go at will, while the social worker was left holding the baby.

Other social workers in case conferences were constrained in a different way. One team leader reported that his main concern at the case conference he was chairing had been to prevent "all the agencies ganging up" on the clients. Here the propensity to do more harm than good was attributed to the entire network of statutory services. His defensive reaction to this aggravated anxiety was to control the case conference discussion so heavily that there could be no free exchange of views and no development of a strategy for the responsible agencies to take forward. Instead, all hope was placed on the idea of suggesting to the clients that they should approach two different voluntary agencies, whose work would be confidential and untainted by statutory powers. The implications of this idea were not thought through, however, and the suggestion was indignantly rejected by the clients.

Short-term joint intervention

Although half their cases had been referred in by other agencies, the social workers in turn managed to refer out only one case (apart from the special instance of a colleague-client who was referred to marriage guidance). In this one case a senior social worker, acting in concert with the GP, secured a place in a special mother and baby unit for a depressed young mother who was not 'bonding' with her month-old first baby, and was referred to social services by the health visitor. The collaborative action with the GP and the hospital was prompt and effective but the emergency revealed a whole family at risk, with the recently married couple having reluctantly taken over the care of the husband's three children by a previous marriage, one of them manifestly disturbed and behaving disruptively at school. The senior social worker, having contained and stuck with the couple over the crisis, felt impelled to take on long-term responsibility for what had initially been only an office duty assignment. Thus, to secure resources from another agency by way of referral was in no way to be relieved of responsibility. The 'output' boundary was as closed as the 'input' boundary was open. Such were the dynamic pressures behind the 'dustbin' experience.

At the same time, this was not the only reported instance of successful collaboration. What was noteworthy was that most, like this one, consisted of short-term or 'one-off' concerted action focused on a single specific issue, where the social worker and the other practitioner were agreed about their strategy and their respective agency tasks were not in conflict. They were therefore unlikely to be split by the influence of the clients' anxieties and defences. Indeed, one purpose of the joint action in two cases was to show the clients they could not achieve such a split; the practitioners, together, clarified to the clients their different responsibilities whilst at the same time demonstrating their common purpose. In another case the social worker arranged a joint interview with the psychiatric consultant to a residential unit for mentally handicapped adults, with the aim of reassuring the client's devoted elderly parents that she would be well cared for. Here the social worker consciously invoked the added authority of the doctor to supplement her own, in a delicate situation where the parents could not acknowledge unaided that they were now too infirm to care for their daughter securely any longer.

Each of these short-term joint interventions was instigated by the social worker, seemed well timed, and proved a turning point in the work. The social workers were not for the moment assailed by the extra anxiety of doing more harm than good; the concerted action did not have the quality of a defensive collusion or 'ganging up' against the clients, but rather functioned to contain anxiety and enable unpalatable truths to be faced.

Long-term collaboration

The picture was more mixed in those cases where social workers attempted longer-term concerted action with other practitioners. Regular joint interviews were undertaken in three cases, all involving clients who were emotionally very damaged. Much depended on how the anxiety of working with these clients was coped with.

A middle-aged single mother whose older children had all been taken into care or adopted had received help on a massive scale to enable her to bring up the youngest two. However, in adolescence the older remaining child persuaded the department to take her into care. The mother became depressed and agitated; the younger child, delinquent. The social worker noted that she now had "three clients, each with separate needs and often pulling in different directions". Recognising that the mother "has a tendency to split and is very manipulative", she managed to work on all three fronts whilst holding on to a systemic view of the whole family. In particular she linked up with their GP, who had some psychotherapeutic training, and jointly with him offered the mother regular fortnightly interviews for three months. This structure proved containing, not least for the social worker's pessimistic anxiety; the mother recovered and her care of her youngest became more effective. Thus the GP's mental health task and the social worker's child-care task were both served.

In the second case, the primary task issue for the social worker was again a lone mother's parenting of her early adolescent children; this time it was she who wanted them taken into care. Convinced that they would suffer if this happened, and that the mother did not really mean it, he linked up with a child guidance psychiatric social worker who was involved because of the children's truancy and under-achievement at school. At first presentation, the two practitioners had been making weekly home visits together for five months. Little had changed and each of them had privately come to dread the visits. The two main features of their joint presentation were the near-psychotic behaviour and relationships described in the family, often with no apparent psychological boundaries between its members; and their own chaotic account of their work, often with no differentiation between the two of them. Asked what their aims were, they could remember no stated plan for embarking on the joint visits; "it just happened". They seemed to be working on an unexamined belief that the situation could be contained without removing the children from home (contrary to the views of the school and the social worker's area director). It emerged that the social worker was assuming that the PSW's superior psychiatric skills justified this approach, while she was deferring to his statutory authority; but in fact *both* felt de-skilled and powerless. It was debatable whether the workshop proved a good enough container for their anxieties. At the second and last presentation the PSW (not a member of the programme but attending by invitation) withdrew the written material she had supplied, on grounds of confidentiality. This at any rate suggested a belated drawing of boundaries, and it was she who was able to reflect that they must have been "clinging together for survival".

The third case was the one referred to earlier in which, to the social worker's dismay, the probation officer 'failed' to have an abusing father sent to prison. Their joint initiative to get marital interviews going is discussed fully in chapter 9. As in other attempts at marital work, the social worker's focus was diverted by resurgent anxieties for the children's safety. This case in fact combined both the characteristic limitations on social workers' ability to pursue a holistic or systemic approach. They seemed unable to sustain a focus on marital interaction if there was anxiety about children, or to sustain a long-term collaborative interaction in the interests of children if there was a marital dimension—i.e. they did so only with one-parent families.

WARDING OFF THE ANXIETIES OF SOCIAL WORK

The social workers gave us a picture of their characteristic anxieties and ways of defending against them which both resembled and differed from Mattinson and Sinclair's (1979) account of an inner London borough social services department.[4] On the intake boundary, as in that study, the fear of being swamped with human problems for which there was no solution, saddled with other workers' unwanted anxieties or (conversely) blamed for failing to come to a child's rescue was dealt with by careful but bureaucratic sifting. Except in the rural team where there was time for non-statutory work, the assessment of clients was often confined to deciding whether they were eligible for one or other category of practical help or mandatory intervention. The reductionist defence thus started at the very beginning and was rooted in institutional procedure.

On the other hand, we did not hear of office duty rotas or allocation systems being operated in a way which enabled the social workers to avoid sticking with clients. On the contrary, they mostly sustained regular and consistent contact, though keeping their distance emotionally. From our vantage point, there was little evidence of the crisis-ridden atmosphere described by Mattinson and Sinclair, in which the excitement of hectic activity warded off one anxiety but generated others. Our impression was rather of dour persistence and painstaking thoroughness within the limits of the narrowly defined task

The citadel

Above all, we found that the social workers tended to make defensive use not only of their procedures and task-definitions but of their entire institution. This had two aspects, internal and external. As their employing body the department was regularly the butt of their complaints. It withheld resources, harrassed them with red tape rather than meeting their need for support and was incompetent at management whilst expecting more and more work from them. Its demands prevented them from doing the good work they would like to do and deprived them of professional autonomy. 'It' (or 'they') became impersonal and monolithic; it could be safely and freely blamed.

However, when they faced outwards towards other agencies, the courts and the demanding public it was this very monolithic quality that became their protective stronghold. The hierarchical organisation (internally the bane of their lives) enabled them to shelter behind decisions made at a higher level, or to put off urgent demands by explaining that they would have to refer upwards for such decisions to be made. Our own relationship with the department over some five years remained more distant and formal than with any of the other participating agencies. And our experience of the social workers themselves was quite different according to whether we were relating to them individually or *en bloc*. As individuals, especially when discussing their cases, they could be lively and expressive at times or wooden and stolid at others, but they could change in themselves and differ from each other. As a group they tended to solidify into one unchanging stance with which there could be little creative interaction. Thus, in the inter-agency world of the study programme, their individual interest in participative learning was limited by the citadel they collectively brought with them.

SOCIAL WORKERS, PARENTING AND SOCIETY

Just as we said at the outset that social work can hardly be considered except in relation to other agencies, so in the end it cannot be understood except in the context of society as a whole. This is true of all helping services (see chapter 10), but social work above all was at the eye of the storm in the 1980s. In the prevailing political rhetoric as well as less sophisticated public and media opinion, social workers have been singled out as the epitome of the 'dependency culture' upon which contempt has been heaped. The opposing rhetoric has castigated such attitudes as the uncaring and punitive ethos inevitably let loose by a ruthless market ideology.

In the middle, social workers who have typically approached their training and entry into the profession with idealistic enthusiasm find themselves in a job which is increasingly nasty, exhausting and frightening. Violence towards social workers has increased, and threats of violence are commonplace; it was reported in 1987 that more social workers had been murdered on duty than police in the previous three years.[5] Some of the most skilled social workers have migrated to the newly expanding professions of counselling and psychotherapy (as indeed have those in need of help with personal and relationship difficulties if they have the means to make an informed choice).

In the social workers' (internal) view of their own employing organisation which we described above it is easy to see the image of a bad, abusing parent, betraying the duty of caring; in the wider context, the state itself (and the society which it represents) partakes of the same image. The social workers in the study programme conveyed their dwindling sense of job satisfaction under the attacks they felt were made on them and on the professional image they once had of themselves. In their individual evaluations of programme learning, one wrote of 'a greater understanding of how in very complex and deep ways the structure and function of a social services department affects the social worker's relationship with the client, especially where there is a 'punitive' statutory involvement which may detract from the therapeutic role to which *we* might aspire'.

Since our study was completed, new legislation is bringing about a more 'mixed economy' in the way social work is to be organised, with greater emphasis on social services departments and social workers as purchasers and co-ordinators of services as well as providers. Meanwhile the Central Council for Education and Training in Social Work is introducing new schemes at both basic and post-graduate levels designed to raise standards, validate proven competence and relate academic training more closely to field requirements. Whether such initiatives will help raise the morale of the profession and clarify its role and objectives on society's behalf must remain an open question, especially so long as finance continues to be restricted. Indeed, all these developments have the potential to push forward the transformation of social work into an emotionally-distanced way of 'managing' people in need, which was already visible in our study.

Social workers are caught up in society's own profound ambivalence about the care of its dependent members, be they children or adults. Their own conflict between the 'good' parenting which they aspire to and the 'bad' which they shun (but fear being identified with) must be seen as reflecting not only the conflicts of their clients but the conflicts of the nation which employs them.

Notes

1   Those concerning Maria Colwell (1974), Lisa Godfrey (1975) and Steven Meurs (1975).

2   The term 'child protection' was replacing 'child care' at this period and has since become universal: one indication of a changing emphasis in the perceived social work task concerning children (Parton and Parton, 1989).

3   Again, this locates our study in the transitional period before the emphasis swung more towards removal of children from home following a new spate of inquiries into

child deaths (Jasmine Beckford, 1985; Tyra Henry, 1987; Kimberley Carlile, 1987) and the surge of concern about child sexual abuse (see Appendix).

4   Not only were we working in a county area a decade later, but our different vantage point gave us different kinds of subjective and objective data. The earlier researchers' immersion in the department included carrying caseloads as part-time members of social work teams; we were located in a 'temporary institution' outside the boundary of any one agency, and relied on workshop study of practitioners' case presentations. Both approaches were different from that of Menzies Lyth (1970) whose ideas both were using (and whose own approach went on evolving in later studies: Menzies Lyth, 1989, pp. viii-ix). This shows one aspect of the relativity of research findings in the field of human relations (chapter 1); whilst these studies clearly form a related sequence, there is no straightforward way in which they either validate or falsify each other as in conventional 'hard' science.

5   Presidential address by Brian Roycroft (1987) to the Association of Directors of Social Services.

Part III

THE NETWORK OF SERVICES

9

Partnerships in practice and the collaborative triangle

In the first part of this chapter we discuss four examples of attempts at collaboration between various combinations of professional disciplines. In each case problems arose in which the respective practitioners' use of institutional defences related to their different settings and tasks appeared salient. The main emphasis will be on these professional defences. But as practitioners are also influenced by their own and their clients' or patients' anxiety (and defences against it) it is the interplay of processes at work in the principal interdependent relationship systems concerned that shapes the picture in any given case. These systems are: the client's or patient's system; the 'caring system' (i.e. the task-oriented relationship between client or patient and practitioner) and the agency or professional system. In our study the influence upon interdisciplinary collaboration of defences at each system level was most clearly seen when practitioners attempted joint work on a case, and it is the ensuing variable and complex mix that we now explore.

DIFFERENT AGENCY DEFENCES IN A CHILD-ABUSE CASE—PROBATION AND SOCIAL WORK

Child abuse cases are notorious for the anxiety they raise. This was true for Mr Roberts and Mrs Winters, the probation officer and social worker involved with the Bennett family. They presented their work jointly on three occasions to the mixed workshop of which they were both members.

> Garry and Tracey Bennett, both in their early twenties, had parents who were well known to the probation and social services—hers because of marital and financial problems; his, divorced for some years, on account of his

father's offences and attendant social difficulties (his family was said to be "very aggressive").

Garry was likened to "a sixteen year-old skinhead", disarming, placatory and flirtatious with the social worker. Both practitioners agreed that he was not very bright. He was unemployed. Tracey, a big, motherly looking young woman, had become grossly overweight since marriage. She talked freely and, though the more intelligent, was disorganised in their home and in child care, both of which Garry left her to cope with.

The couple had met through talking to each other on citizens band radio, in which Tracey was a 'leading light'. When they married they had both been on probation to Mr Roberts for separate offences. His relationship with them was benignly paternal. He had been "rather touched by their affection and loyalty" and the way Garry was not averse to fathering another man's baby with which Tracey was by then heavily pregnant. When this child was three months old, however, she was found to be injured after the police were alerted by an anonymous 'phone call. The injury was not explained but the baby was registered as 'at risk'. The family's first social worker left after six months and Mrs Winter took over, at her own request, because of her interest in working with such families. Meanwhile Mr Roberts got the probation orders discharged on the grounds that the Bennetts had not been re-convicted and social services were now involved.

The couple's own baby (a boy) was born a year after the first; three months later the little girl was again injured. This time Garry himself showed Mrs Winter the bruises and (after some prevarication) admitted causing them. He was not prosecuted, but "got himself arrested" some weeks later for taking a car and driving without a licence. At Mr Roberts' suggestion he was given a community service order, but he was soon back in court for not complying with it.

Garry was now in danger of a prison sentence, and at this point Mr Roberts re-thought his policy. Though still "reluctant to be involved again because of suspected abuse of children", and "mindful of the difficulty of working with social services in such cases", he saw a twofold opportunity: to pursue the probation service aim of keeping offenders out of prison, and the study programme aim of trying to improve collaborative work. He consulted Mrs Winter, and successfully recommended a probation order to the court on the basis that they would be working closely together with the Bennetts.

Meanwhile the family was frequently in various minor crises, with a persistent shortage of money and sometimes of food. Not surprisingly, Garry and Tracey's relationship was increasingly under stress. There had been talk of divorce and several brief separations. Tracey was vociferous in her complaints about Garry's limited and inconsistent help in the house and about being left to cope with the children. Mrs Winter reported that she managed rather better when they were separated but seemed determinedly helpless when they were together, as if to keep him there. She was sometimes explicit about her need of him and her dread of living alone. Garry complained less. He mostly went out instead. But he got frantically jealous and could be violent if he felt Tracey's faithfulness was in question. As a parent (according to Mr Roberts' workshop notes) it was 'almost as if he seeks nurture from his own babies/children—unable to tolerate frustration of his needs/desires'.

The Bennetts presented a picture familiar to probation officers and social workers. As a family they epitomised what has been called the 'cycle of deprivation'. Their relationship with its background of disturbance exhibited the same ambivalent attachments and impulsive behaviour as Mattinson and Sinclair (1979) found in their core sample of exacting and time-consuming social services department clients. They were bound to make the same heavy demands on the practitioners involved with them, not least for consistency and reliability in the face of their chaotic and phantasy-ridden lives and relationships which put the children in jeopardy. They were also likely to react to anxiety predominantly with the primitive unconscious defences of splitting, denial and projection.

Mrs Winter visited the home more or less weekly; it was not clear whether by appointment. She always saw Mrs Bennett and the children, and Mr Bennett if he was there. Mr Bennett attended the probation office and saw Mr Roberts regularly as required by the probation order. In effect the social worker became the wife's confidant, the probation officer the husband's. The practitioners planned to keep in regular contact with one another though they said that the claims of their other work often made this difficult. In addition they had agreed with Mr and Mrs Bennett to hold monthly joint interviews at the social services office, in which the couple together with both practitioners would work on difficulties in their marital relationship. Since this was the family's main resource system but was not coping with the practical and emotional demands of caring and providing for the children, the joint aim was 'to see if the couple can be helped to understand further what is the matter, and if so whether they are able to effect some improvement towards their (apparently) shared goals of keeping the children and (with more ambivalence) staying together' (Mr Roberts' notes). However, only two such meetings took place, and we shall concentrate on these for the light they throw on the difficulties of collaboration in such a case.

Before they first met as a foursome, Garry had told Mr Roberts that he wanted clarification of the legal position arising from the children being on the 'at risk' register. The demand had been passed on to Mrs Winter, and the first joint interview opened with her explanation. She made reference to Garry's violent behaviour as well as the purpose and powers of the child-abuse case conference. Tracey wanted to attend, Garry did not because "it would be boring". Mrs Winter made it clear that they would not be invited to the conference, but undertook to tell them about its meetings and decisions. Both workers felt that so far, with only a bit of "sniping" at each other, the couple were joining forces to present themselves as "good parents".

At this point Mr Roberts intervened to change the focus of discussion away from the children and onto the Bennetts' relationship. They then revealed aspects of their collusive interaction; for example, from what she said, Tracey showed she was well aware that Garry's absences from home would be prolonged when he said, "I won't be long". She saw him off with a smile—and then "stewed" over his duplicity, scolded and provoked a row and often an outburst from him when he did get back. Untrustworthiness was the theme, imputed to one another and to other people—for instance the health visitor of whom Garry was very suspicious. No doubt there was also distrust of these two practitioners, and especially of the way they had now joined forces. As the session ended the

clients contrived to separate them. Tracey left the room
with Mrs Winter, whilst Garry button-holed Mr Roberts.

This was the first time the Bennetts were met face to face by both the
practitioners with statutory powers and responsibilities. Each worker represented related aspects of the clients' lives which had hitherto been kept separate.
Meanwhile, though Mr Roberts and Mrs Winter were in the same workshop
and had had a chance to appraise one another, the foursome was just as novel an
event for them as for their clients. In part, their difficulties and anxiety arose
from their lack of experience and technique in joint interviewing at that time. It
could scarcely have been otherwise given their training and the traditions of
their respective agencies described in chapters 7 and 8. The noteworthy point
however is that, just as they were separated physically by the clients, their
handling of the interview ensured that 'statutory' issues concerning care of the
children were partitioned off from the Bennetts' relationship, despite the stated
intention of linking them.

The practitioners' behaviour in the workshop discussions was also revealing.
They demonstrated how strange was this degree of shared responsibility and
how anxious-making the mutual exposure in joint sessions was in itself. They
were excessively polite to each other and at the same time distant in their flat,
heavy and sometimes barely audible presentations. The workshop logbook
noted that their material was 'parcelled up—His and Hers'. Mrs Winter was the
more pessimistic, emphasising Garry Bennett's lack of co-operation and
evasiveness, especially regarding her plans for the family as a whole to get
intensive help at a local centre for 'child-abuse' families. Mr Roberts was more
sanguine and his factual and well documented presentations, typical of
probation officers, revealed 'his nostalgia for a period when both clients were
on probation and courting each other under his benign eye' (as the logbook put
it)—a time when he had seen no overt hint of Garry's capacity for explosive
violence.

Mrs Winter said that in the interview she thought Garry was upset when she
discussed his violence in front of Mr Roberts, but Mr Roberts did not confirm
it. In hindsight, it was as if Mrs Winter herself was anxious about her own wish
to draw Garry's violence to his 'indulgent' probation officer's attention. For his
part Mr Roberts disclosed that when Mrs Winter left at the end of the interview
he had second thoughts about the propriety of giving her a sight of the court
report he had written on Garry. Thus their uncertainty about each other was
underlined.

In the workshop discussion, however, there was no 'mental space' to note
how the practitioners were re-enacting the clients' mistrustful relationship.
Given the evidence before them, the other members too dealt with collective

anxiety about destructiveness by denial and splitting—as if to make connections was to be critical, hostile and damaging to their colleagues. Much time was devoted to a suggestion that the marital work be hived off altogether and referred to the 'confidential' setting of marriage guidance (until the marriage guidance counsellor present rejected the idea).

The second joint meeting took place as planned. In the month since the first session the Bennetts' gas supply had been cut off, Tracey having broken into the meter. She was conditionally discharged for this while Mr Roberts, Mrs Winter and her senior "moved heaven and earth" to get the gas re-connected. During the week when they had no means of cooking, the Bennetts asked for their older child to be taken into care. Despite Mrs Winter's feeling that this was "blackmail" (and the speedy restoration of the gas supply), she had in fact acceded to the request a few days before the second joint interview.

Mr Roberts reported that Garry Bennett started off the session by saying that the older child "makes me lose control" because of her head-banging which he was powerless to stop. Tracey said she was similarly affected by her daughter, and Garry went on to talk of his mixed feelings for the girl because she was not his child. His wife associated to what he was saying with material about her mother's ambivalence to herself, talking in a way which led Garry to add that the younger boy "gets away with murder" by comparison to his half-sister.

Garry recounted how in his own childhood he was "just fed and that's all ... pushed from pillar to post", turning to each of his warring parents in turn but being rejected first by one and then the other. But at least "I am not spending all my time in prison like my father". Tracey, on the other hand, said that (for all her mother's ambivalence) she was never in want materially. In the exchanges that followed, Garry conveyed clearly that he regarded her as if she were his mother, longed-for but often neglectful. Taken aback and pleased at first at what seemed like a compliment, Tracey soon went on to complain of being "used" by him. She thus responded with a double message—as her own mother (and no doubt his) had done.

Mr Roberts could not remember the sequence, but at some stage the couple got together to complain about their lodgers (Garry's younger sister and her boyfriend). The repeated theme of being used and exploited was recognised in the workshop, but the two practitioners were at pains to emphasise a different aspect. Mrs Winter stressed that she and Mr Roberts "were on the same lines at this point"; they both pointed out to the Bennetts the need "for a united front and compromise ... [but] Garry and Tracey found our reaction very odd". What was said and the way the practitioners related to one another was strange to the clients, each practitioner picking up from the other, "finishing each other's sentences". It was so different from "their all or nothing approach to things ... they were very puzzled". Mrs Winter added that Garry's deprivation was very obvious, as was his need for "material goodies" and his envy of the children. Mr Roberts said he was encouraged, and both workers felt they had got the clients engaged.

Their hopes were not realised, however. The couple failed the next appointment (delayed by the practitioners' holidays) and a further date was missed because it clashed with a hospital appointment for the youngest child. Mrs Winter reported that Tracey eventually told her she wanted no more foursomes; she and Garry now found it easier to talk together "without someone else present". Garry, less explicitly, indicated the same to Mr Roberts in his interviews, which were mainly taken up with a further offence he had committed and its sequel (a suspended sentence rather than the immediate imprisonment Mr Roberts feared). Mr Roberts was "very disappointed ... found it very difficult to come to terms with [the joint interviews] tailing off ... but if they don't want to come, OK, I have to accept it".

So probation officer and social worker continued the work separately; the matter was left there. Neither of them at this stage explored with their respective clients, or each other, what might lie behind the couple's antipathy to joint interviews—after one in which the practitioners' differences were plain and they felt themselves to have been split, followed by the second in which the practitioners were in unison.

The workshop did not investigate the issue either. Nor did its members go into what Tracey might have meant when she talked of third parties as a hindrance to talking with Garry. These intriguing questions to do with the couple's interaction and their relationship with the practitioners were eschewed.

As on the earlier occasions, the presentation was *sotto voce*, the atmosphere in the workshop heavy and depressed. The mood then changed dramatically and became angry and accusatory. As it was put later, "it was as if a hope suddenly emerged in the group that some life might be found in conflict". The change followed Mr Roberts' expression of "despair that Mr Bennett was likely to go to prison". This would have marked the failure of his work for, as a probation officer, "my prime task is to keep him out of custody". His stance was forcefully challenged, principally by another social worker, an experienced senior (not from Mrs Winter's office). Her view and that of other women in the group was that he should be confronting his client with the choices he was making, encouraging understanding and responsibility for his actions which jeopardised the family, instead of (as she put it) "sticking up for him [to] keep him out of prison . . . one can be too passive. I would have said to him this time: 'stop it—if you go to prison, you go to prison'."

The men in the workshop disagreed. The value of prison in cases like this was disputed by a male GP; Mr Roberts defended his work with Garry; the TIMS consultant affirmed the probation service's responsibility to achieve alternatives to prison. The sexes were split. There was a fleeting recognition that this might reflect the fact that the couple too were influenced not only by their own psychopathology and interaction, but by social and environmental pressures. Mrs Winter ended consideration of this theme by bringing material to condemn Garry for his view that "the children were her [Tracey's] job". A further desultory effort to understand why this should be so was halted by Mr Roberts. He was "very uneasy. . .so many assumptions are being made" and he later commented in his notes on the "uphill task of representing Garry as not all bad to members of the workshop who seemed to be against him".

Mrs Winter then acknowledged mixed feelings about the prospects of work with Mr and Mrs Bennett. "I see my prime task as the children. I'm doubtful if any work can be done with him to help him cope with the kids' needs for many years to come; I don't think he's got a lot of potential for growth. I think she's got slightly more, but I don't think she can do it without a very supportive partner . . . I would like things to break down in order that I could make firmer plans for the children by getting them into care. But . . . how far can I take the risk of letting that happen, with goodness knows what consequences? Therefore I compromise, I suppose, with very uneasy feelings about [the supportive and relief arrangements she had made] and their usefulness, if he's not partaking of them as well." Mr Roberts firmly disagreed with his co-worker's assessment of Garry.

Now that the conflict between the practitioners was out in the open, the workshop members recognised their own strong tendency to react to complexity with thoughts of separating things out; if only Garry was firmly held in prison, Tracey and the children could be attended to; if only the children were safely in local authority care, the couple might be worked with. Such defensive splitting had lost sight of the whole—the price paid for an attempt to avoid anxieties inherent in the practitioners' difficult tasks with this family.

This more thoughtful phase of the discussion was again short-lived. Distancing himself from Mrs Winter's difficulties, Mr Roberts said, "one major difference, and it's a luxury I know, is that I'm free of the anxiety about the children. That's your responsibility." Loud protest greeted his remark. How could he entertain such a view? All those involved with the family *must* accept responsibility for the children, etc. Eventually a quieter atmosphere did prevail and it was seen that Mr Roberts' identification with his client and with his 'prime task' (as he defined it) led him to mirror Garry's attitude: "the children are her job". Equally, the workshop's furious reaction mirrored that of Tracey — and indeed that of Mrs Winter once she in turn fell back on the narrow definition of 'my prime task is the children'.

As this part of the discussion recognised, the splitting (men from women, practitioner from practitioner, agency from agency as well as husband from wife) and the violent feelings were being acted-out and reflected by the workshop. The fight was mobilised by the senior social worker who had no responsibility for Mrs Winter's work but nonetheless was identified with the social service culture, spoke to its task-related anxiety and dealt with it in characteristic fashion. She succumbed to the temptation to blame—just as social workers are so often blamed by others. In the polarised climate, one valid point she did make was lost, i.e. that the probation officer's task was not only to keep an offender out of prison but also to confront him with his responsibility for offending (and to work to reduce it). We now look more closely at both practitioners' task-related anxieties and agency-specific defences.

Mr Roberts was frank concerning his anxieties about child abuse and about collaborating with social services. When these had originally come up, with the first injury to the Bennetts' daughter, he had dealt with them by opting out and getting the probation orders discharged early; though bound by his mandate he could use that procedure to free himself from it. He could also use the social inquiry report on Garry Bennett's next offence to suggest a community service order—which would not be his responsibility. Though both these moves could be justified in their own terms, they could also function as defences against the anxieties he acknowledged.

Anxiety about Garry's offences themselves probably played only a minor part. He was never charged with injuring the child, though he admitted it to Mrs Winter. The inference she drew—that he 'got himself arrested' on car offences (i.e. to draw attention to his feelings of guilt or of being out of control) — was unlikely to impress a probation officer. It would hardly be justice for an offender to be imprisoned ostensibly for one offence but really because of an offence he had not been charged with, even though it might have been a relief to those, like Mrs Winter, concerned mainly with the children's safety. On the other hand, it was Mr Roberts' anxiety about child abuse and collaboration that led him to avoid suggesting a new probation order as the means of keeping Garry out of prison at this point.

When the danger of prison reappeared, with Garry in breach of the community service order, Mr Roberts was mobilised to re-think his policy of opting out, and was encouraged by his and Mrs Winter's membership of the study programme to hope that support would be available for their collaboration if, after all, he took Garry on probation again.

For her part, Mrs Winter took over responsibility for the Bennetts willingly, but she expressed the characteristic anxiety and dilemma of her profession when she admitted she would 'like things to break down' in order to get the children into care, but in the next breath expressed her fear of 'goodness knows what consequences'. In the uncertain 'wait and see' situation she was first anxious for the children's safety and wished she had a good reason to remove them; but this implied attack on blameworthy parents aroused a second anxiety of doing more harm than good by intervening.

By turns inclined to take blame on herself and put it elsewhere, she kept losing sight of the whole; blame seemed to offer more certainty than the complex holistic view. When she in effect echoed Tracey Bennett's complaints about Garry (and by implication his probation officer), she forgot her own observation that her client was determinedly helpless in her husband's absence, and ignored or overlooked the powerful influence of the contradictions in Tracey's make-up—her need of Garry (dreading to live alone) as well as her rejection of him.

In short, faced with the conflict and anxiety engendered by the couple's ambivalent attachment to each other, the practitioners too dealt with it by splitting. At Mr Roberts' instigation, they had set out together to pay attention to and work with their clients' marital interaction, seeing this as relevant to *all* their objectives—safeguarding the children without having to remove them, *and* reducing the parents' delinquent acting-out without having to resort to imprisonment. By the last presentation this joint quest had run into difficulty. With the joint sessions interrupted, a child taken into care and both parents re-offending, the social worker for the time being could focus only on the safety of the children, the probation officer only on the avoidance of prison and the demarcation of his responsibilities from hers.

Probation officers and social workers are familiar with clients whose predominant defences are those of splitting and projection. The caseloads of workers in both disciplines are heavily weighted with them. But as we saw in the preceding chapters, the socially organised defences of their respective agencies have evolved in relation to the different tasks and responsibilities they have been assigned and the anxieties inherent in them. This case exemplifies vividly the propensity not only for the client system's defences to 'get into' practitioners, leading them to reflect opposite aspects of the clients' conflict and ambivalence, but also for their entrenched agency defences to support these opposites. In fact *both* Tracey and Garry Bennett had mixed feelings about the eldest girl which they tended to split; both identified alternately with the 'bad', rejected child and with the 'good', indulged one; both were caught up in a shared dynamic of provocation and jealous mistrust; and both had acted-out their conflicts by offending. The unconscious forces at work, however, made it difficult for the practitioners always to keep the collusive aspects of their clients' interaction in the forefront of their minds. And their own differences and those of their agencies were just as difficult to encompass in the interaction between themselves. They were either 'at odds' or behaved as if they were 'the same'. They, too, became enmeshed in the all or nothing view of the world that was their clients'. Under pressure each fell back defensively on irreconcilable definitions of their 'prime task'. Mutual understanding which encompasses differences—the essence of collaboration—seemed out of their reach at the point where their account of the work broke off.

But collaboration was not thereby rendered impossible. It turned on whether the anxieties affecting the practitioners could be contained and mastered. In our own institute's practice of marital psychotherapy it has become axiomatic that the two therapists assigned to a couple have to be able to expose their conflicts and differences—'have their own row'—in contained conditions before they can help their clients to confront theirs. Mr Roberts and Mrs Winter did have their row in the workshop. Although other members also joined in, fiercely at times, this group did provide an environment in which differences and anxiety could be exposed; time and space in which lost wits could be recovered. We do not have a follow-up on this case; Mr Roberts took on another role in the probation service a few months later (one in which he extended his experience of joint interviewing). But his notes recorded 'an amber light from the workshop to raise the possibility of further joint sessions with Mr and Mrs Bennett'. Whether or not that particular strategy was renewed, conflict had been survived and the practitioners' resolve had been strengthened to stick with their collaborative task rather than give it up in despair and acrimony.

Just as the viability of a marriage largely depends on how far the partners' unconscious defences against anxiety are mutually supporting and flexible, so the same is true of a collaborative relationship between practitioners, and the socially organised defences of their respective agencies. The more threatening the anxiety, the more rigid the operation of defences—by practitioners as well as clients—and the greater their need for a containing environment in which to confront and understand the anxiety and modify the defences. Given such a favourable context, practitioners can learn to use their subjective experience to understand their clients' or patients' problems and their own responses as individuals—though not without a struggle. It is more difficult to modify organisational practices and attitudes, or for practitioners to stand out against their agencies' well-established socially organised defences. We return to this crucial question in the final chapter.

THE INFLUENCE OF THE CLIENT ON COMPATIBLE SOCIAL DEFENCES—HEALTH VISITING AND SOCIAL WORK

What has been said about the role played by task-related, institutionalised defences in inter-professional collaboration helps to explain the generally positive attitudes social workers and health visitors had to one another in the study programme. Both were oriented to children; social workers were the agents of their protection from inadequate or harmful parenting, health visitors had a traditional concern for their health and welfare. But this 'compatible' combination of practitioners could nonetheless be vulnerable to the interplay of their clients' and their institutions' defences. As an example, we look again at the case which we called *Abstinence and greed* in chapter 6. This was contributed by the health visitor, Mrs Hunt; the social worker involved was not a participant in the programme, so her point of view is missing from the account and we do not have a full picture of what dilemmas she may have experienced and how she dealt with them.

We noted in chapter 6 that the characteristic anxiety in health visiting stemmed from the conflict between dependency and autonomy; their resultant defensive preoccupation was with distinctions between their 'normal' and 'abnormal' families, seeking to refer or share responsibility for the latter. 'Abnormal' families not only heightened anxiety, they highlighted the issue of dependency that resonated with the health visitors' own uncertainty about professional autonomy. As one of the health visitors in the group discussing the work with the Bennetts (above) put it, "we are also concerned with the children, but we're very glad to have social services behind us when it comes to child abuse". We also saw how health visitors tended to project skill and competence into other professionals and then resent their reluctance to accept the burden and mantle of 'the expert'. And there was their opposite tendency to resist appropriate referral or joint work rather than relinquish rewarding and exclusive 'mothering' relationships. Meanwhile the health visitor's focus on mother and child made for problems in relating to both parents and the adult world of marriage.

The themes from chapter 8 which seem relevant here are: the insistent anxiety for social workers of the child-protection task; their tendency to react to this with a reductionist approach that included viewing the couple at the core of the family primarily as parents rather than spouses; and their institutional defence of the citadel.

It will be recalled from chapter 6 that Mrs Hunt's first move when the Grays' explosive marital situation became apparent (in the course of routine checks on their daughter) was to suggest the couple go to marriage guidance. When the suggestion was rejected she involved a social worker to help with their housing and financial difficulties—which were also linked with the marriage problem. In this way she sought to share the anxiety of working with the Grays; envy and resentment were unlikely to arise, since she had channelled the request to a social worker she knew and got on well with. The absence of apparent conflict between health visitor and social worker also owed much to the fact that the assigned tasks of both practitioners were congruent. However, in the event, the course their collaboration took was effectively determined by the clients rather than themselves.

The social worker came into the work shortly before the legal process removed Mr Gray from home; thereafter the practitioners worked only with the wife/mother. They defined their respective roles clearly to each other and to her; but these differences of task did not seem divisive in themselves, and (as we noted before) because both of them engaged with the emotional and relationship issues raised by Mrs Grey the net effect was that sameness seemed to predominate over difference.

They kept in close touch with each other and, as Mrs Hunt put it, 'formed our own little support group' in the face of the client's explosive and demanding behaviour and the anxiety she generated by her emotional state and contradictory feelings about her husband. Their cohesion was facilitated because they were working with only half of the marital system. There was no live input from Mr Gray. He was not in the work as a real person, only being present through the distorted images and attributions of his wife and those of the neighbourhood with which Mrs Hunt at least was at pains not to collude. Had he been there 'in the flesh' the practitioners could hardly have failed to pick up and reflect the couple's divisive interaction—as indeed the workshop did.

Even so, Mrs Gray's predominant defence of splitting and denial came increasingly into play. She showed her propensity to put people into rigid categories and distance herself from those whom she felt to be hostile, into whom she projected her own destructiveness. Relationships in the outer world were coerced into confirming the pattern of her inner world in which tensions between opposites could not be tolerated and differences were experienced as irreconcilable. And from her point of view there were real differences between the practitioners. The social worker, who had helped her to be independent of her husband as if a single parent, was thereby associated with her rejection of him. When Mrs Gray was no longer able to sustain that rejection against her need of him—sexually and because he had been the receptacle for projections of her greedy, infantile self—she rejected and excluded the social worker. 'Now I've withdrawn my statement [that he had threatened her life] there's no point in her coming.' Meanwhile, the health visitor was associated by the client with mothering and with an asexual image, but at the same time had never shared the social worker's implied acceptance that the marriage could be finally written off; and she continued to be welcomed—for a time.

However, as Mr Gray duly came back into his wife's life and their sexual relationship resumed, the health visitor's experience was of becoming inquisitive and intrusive like a prying mother; of being fended off; of not being autonomous; fearful of making connections between the 'infant' and the 'adult' in her interviews with her client. It was then her turn to be rejected.

With John Gray back home for a while, then ejected in favour of a new sexual partner, Mrs Hunt found her role as health visitor progressively less tenable and agency rules could be invoked to justify her withdrawal, even though she was still anxious about the child's emotional state and her mother's relationship with her. The little girl with her sleep problem was now the one intruding on Mrs Gray's new sexual relationship. She too was eventually ejected and went to her father as a prelude to divorce. The social worker then replaced the health visitor, re-engaging this time with statutory authority as an agent of child protection.

Just as there were rigid boundaries between conflicting aspects of Mrs Gray's personality, so rigid boundaries were induced into the working relationship between the two practitioners. The 'one in, one out' situation in the caring system reflected the dynamic of the client system, but the task-related anxieties and institutionalised defences of the two practitioners were so congruent that they believed themselves to be working in harmony when in some respects they were not. Anxiety for the child progressively led them to diverge in their views of the marital and family system. The social worker, perhaps seeing the Grays primarily as parents, directed her work to helping the mother manage the family without the father (only to find she eventually had to work with him as the custodial parent). The health visitor never lost sight of the couple as marital partners and did not believe Mrs Gray had finished with her husband. But she was also at pains not to relinquish her own 'maternal' relationship with her client, despite having invoked another child-care agency. These differences throw light on why the miniature 'citadel' within which these two practitioners stuck together for mutual support did not in fact stop them being split by Mrs Gray.

ANXIETY AND RESPONSIBILITY: BOUNDARIES AS A
PROFESSIONAL DEFENCE—GENERAL PRACTICE,
HEALTH-VISITING AND CHILD AND FAMILY
GUIDANCE

Dr Sanders' case, the start of which was outlined in chapter 2, also involved a
health visitor. Across a period of more than two years Alison Wright, known to
be able and competent in practical matters, had consulted the GP because of a
series of physical symptoms which proved to have no organic cause. She
eventually revealed what lay behind her evident tension: the desertion of her
husband. To her this was quite inexplicable; she was an exemplary wife. She
became anxiously invasive of the practice, turning sympathy and concern to
exasperation when nothing that was said seemed to make any difference, lessen
her incomprehension or help her even to entertain the possibility that her
marriage was over.

   However, she gave up her frantic surgery visits and when, six months later,
she presented her ten year-old's problem of school refusal, Dr Sanders sought
the help of the practice health visitor because of her expertise with mothers and
children. In our earlier brief comment we noted that Lisa's behaviour was
clearly bound up with Mrs Wright's anxiety, manifest following her husband's
departure, and that the child's recovery and emotional development largely
turned on the extent to which her mother could face what had seemed
untouchable when she had shown her distress to the GP more directly. It
seemed that it was the same fear of cruel desertion the doctor experienced when
she turned to her own health visitor, rather than 'abandon' mother and
daughter to a specialised psychiatric agency. We captioned the case: *Which
patient? Which practitioner?* and we now re-examine it with a focus on how the
patients' salient defences against anxiety interacted with the socially organised
professional or agency defences of the two practitioners.

   It was Mrs Kerr, the health visitor, who first introduced the case into the
study, though with Dr Sanders' active participation.

> Describing her home visits, Mrs Kerr said Lisa impressed
> her as a babyish, clinging child who constantly touched
> and was touched by her mother. It was the same picture as
> Dr Sanders had given her from the recent consultation
> with her mother which Lisa had attended. On the health
> visitor's first visit, the child came into the room back-
> wards; her attitude seemed to Mrs Kerr "like an ostrich, as
> though if she couldn't see me I couldn't see her". After
> this behaviour was ignored by Mrs Kerr she acted more

normally. Her mother was unable to distance herself from Lisa in this way.

Meanwhile Mrs Wright once again talked volubly about her marital situation but was unable to entertain any suggestion that she might have been involved in the difficulties that had arisen; no blame or fault could possibly attach to her. Mrs Kerr summarised her experience: "Alison conveyed a lot of anxiety and tension which was transferred onto me. I felt exasperated, but was quite unable to tell her that I felt her handling of Lisa was not helping the situation."

The health visitor then contacted Lisa's school and was surprised that the head teacher seemed unaware of the girl's absences or of any difficulty with her in school. On hearing the story, the head suggested that if only Lisa's mother "pushed her into school it would be okay". Mrs Kerr felt discouraged by this seemingly simplistic response.

In her notes for the study, Mrs Kerr recorded that her initial reaction to Dr Sanders' request had been: 'a straight referral to the child and family guidance service might be most appropriate as Lisa is well above the age range [of children] who are my first priority'. She had not voiced it at the time, but after her fruitless home visits she got Dr Sanders' agreement to an attempt to involve that agency, which was under the auspices of the local education department. When their principal social worker (a psychiatric social worker by training) saw Lisa, "he got the same impression; he was quite alarmed by her and thought her very disturbed".

After some further weeks it was learned that formal notice had been given to the authorities of Lisa's absences from school. A place of safety order was being considered; if necessary, the girl could be sent to boarding school. Both health visitor and doctor were alarmed by the news. "We thought it would be the worst thing possible for the family. Lisa had lost her father; to separate her from her mother is not the way to help the family situation." It transpired however that these possibilities had not been conveyed to Mrs Wright; only to Mrs Kerr and, through her, to Dr Sanders.

Neither intervention in fact materialised. Instead, a change of school was decided on. Lisa settled in and began

attending well—until she broke her collar bone. She was
kept at home again in spite of assurances to Mrs Wright
that her daughter could safely go to school with her arm in
a sling.

Meanwhile continuing work with Lisa was undertaken
by another social worker from the child and family
guidance service, a woman who made a good relationship
with her. She told Mrs Kerr that the girl had confided: "I
just can't say goodbye to Mum. She cries and gets upset so
I stay at home. School is fine once I'm there." This
practitioner seemed to have got through to Lisa, but she
was also made to feel uneasy. She told Mrs Kerr that she
feared she might develop a better relationship with Lisa
than her mother had. "I can't get into a position where
she'll go [to school] in my car and not on the school bus.
Mother's the problem, not Lisa."

Reporting this exchange to the workshop the health
visitor again made the point that she herself had "wanted
to be harder [on Alison Wright] than I actually am. She's
so upset. She says she doesn't want to cause any problems,
yet she knows she does. I feel it's stalemate."

Mrs Wright applied to the court for maintenance and a
separation order, but even this partial step towards
confronting the end of her marriage greatly increased her
anxiety. Dr Sanders reported that she managed to circum-
vent the removal of her intra-uterine coil (recommended
when she complained of heavy periods); the idea could
not be contemplated with the court appearance looming.
The patient wanted tranquillisers to help her get through
it for fear of "lashing out and making a scene".

For her part, Mrs Kerr suspected that recourse to the
matrimonial court might well have the effect of drawing
in yet another agency, the probation service. She thought
there were too many practitioners involved; there were
bound to be complications. She therefore put it to a
practice meeting that she "should stand back and leave it
to the social worker—see if they get anywhere". And so it
was agreed.

From this point, Mrs Kerr increasingly 'stood back' in the workshop discussion
too, leaving Dr Sanders centre stage. The GP became preoccupied with why
she found it so difficult to take things up with the patient. "There's something
of the martyr in her; that's irritating, but there's something else. I don't know

what it is. We've been talking about it in the practice. It's very interesting how she's come to different members of the team, including the practice manager . . . she's got everybody going and we're all unable to say wait a minute."

Asked what she would want to confront the patient with, Dr Sanders said it was her denial of the real situation and her part in it, "but there's also the fear that she might 'go over the top'—have a complete breakdown. Alternatively, I think she'd just go round to someone else. Everyone would need to take the same line. But I doubt if she could take it, that's what worries me."

Members of the workshop responded to different aspects of the situation: the patient's propensity to involve all and sundry, and her vulnerable mental state. On the first issue, a social worker thought Mrs Wright was implicitly appealing for a relationship with one practitioner, who should "grab hold of it . . . see her regularly at a regular time". A marriage guidance counsellor spoke on the second: she needed "something for herself from someone who can follow things through with her . . . she's lost so much . . . I think by seeing the same person you'd begin to strengthen her own identity". One member was concerned about fragmentation of the practitioner network, the other about fragmentation within the patient; their prescription was the same.

Dr Sanders countered the advice (for it was clear that she was the practitioner of choice the group had in mind). She listed organisational and practical difficulties and reiterated that both she and Mrs Kerr found Mrs Wright exhausting and emotionally intrusive—"you don't do well by other patients after seeing Alison".

The workshop came back to the referral to Mrs Kerr and the separation of Lisa's problem from her mother's. Dr Sanders explained her request to the health visitor by saying, "I didn't want to go along the medical line by referring to a psychiatrist; I didn't feel that was appropriate . . . I wanted to put it into a different channel . . . split it [Lisa's school attendance] off from the main problem". But she also conveyed yet again what a daunting patient she found Mrs Wright.

A member of the workshop noted how hostility and the fear of it seemed to permeate the case; such a patient could generate great anger in others. Dr Sanders responded forcefully: "I don't feel hostile because she's manipulating me. I feel hostile because I'm not doing her any good and she makes one feel impotent. That's the nub of it. We're not helping her and her distress is so obvious. She's in a most awful state."

Dr Sanders briefly reported the case four months later, Mrs Kerr being unexpectedly absent.

> There had been a lull and Lisa's school attendance would not be an issue during the impending school holidays. But anxiety about the patient persisted as did the doctor's

feeling about her own ineffectiveness. She now felt that a specialist psychiatric consultation would after all be helpful. Although she could not be sure of all the considerations leading her to this view, the previous workshop discussion had certainly been one; and there was also the suspicion that Lisa might yet be removed from home if non-attendance at school persisted—a step to which she and the health visitor remained strongly opposed. She had decided on referral to the psychiatrist at a local children's hospital where she was sure Mrs Wright's difficulties would be taken into account in assessing the child's emotional problems. The child and family guidance service's principal social worker was very much against the idea. Dr Sanders and Mrs Kerr both felt he was "possessive about the case" when the matter was discussed with him. He insisted that he and his agency should continue to handle it. There had been no feedback from him since.

Dr Sanders was called away from the workshop at this point for a clinical emergency, but members went on discussing the inter-professional exchange just described, without either her or Mrs Kerr present. They speculated that perhaps neither practitioner was aware that the child and family guidance service included a child psychiatrist; or that the agency was under threat because of restrictions on public expenditure. There was unanimity among those remaining, all from non-medical settings, that the social worker was probably affronted by the decision to refer, seeing it as "an undermining vote of no confidence".

Although Dr Sanders, who had the longest relationship with Mrs Wright and carried the major responsibility for her care, was the most obviously affected, all the practitioners in the case were constrained by the patient's anxiety and defences against it. Different as were their personalities, neither GP nor health visitor could be straightforward and direct with her, but both were perturbed by her and Lisa.

The other practitioners were also apparently affected by Mrs Wright. The education authority's principal social worker conveyed to the health visitor and not her the possibility that Lisa might be removed from home. Meanwhile, the social worker in continuing contact with Lisa was made to feel anxious too. She feared she would emphasise Mrs Wright's failure by doing better than her with a child whose difficulty she saw as reactive; mother was the problem, but a problem that could not be tackled.

Mrs Wright's defence of denial was pervasive, but it was the associated defence of projection that had an even more powerful influence. Her demand for tranquillisers to prevent 'lashing out' in court revealed for once her anxiety about hostile feelings and their potential for damage—an anxiety which was usually denied in herself (the 'perfect wife') but experienced by those in relationship with her. Thus, Lisa was afraid to leave her mother 'in a state', and there was a general tendency among the practitioners to fear doing an injury—whether through sins of omission or commission. Mrs Wright's denial was reinforced; others tended to confirm her worst fears; any attempt to engage with her evoked the unconscious aggressive and sadistic impulses alive at some level in the minds of everyone—and simultaneously the fear of giving way to them. The omnipotent phantasy which resulted was the mirror image of Mrs Wright's: that to address anxiety directly would constitute a dangerous attack —the patient might 'go over the top', be driven mad—rather than a benign process through which disturbed feelings could be contained, detoxified and put back to her in a more manageable form.

It was under this constraint that Dr Sanders passed the problem to the health visitor, and Mrs Kerr took the referral in spite of it being outwith her main responsibility—work with children under five. Only later, and in notes made following the workshop, was she explicit about her view that referral directly to the child and family guidance service would have been the appropriate disposal. In thus joining with the GP in re-enacting Alison Wright's displacement of her problem onto Lisa, Mrs Kerr was influenced not only by the client or patient system's dynamics but also by the characteristic dilemmas of her own profession.

Exposed to the mother-daughter relationship (the part of the client/patient system presented to the practice), Mrs Kerr's own judgement about the source of Lisa's problem was overshadowed by the transfer of anxiety and tension from Mrs Wright onto herself, inhibiting what we knew from her other work to be her customary directness. She could neither address Mrs Wright's anxiety and anger about her husband's desertion for a younger woman, nor confront her denial of the part she must have played in the apparent failure of her marriage and was certainly playing in her daughter's disturbance and school refusal. Nor could she bring to bear her health visitor's expertise with mother-child relationships, the attribute that led Dr Sanders to invoke her help. 'De-skilled', she lost personal and professional autonomy. The dynamic at work in her relationship with Mrs Wright left her with her sense of competence undermined, while her relationship with the GP highlighted the ambivalence in health visiting about the exercise of professional authority. Thus both the case and her working environment epitomised for Mrs Kerr the conflict between dependency and autonomy noted as a characteristic dilemma of her profession in chapter 6.

The situation she was caught up in was redolent of ambivalence, not least about psychological and task boundaries. There was first a conflict of feeling between allegiance to her medical colleague and to her role as health visitor, with the professional defences against anxiety integral to it—among which is the injunction to refer problematic cases. Later, although referral to the appropriate agency shifted the onus for Lisa's problem, it caused Mrs Kerr further alarm and left her neither in the case nor out of it. Eventually conflict was ameliorated by 'standing back', prompted by the assumed advent of yet another practitioner. But her most difficult inter-professional dilemma was with the GP, portrayed by the way she brought the case to the workshop—effectively passing the problem back to Dr Sanders.

For her part, Dr Sanders too was doubly affected, by Mrs Wright and by her own professional dilemmas and defences. She vividly expressed both her bewilderment and her subjective experience of the patient. She felt impelled to assume a responsibility greater than that inherent in her role as physician. Such an impossible burden generates resentment—but it was being rendered impotent that was the conscious source of her hostility. There was bound to be a conflict of feelings towards her patient, between hostility (with an impulse to reject) and sympathy (with the urge to relieve distress). Defending herself from this conflict, she was made all too aware of helplessness and inadequacy.

In chapter 5 we drew attention to the paradox in the doctor-patient relationship arising from the need to maintain a firm boundary between doctor and patient at the same time as preserving the boundary around them as a pair and their relationship from intrusion. We also quoted Balint to the effect that medical referral represents a 'crisis of confidence' at some level.

Mrs Wright's invasiveness threatened the emotional boundary between the doctor and herself. Few practitioners would have been immune from influence, even if they had been consciously determined to 'keep their distance' (Mattinson, 1975). Meanwhile, Dr Sanders was explicit about the crisis of confidence that had arisen in her treatment of this patient. When Mrs Wright brought Lisa into the consultations, the burden of therapeutic responsibility became heavier; the treatment task more complex. There was increased pressure to adopt a reductionist medical stance and break the problem down into its component parts. As the doctor put it, her intention was to split Lisa off from the main problem, her mother—rather than address them as an interactive pair, and their relationship as 'the patient'. In this situation, invoking the practice health visitor had a number of purposes. It eased the burden of responsibility, and Mrs Wright's emotional invasiveness of the boundary *between* doctor and patient; it kept the work within the practice team, minimising disturbance of the boundary *around* the doctor-patient relationship; it avoided the intrusion of outsiders.

An important special factor here was the nature of this particular primary care practice. Every working group has a distinctive identity, partaking of the character of the larger institution of which it is a part, but crucially shaped by the personalities of those comprising the group, and especially its leadership. Nowhere was this more evident in the study than in general practice. The senior partner seemed to us to influence the tenor of a practice more profoundly than the leaders of any other working groups of which participants were members. And as we noted earlier when discussing GPs' cases, the structure, organisation and culture of a practice embodied techniques to cope with anxiety.

Dr Sanders effectively ran the practice single-handed at the time; our impression was that she, Mrs Kerr and the all-female practice staff were mutually supportive and obviously caring of each other, as indeed they were of the patients. Dr Sanders set the tone. Energetic even though under pressure, if anyone was a 'patients' doctor' it was she, and the practice showed very considerable tolerance of patients like Mrs Wright with her often aggravating distress. Our impressions were formed not only from the cases the two practitioners presented but also—because the practice hosted this workshop —from our own observation and experience. Though no more than impressions, they were strong ones which we take account of in attempting to understand the inter-professional relationships in the work with Mrs Wright and Lisa.

As a member of the practice team, Mrs Kerr was part of its mutually supportive culture, but she brought into play a pattern of professional defences against anxiety which were at variance with those of the doctor. Health visitors too, as we have noted, tend to use referral as a means of relieving anxiety, but unlike doctors they are under no pressure to 'keep it in the (medical) family'. Mrs Kerr's allegiance to Dr Sanders and the practice culture played a part in her accepting the request to tackle Lisa Wright's school refusal, but before long her own professional culture reasserted itself and she referred the problem 'out' to the child and family guidance service.

Faced with that service's tough line, GP and health visitor re-united in opposition; but then they divided again. Mrs Kerr 'stood back', and in the workshop discussion Dr Sanders became more conscious of her dilemma in reaction to the patient's transference, but still unable to resolve it. Her urge to 'dilute responsibility' must then have increased and with it the feeling that it would be safer to do so by a referral within the medical network. Her proposal to send Lisa to a hospital child psychiatrist was not, as it turned out, made in ignorance of the similar expertise available to the child and family guidance service (nor of the survival threat to that agency). But it was uncharacteristically tactless and seems likely to have been defensive.

Other studies of work with school refusers have emphasised the confusion they and their families can generate in practitioners. As Will and Baird (1984) point out, for example, 'the school phobic is both *a victim of separation anxiety and* an omnipotent child and these dual characteristics tend to generate quite profound ambivalence'. Practitioners tend to respond to the victim with 'a desire to provide care and nurturance, and to the omnipotent child with a conviction of the need for firmness and reality testing' (ibid., p. 279). This not only describes the conflict of feeling among the various professionals in relation to Lisa but also epitomises the experience of Mrs Kerr and Dr Sanders in relation to her mother. In the face of such ambivalence, splitting is the common defence. Care and firmness are felt to be mutually exclusive as are the positions taken up by those in different camps who contrive to push each other to extremes. Will and Baird also comment on the marked tendency for different professionals working with a school phobic family to become involved in conflict with one another—as the two primary care practitioners did with the education department workers in this case. However, although these authors point to lines of vulnerability in the various professions, related to differences in prestige and power, they do not link these with practitioners' anxiety and their use of institutional structures to defend against it. The next case vividly illustrates this link.

ANXIETY AND THREE-PERSON RELATIONSHIPS— MARRIAGE GUIDANCE AND THE PROFESSIONAL NETWORK

We noted in chapter 4 that collaborative work was as rare for marriage guidance counsellors as it was for GPs. Other professionals tended to keep clear of counsellors even though they had responsibility for the same clients, thereby collusively sustaining the counsellors' own defensive insularity. The triangle of collaboration had special significance for counsellors. And it posed them special problems.

Such joint work with other professionals as they brought into the study was nearly all undertaken in health centres, where the attached counsellor became an operational part of the practice system and had to adapt to its established culture. Mrs Lambert's case in chapter 2 and Mrs Rogers' in chapter 4 illustrated some of the inter-professional difficulties which could arise there. The only marriage guidance centre case in which there was significant engagement with outside practitioners showed some similar difficulties and some additional ones related to the counsellors' own institution. Again we see the phenomenon of the reflection process at work.

> Mrs Hargreaves had been seen for some months during which she had been divorced from her husband. Her counsellor, Mrs Sale, became increasingly worried by the accumulating evidence of the children's disturbance (including the adolescent son's truancy) as well as Mrs Hargreaves' very violent emotions towards the youngest child onto whom, it seemed, she was displacing her feelings about her husband. She seemed insistent that Mrs Sale should know this, but at the same time put an embargo on her contacting the statutory agencies who might have helped—but whose power to intervene she feared. Mrs Sale, anxious about the risk of child abuse, felt she ought not to keep this information to herself. She knew that it was specifically exempted from the normal marriage guidance rule of confidentiality, but she still felt immobilised. She tried encouraging Mrs Hargreaves to get in touch with a doctor or social worker herself, but the client resisted. As it was put in the workshop, the anxious stalemate affecting both client and counsellor could be expressed as: "I *can't* let anyone know but I *must* let someone know".
>
> When Mrs Sale presented the case a second time, she had found a way to resolve the dilemma. With considerable misgivings she modified the non-directive counselling approach and insisted that Mr Hargreaves attend a joint interview. Her strong feeling that both parents should be mustered in the children's interests overcame her reluctance to take this kind of initiative. The move broke the 'log jam'. Before the joint interview had even taken place, Mrs Hargreaves got in touch with her GP practice where she managed to see a locum, a woman doctor "who doesn't know us". This led to referral to a clinic for children and families.
>
> Meanwhile in the joint interview Mrs Sale became convinced of Mr Hargreaves' genuine concern and worry about the children. Still uncertain about her newly adopted directive stance and whether the kind of work she was embarked upon fell properly within her agency's

remit, she got the couple's agreement that she should seek a meeting with the staff of the clinic, to include Mrs Hargreaves as well.

The meeting was arranged, but Mrs Hargreaves took virtually no part in the discussion and was obviously apprehensive. The counsellor's experience was of being treated by the clinic staff as if she herself was the problem client. For her part, she felt highly critical of what she thought was their limited appreciation of the boy's difficulty in getting to school and the poverty of their response to the emotional problems of the other children.

In the event, however, the clinic arranged an appointment for the Hargreaves at a psychiatric unit which offered family therapy; the school was also alerted and responded positively. The counsellor then decided to focus her work on helping her client (and through her, she hoped, the children) to use the family therapy rather than sabotage it, which she thought was likely otherwise.

The workshop log noted, 'the treatment of the counsellor as a client was no doubt a collusive [process]—and she acknowledged [her part in] this ... the splitting/ fragmenting dynamic in the marriage bedevils the network of practitioners ... [and there is] the recurring problem of the voluntary MG worker versus the statutory and professional status of the other helping agencies'.

This is a summary of reports whose main emphasis was on Mrs Sale's subjective experience, particularly of the clinic meeting in which she felt she was treated contemptuously by its practitioners. But the presentations were sufficient to show that all three parties—client, herself and clinic staff—encountered reciprocal difficulties. In the workshop, she could see that she and her opposite numbers had acted-out a reflection of the client couple's interaction in the meeting by a three-cornered collusion. It was a collusion which ensured the mother was left out, just as in the Hargreaves family someone was always left out in the triangle, husband, wife, children. The counsellor believed she was turned into 'the problem' and, feeling demeaned, underrated the clinic's response to her anxiety and to the family.

Like Hornby (1983) we have met this phenomenon in other encounters between practitioners where skills and status are felt to be in question and there is an element of competitiveness. We agree with her that the projection and identification serve as a defence against depressive anxiety (p. 48). As she suggests, 'it is so used by professional workers when their capacity to help is in doubt. The defence is unconscious and the cause . . . not so much self-doubt as an unrecognised fear of losing all capacity to repair damage or change things for the better.'

In this case, notwithstanding the defensive behaviour, resources were eventually mobilised in the service of the family as a result of the counsellor's initiative. The task-oriented workshop discussion probably played a part, for it was after she had first voiced and sought to understand her own doubts and discomfort in this context that she made her initiative, and the couple responded and were able to co-operate as parents in the aftermath of their divorce. Subsequently, by aiming to focus her counselling work on the anticipated resistance to family therapy, she recovered confidence in her capacity to help the mother and could envisage an appropriate collaborative stance.

In her struggle to achieve these developments Mrs Sale had first to contend with her anxiety about being proactive—which meant departing from her agency's customary counselling style. Having extricated herself from the couple's shared defences of splitting and exclusion in the counselling, she then had to cope with more uncertainty. She moved into unknown territory where her agency's socially organised defence, which fosters the security of a tight boundary round the counsellor-client relationship, was no longer available. This exposed her vulnerability as a voluntary worker in dealings with more 'prestigious' professionals.

All marriage guidance counsellors attend case discussion groups throughout their service because of their agency's awareness of the emotional and technical problems inherent in marital work. However, focusing as they do on the exclusive counselling setting and therefore inevitably embodying the agency culture and its dominant defences, these can provide little opportunity for counsellors to experience, work-through and master the anxieties engendered for them by the triangle of collaboration. The counsellor in this case, however, was able to engage in such a process with her inter-disciplinary workshop colleagues.

The foregoing examples lack uniformity. Any set derived from actual practice would do so because of the variable contributions made by clients or patients, practitioners and institutions as an interacting series of open systems. Within and between these three relationship systems, each time with a unique pattern, defences against anxiety impeded collaboration. But whatever the pattern in any given instance, we believe there is a further dimension of anxiety, largely unconscious, which is stimulated and objectified by the collaborative mode itself. We must now bring this dimension into focus.

THE TRIANGULAR DYNAMIC

Triangular configurations are ubiquitous, and the dynamic forces they generate exert a powerful influence on human interaction. Third parties, actual or alive in phantasy, can undermine inter-personal relationships. We saw in chapter 4 that spouses in marital difficulty, for example, are often caught up with inner world residues of the early developmental task of being 'related as a human being to two other human beings ... at one and the same time' as Winnicott put it; the advent of a child, though longed for, can also reawaken old feelings and images for couples and may make the transition from two to three stressful, sometimes hazardous (Clulow, 1982).

Practitioners are no less subject to the dynamics of three-way relationships than those they seek to help. They may find them arising in any area of their practice (not only in specialised marital work). But they will always find them in collaborative situations. What we called the 'triangle of collaboration' in chapter 4 is manifest whenever two practitioners, or coalitions of practitioners, have to deal with each other in relation to clients or patients. Dr Sanders and Mrs Kerr, for example, became such a coalition over against the child and family guidance service concerning the Wright family. This helps to make it clear that triangular dynamics are by no means confined to relationships literally of three individuals. Besides the other cases in this chapter, Mr Webster's in chapter 7 was also a particularly vivid example.

Three-way relationships and the study programme

The programme was itself an exercise in collaboration. As a temporary institution with closely related and formally agreed tasks, it contained numerous sets of triangular relationships which are relevant to our present theme. They have many analogues in other organisational situations in which individuals or multiple groupings are required to collaborate to achieve institutional tasks. A few examples will suffice to illustrate how the triangular dynamic exerted a persistent influence on the multiple relationships all concerned had perforce to maintain within the programme institution.

In the workshops, there was always a potential triangle between different members, or sub-groups, and ourselves as third party. Conflicting feelings about the experience of collaborating tended to be sublimated or repressed when there was conscious preoccupation with the workshops' primary tasks, but emerged in the periodic review sessions, when members were relieved of concern with their work on cases for the time being. Then we were described as powerful, influential, expert; we suppressed differences and were intolerant of opposition. Conversely, we were misguided, irrelevant and ineffectual, especially because we did not teach enough and withheld practical advice. Nor, of course, were we immune from reciprocal feelings. Sometimes our experience in the workshops was of doing too much and sometimes not enough. We frequently felt invaded and often anxious. Like parents, we could oscillate between a conviction that we 'knew' and that we would never understand, between feeling gratified and exasperated.

But there was also evidence that in members' relationship with each other anxiety was prevalent about hurting and being hurt; about doing damage to 'vulnerable' colleagues with no time for reparation or to 'pick up the pieces'. In one workshop which met at lunch-time, a short-lived ritual of bringing wine was clearly intended to defuse hostility and was eventually recognised as such by members. There was much reference to the need for a common language, but this seemed less to promote communication than to avoid the struggle with difference. 'Sameness'—of attitude and purpose—was repeatedly invoked. The danger posed by differences could be dealt with by a unified attack on a third party—ourselves and the programme—the joint task of exploration and learning being seen with complete conviction at that moment as our sole responsibility. But such attacks could provoke renewed anxiety about destructiveness. One episode of this sort brought eleven individual enquiries about our well-being—after the meeting. More safely, if the case under discussion involved another practitioner or agency not participating in the programme, these third parties could be held responsible for all collaborative problems—especially if they were psychiatric practitioners of any kind.

But it is important to emphasise, as we did in chapter 3, that such conflicts were inevitable and developmental, and there were perceptible changes over time. Dependency, fight and flight gave way to an assumption by most practitioners of greater personal autonomy and appropriate responsibility for the work of their groups and the programme's objectives. For our part, with the level of anxiety in the workshop 'triangle' reduced, we could become more receptive to the material and freer to allow understanding to evolve.

A further triangular configuration was comprised of ourselves, the practitioners, and their organisations. The potential for tension in this triangle is obvious. Agency managers (or the partners of a GP member) who did not have first-hand involvement with the programme were prone to see us as an embodiment of intrusive and sometimes unwelcome change. Those at senior level who did have continuing involvement and had helped to mount the programme and evolve its form and objectives could not but be uncertain if not ambivalent about its implications. The practitioners were in the middle, between ourselves and their organisations, and had to try and manage a double allegiance. Some responded to this dilemma by tending to keep the programme experience encapsulated within themselves while they grappled with its personal and professional repercussions. This made for more uncertainty among managers—for example the chief officer who reported that his agency's teams seemed not to be influenced by their members who were participating in the programme; they were aware of it because of their colleagues' periodic absences, but there was no feedback. On the other hand, the practitioners often conveyed to us that such influence was made impossible because of the way their agencies operated, the pressure of work and the kind of tasks they had to undertake. One social worker acknowledged the relevance for his work of paying attention to marital interaction, but added that as far as his agency was concerned it was "a luxury, just icing on the cake". So either there was a secret from which third parties were excluded, or the third parties were held responsible for preventing the development of creative pairing (between practitioners and ourselves).

As a final example of the triangular dynamic within the study programme we can cite the relationship between the participating agencies, ourselves and our own parent organisation—on behalf of which we initiated and conducted the fieldwork. As in the last illustration, one member of the triangular relationship was the link between the two. There it was the practitioners. In this instance we were the intermediaries; we too were subject to conflicting claims on our allegiance, and encountered suspicion from both sides. Thus, in the field at times we were believed to be furthering our own institute's interests at the expense of the participating agencies; back home, on the other hand, we were sometimes felt by our TIMS colleagues to be sacrificing the institute's well-being to that of the programme and local agencies. It was as if we were suspected of 'going native'; such can be the fate of plenipotentiaries.

Anxiety in the triangle of collaboration

The foregoing simple examples are of behaviour with which most readers will be familiar. Few who work in groups and institutions will not have had similar experiences. But the study programme was particularly apt to generate anxiety concerning three-way relationships. Because of its subject matter this was its own task-related anxiety, and it also produced its own institutionalised defences.

The fact that the participants and ourselves had embarked willingly on a study of marital work and collaborative work (out of a shared conviction that both were important and a shared concern that both seemed so difficult) was no guarantee against the anxiety that they stirred up. Many of our experiences together confirmed that people can combine to frustrate their own conscious wish to tackle a problem; not out of malice or stupidity but because the problem, though painful, is itself the product of unconscious defensive strategies against anxiety. Areas in which this might be discovered tend to be avoided, as the wish to resolve the problem struggles with the need to preserve it.

Just as, in their practice, members hesitated to open up issues of marital stress (often referred to as a 'can of worms') with their client/patient couples, so in the workshops the collaborative practitioner couple hesitated to let their 'can of worms' be opened up in front of fellow members and ourselves. Both situations evidently touched off anxieties about the exposure of unconscious, irrational aspects of relationships in a third-party context. We believe that all concerned in this programme institution—practitioners, managers and ourselves—were subject to powerful forces stemming from this source that could interfere with the capacity to work on the problem of interprofessional collaboration.

Because of our involvement in this dynamic, it was some time before we connected these phenomena with similar experiences which had already been described by a TIMS colleague. In workshops for social work supervisors, Mattinson (1979) had found that the participants were unaccountably loath to fulfil the basic requirement of the course they had willingly joined, i.e. to present in detail what transpired between themselves and their supervisees. Supervisors who did manage to do this turned out to be having the same difficulty in getting supervisees to reveal what actually went on between them and their clients; and also in judging when (and how) to intervene and when to allow the supervisees space to get on with the work. Concluding that these problems were linked, and that their roots lay in the original three-person oedipal situation, Mattinson commented:

> the encompassing of a third person in what was a two-some demands a flexibility of movement between the three. One party must be able to allow temporary pairing of the other two and there must be freedom for one party to be in or out of the various transactions between the three at any time . . . it is only possible for a person to be able to allow himself this freedom of movement if, first, he has come to terms with his own difference (p. 99).

The struggle to find that kind of flexibility, with recognition and acceptance of difference, posed similar problems in this programme, especially when practitioners were faced with the task of disclosing their own collaborative relationships in the workshops. We believe it was this potentially disturbing experience that was often avoided by tacit agreement, and accounted for the comparative dearth of joint work jointly presented. The study programme itself was therefore no exception to the rule that institutions are characterised by task-related anxieties and socially maintained defences.

Mattinson stipulated that her formulation needed further testing. The evidence from the present work provides strong support for her hypothesis. We would extend it to the proposition that *behind the specifics of any given case or circumstances calling for collaboration there is invariably a general anxiety arising from the stress of triangular relationships—a dynamic field of unconscious forces liable to inhibit collaborative endeavour*. If we are to understand why collaboration is so often advocated and so often fails to materialise or breaks down, we believe due weight must be given to the divisive implications of this stressful field.

10

Anxiety, interaction and impediments to collaboration

Realistic co-operation with others in a joint task is always liable to involve struggle—within individuals and between them. Recalling Bion's (1961) contribution to the understanding of group behaviour and his description of the human being as a group animal, Menzies Lyth (1986, p. 27) commented: 'as such he cannot get on *without* other human beings. Unfortunately, he cannot get on very well *with* them either ... This is his dilemma.' In this summary chapter we review what was learned about the collaborative dilemma from the sample of their practice contributed by our colleagues in the five participating agencies and from our own experience of the training-cum-research programme. In the Appendix the way of 'reading the situation' developed from it is applied to the sexual abuse crisis in the county of Cleveland in 1987, an episode notable for failures in communication and collaboration in a local service network.

PRACTITIONERS' CASES AND THE PROGRAMME EXPERIENCE; COMMON FEATURES AND RECURRING THEMES

In the series of 132 cases, selected by practitioners themselves, the difficulties or symptoms they had to address were bound up with stress and tension in marital and family relationships, but (except those from marriage guidance centres) few indeed were conventional 'marital' cases. Other practitioners were known to be involved in most of the cases and, despite the marked reluctance to examine it, there was in fact active collaboration in a third. The series represents a qualitatively significant segment of the practice of experienced professionals in the participating agencies, a sample of working problems liable to crop up day-to-day. Those chosen as exemplars in Part II, discipline by discipline, could have confronted any worker in the fields in question. The series confirms that practitioners in organisations with different primary tasks and concerned with different presenting problems are faced with the same underlying phenomena: interactive processes within and between open systems of relationships. Those in difficulties arising from these processes do indeed find their way to many different doors (Home Office/DHSS, 1979).

A variety of motives will have led practitioners to present cases,[1] but the great majority of clients or patients they wanted to discuss perplexed and worried them and increasingly, as the workshops progressed, there could be several people waiting to bring or bring back a case. In this process they revealed their working worlds to each other along with their constraints and opportunities. And with varying degrees of awareness and apprehension they also revealed their own as well as their clients' or patients' difficulties.

As was evident from the cases reported in Part II and chapter 9, however, the responses of workshop colleagues to presenting practitioners and their 'failings' could be condemnatory, dismissive, or otherwise rejecting insofar as they were felt to be intolerable by the group; or the anxiety evoked could induce members to split into conflicting factions, to be silenced, or to withdraw; collaboration in the service of understanding was then impaired.

Such processes, emanating from the practitioner's encounter with the client or patient system, channelled into the learning system of the workshop and focused by the presentation, underlay the enactment of a 'reflection' from the case. Given time, practitioners could learn from their experience of these phenomena in an environment where task-related conflict and anxiety were accepted and contained rather than condemned or avoided. This facilitated their mastery. Practitioners need such 'detoxifying' conditions if they are to modify or appropriately relinquish defences of their own which hinder the work; this kind of learning was the aim of the workshops. When it was not achieved—for example, if we as consultants colluded in the avoidance of conflict and anxiety and got caught-up in 'anti-work' group processes—collaboration on the case-focused task was undermined. When it was achieved, practitioners tended to gain in autonomy and imaginative capacity in their interplay with each other as did presenters with their clients and patients.[2]

It was universally difficult to shift to the 'mind set' needed to focus on interactive processes. They can be hard to delineate because they operate between people who are both subject and object at the same time. This uncomfortable duality did much to encourage what we came to think of as 'one-person psychology'. The phrase was coined as a shorthand way of describing the common tendency to construe couples' relationship difficulties in terms of the problems and psychopathology of one partner and their effect on the other —leading to a given reaction, unfortunate but generally assumed to be predictable. The emotional pressure was to 'take sides' and lose sight of the system as a whole. Among the notions hardest to grasp and apply was that the feelings, attitudes and behaviour of each could have a meaning and purpose for both, in a largely unconscious and collusively defensive process in which what was denied and disowned by one was projected into the other and related to there. Such interactive themes are most clearly stated in the close interpersonal relationships of couples and families, but are present with variations in other relationships and in the working environment; in particular in collaborative relationships. The mode of thought inherent in one-person psychology invokes a mechanistic model of action and reaction as opposed to a dynamic one of interaction, interpenetration and interdependence in accord with the actual state of affairs.

True, intellectual difficulties can arise when practitioners are confronted by such dynamic interrelations—the mechanistic Cartesian world view and the logic of Newtonian physics with its emphasis on linear processes remain immensely powerful influences on the way most of us have been taught to think. Our study confirmed that the problem was more than an intellectual one, however. The interpenetrative aspects of human interaction can have threatening connotations relating to the earliest of struggles: to distinguish the 'me' from the 'not me', between what is 'inside' and what 'outside'—the most primitive of our uncertainties. The fact that boundaries between human systems at any level are not sharply defined can itself stimulate anxiety and defensive denial. Herman (1989) was addressing this denial when she said (p. 339), 'if such intense hobnobbing by a process of osmosis still seems questionable to my readers, let me once again quote Freud: "It is a very remarkable thing that the unconscious of one human being can react on that of another without passing through the conscious" (Freud, 1915a, p. 194)'. In our experience, resistance to the idea of unconscious mutual influence, in any case a strange one to most practitioners, was strengthened when they experienced the clients' or patients' difficulties as touching a raw nerve of their own in some way.

Nor were we unaffected by anxiety. Previous experience of work with allied professionals over many years could offer no immunity to the inevitable conflict and uncertainty of moving into the unknown territory the programme represented. We, too, found ourselves resorting defensively to simplistic explanations under pressure from the complexity of processes that had been set in train. However, as in therapeutic situations, we valued our subjective experiences, both positive and negative, and gave them due weight as evidence along with other kinds of data. Writing this book not only revived these experiences as we reviewed our material, especially the tape recordings of all workshop and other sessions we had assembled; it also made us aware of what we had missed at the time through the unconscious impact of anxiety, the defences aimed at dealing with it and the conflicts of feeling it generated which undermined the ability to think and to work collaboratively.

Thus, in attempting to learn what actually happened in work with difficult, worrying cases and to understand problems in partnership better, we and the practitioners encountered the reality of the unconscious mind, and the marked tendency for anxiety and conflict in the inner world to be externalised and acted-out in interpersonal relationships, through processes which were also unconscious and often mutual. For while personal boundaries serve to distinguish one from another, and without them there can be no relatedness (Lawrence, 1979), they are also permeable. Practitioners could no more escape such interpenetration than their clients and patients.

To underline characteristics practitioners have in common with clients and patients, and the mutuality of influence, does not carry the implication that they are in like case and, being 'the same', are unable to help. Personal qualities apart, their training (which serves to discipline reparative drives as well as providing a relevant knowledge base), their role and relative position in what may be called 'social space', all help to establish crucial difference and, in favourable circumstances, a location from which objectivity may be regained. But it is to emphasise what is obvious, though too often out of mind: that the humanity of practitioners makes them subject to primitive emotional processes just as their clients or patients are.

DYNAMIC IMPEDIMENTS TO TASK PERFORMANCE AND COLLABORATION

Anxiety and defences in the caring system

The conflict and anxiety activated by encounters with clients or patients were objectified for practitioners by their own roles and tasks. In pursuing them, they inevitably colluded at times by enacting defences which were the same or opposite to those of their clients or patients. As long as this process was unconscious, their task performance was impeded. Their potential strength lay in the capacity to struggle to understand what was covertly happening in their interplay with those they were attending. But, as the cases we have reported testify, the work could give rise to experiences of a kind and quality capable of threatening their sense of professional adequacy and personal autonomy. The potential for invasiveness was most commonly warded off by the defensive use of personal boundaries—'keeping one's distance' from the patient or client. But whether 'too close' or 'too far', when they were not able to find what, for them, was an effective working distance (Mattinson, 1975) they tended not to get confirmation of themselves as skilled and concerned workers; the realistic sense of an informed capacity to help was all too often undermined.

In collaborative work their effectiveness could be restricted by similar defensive responses which came into play in their relationships with other practitioners. A range of these were variously enacted in the work presented and in the programme generally: denial and avoidance (not least of their own envious and destructive feelings towards the opportunities and skills of others); splitting off and projecting feelings of inadequacy; 'coalescing' in the face of disturbing clients or patients or of hostile third-party agencies; and mutual projection and projective identification which could ensure that competence or responsibility was vested in one, uselessness and irresponsibility in the other. These processes could link practitioners either in amity or hostility, but without the separateness and autonomy that encompasses both knowing and not knowing. Here too the defensive use of personal boundaries was a prominent feature. Testing of mutual perceptions through working relationships was generally avoided, and the way practitioners tended to isolate themselves from others in the field was evidenced in case presentations which showed them behaving as if colleagues in other agencies did not exist or were unapproachable.

The powerful impact of the clients' or patients' anxiety and defences; the phenomena of transference and counter-transference underlying the reflection process; and sometimes the enervating pressure of events (whether in particular cases, over-heavy case-loads or other demands in the workplace) could serve to inhibit practitioners' understanding of the clients' or patients' difficulties and of the problems they encountered in collaborating with each other. The capacity to use themselves and their knowledge wisely, think imaginatively, be curious, questioning and self-observant could desert practitioners in such situations.

The agency as defence

Most practitioners work in an institutional context. This gives rise to a most important relationship, just as influential as that with their clients and patients. At times it can be more so. The relationship with the employing institution includes emotional elements with origins in unconscious phantasy as well as those based on the objective need to make a living through contractual obligation (Jaques, 1955). The opportunity is afforded to practice one's craft and to extend skills that were sought through training; once qualified, their exercise on the agency's behalf confirms and gives expression to personal as well as professional identity and status. The role occupied sustains the individual's sense of self and self-worth, while membership of the organisation and the profession offers the hope of a sentient group from which the practitioner can get emotional support (Miller and Rice, 1967).[3] The great majority of those in the caring professions are so employed from personal choice. For most, their occupation is symbolic and plays a big part in the individual's psychic economy. Thus, along with the creative and reparative potential of the work goes a means whereby 'old ghosts can be, if not entirely laid to rest, at least appeased and kept in hand' (Mattinson, 1988, p. 39; see also Skynner, 1964). This factor too binds members of a profession together.

Following Menzies Lyth's (1970) findings from her work with hospital nurses, we tested the possibility of recognising distinctive features in the practice of each of the agencies joining us in the programme. For this we relied on practitioners' case material and their presentations, supplemented by our recorded observations and experience (we had no means of undertaking organisational studies *per se*). We found that characteristic anxieties could be identified which were associated with and specific to the tasks of each agency. Practitioners of each discipline were constantly brought into contact with issues which generated these anxieties: marriage guidance counsellors with stress and conflict in intimate heterosexual relationships, involving, as most do, oedipal residues; GPs with illness and threats to life and with death itself; health visitors with dependency and the struggle for autonomy in the exclusive—but ambivalent and often conflictful—relationship between mothers and their children; probation officers with delinquency and the tension between confor- mity and individual liberty, care and control; social workers with the betrayal of dependent children by parental failure. In Part II we listed the specific defences against these anxieties which we found to be characteristic of each service respectively (as well as some which were common to all).

Thus, while practitioners have idiosyncratic anxieties and defences at a personal level and may become enmeshed in those of specific clients and patients at the level of the caring system, they are susceptible to generalised, task-related anxieties at the agency system level; and here they have another set of defences at their disposal. These socially organised defences are embedded in the professional and/or agency culture as expressed in its rules, practices and ways of interpreting policy—its values. The fit between the reality of an institution and what its practitioners personally conceive as desirable patterns of practice can rarely be an exact one. But those whose psychological needs are sufficiently met by the prevailing socially organised defences will naturally support and seek to preserve them. Such defences, developed by succeeding generations of practitioners over the years against the conflict and anxiety inherent in the agency's task, command deep emotional loyalty. Having become integral to the fabric of institutions they are notoriously resistant to change. Attempts to introduce new perspectives on practice, for example, regularly meet with ambivalence or rejection if at variance with established social defences.[4] This was true of the programme; it was endorsed by senior managements as well as the participating practitioners, but its impact on the overall practice of the agencies was questionable (see chapter 9) even though, in their individual evaluations, many participants confirmed the changes in their own practice which were also observable in the workshops.

At each level in the hierarchy of open systems involved in the provision of care, defences find a particular mode of expression which, at first sight, seem to be distinct and unattributable to those at the level below. We have now moved to the level of the institutional system where defences have a social and organisational dimension. Structures ostensibly intended to promote task performance are customarily used to avoid rather than master the anxiety that is an intrinsic component of it. Ultimately however, as we said of groups in chapter 3, what happens in institutions is determined by their members. It is the individual practitioner (or manager) who experiences anxiety; institutions cannot experience anxiety nor operate defences against it. Only their members can do that.

Like Will and Baird (1984), we observed inter-professional dysfunction to be linked with conflict between agencies' perspectives. These were rooted in their tasks and responsibilities, their philosophy and values and the differential status and working conditions of their staff. But we found that what these authors identify as 'real institutional vulnerabilities' were primarily a product of the fact that 'the culture, structure and mode of functioning [of an organisation] are determined by the psychological needs of its members' (Menzies Lyth, 1970 p. 50). In our view, *major impediments to inter-professional collaboration originate in the unconscious needs of practitioners to use the structures of their agencies and professional groups in their struggle to manage task-related anxiety.*

The defensive use of boundaries

It seems universally to be the case that professional and institutional boundaries are difficult to manage. Increasing interdependence between helping services gives rise to more transactions across them. It also draws attention to the experiential threats such transactions can pose to those involved.

This was true within the programme. We noted in chapter 9 the practitioners' reluctance to reveal the detail of their work with colleagues from other disciplines who were also participants—this in contrast to their growing trust and readiness to examine working problems with clients or patients. We did hear from workshop members about successful as well as unsuccessful attempts to collaborate with practitioners who were *not* part of the programme. That is to say we got the presenter's view, necessarily one-sided and often a negative one, of what was happening. This was by no means without value for, when negative explanations of difficulties were not taken at face value, practitioners as a rule proved able to review their own contributions to the problem, its links with the clients' defences and the reflection process, and thus, having regained at least a measure of objectivity, to ameliorate then. But the occasions when the workshops were given access to the processes involved in joint work directly by the two practitioners undertaking it were few. As with their clients' or patients' marital difficulties, so with their own collaborative ones, practitioners seemed reluctant to 'broach the subject'. Either area was evidently liable to evoke kindred anxieties about interaction and exposure of the irrational in relationships. We came to understand that practitioners co-operated, largely unconsciously, in avoiding areas of discussion in which the anxieties aroused by collaboration on a shared task with clients or patients could be learned about.[5]

The cases which did involve inter-professional collaboration, the comparative rarity of their presentation, and our other observations during the field-work lead us to a general thesis about the dynamic processes making for the defensive use of professional and institutional boundaries, and the evident fear of discovering through direct experience the reality of other practitioners' assets and liabilities and those of their institutions:

The socially structured defence mechanisms integral to an agency by virtue of its tasks and embedded in its rules, procedures and priorities are distinctive. Serving crucial psychic purposes for its members as well as being designed to achieve the agency's overtly formulated objectives, the commitment to them at personal and institutional, conscious and unconscious levels is far-reaching. When practitioners seek (or are compelled) actively to collaborate in the interests of clients or patients they have in common, differences in defensive modes of both practitioner and agency are bound to become explicit on the boundary between them. These have to be accommodated as the workers interact with each other and with their clients or patients. Each has to learn from experience. But this is an emotionally hazardous process which there is a pervasive inclination to avoid.

The potential for dissonance and conflict increases the more splitting and denial (i.e. mental partition) is the dominant defence employed by the shared clients or patients, and the more their problems occasion high levels of realistic anxiety, stimulating powerful unconscious phantasies in practitioners and their managers. The more threatening the anxiety, the greater and more rigid the practitioners' reliance on socially structured institutional defences and the more fraught it becomes to enter imaginatively into each other's working world for fear of losing hold of their own. Practitioners may then fall back on the 'bedrock' of a narrowly defined primary task. Boundaries tend to become defensive bulwarks instead of the definition of a secure base for commerce and negotiation; fight or flight are alternative mechanisms of defence. Thus, effective collaboration is liable to be most difficult to achieve when it is at a premium.

At the same time, collaborating practitioners are always involved in a triangular dynamic with their shared clients or patients, in which the residues of unresolved three-person (oedipal) conflicts are particularly liable to become active. They may already be so, more or less intrusively, within a client or patient system or caring system, but will inevitably come to the fore in the combined system established when different practitioners engage with the same clients or patients. Tensions within triangular configurations are thus the general rule whenever collaboration is attempted. The three-party situation then created embodies a potential threat to personal autonomy through unconscious forces, ultimately psycho-sexual in origin, which may come into play in various ways. Salvation may be vested in a powerful 'leader' to whom responsibility is surrendered; it may be sought through the coalescing of two and therefore the isolating of the third party; all three parties may collude in permutations of possessiveness, rivalry, sabotage, seduction and umbrage. Such defensive impulses and their expression must be reckoned with at any or all levels in the array of open systems involved in collaborative endeavour.

ANXIETY AND DEFENCES IN SERVICE NETWORKS

Local agencies become an operational service network only in response to particular clients or patients and it is *their* needs that determine its composition. Agencies may decide to co-operate over other issues, training for example (an important stimulus for the programme), where interests are felt to coincide; there may be a local tradition of working together in this way. But clients or patients are catalysts of a different order. They provide an imperative to collaborate over task performance.

Child abuse

Abused children and their families are one such focus for shared responsibility, prescribing the network's membership and introducing into the resulting systems just the kind of primitive task-related anxieties we are concerned with —in a particularly acute way. The nurture and development of children was frequently at issue in the cases studied in the programme. This was to be expected in a series characterised by disturbed relationships in couples, the great majority of whom had children (well over half had infants under five). There were numerous cases which raised suspicions of physical abuse, with children placed on the 'at risk' register, even though actual abuse had been confirmed only in a few. Meanwhile the capacity of parents, through their mutual defences, to be divisive of practitioners and agencies was by no means confined to child-abuse cases; other presenting problems such as school re-fusal and children who were failing to thrive gave rise to similar technical problems. Anxiety about children affected practitioners from every discipline and agency involved.

The social services department—'citadel' and 'dustbin'

Although child protection did not dominate the programme, it was the major preoccupation for social workers. And when it became a live concern to other practitioners it was invariably to the social services department, with its statutory responsibilities, that they turned. Attention here is not on the quality of response by social workers or other experienced practitioners to child-care problems (some was sensitive and insightful); our concern with child protection is with the anxiety it stimulated in practitioners generally. It was clear not only from the cases but also from the interplay between practitioners within the programme that this anxiety tended to be lodged with social services.

This throws further light on the image conjured up in chapter 8 of the social services department as a citadel under siege whose occupants kept an ever watchful eye on the portal. An important function of its practitioners and managers at field level was to ensure that referrals conformed to acceptable categories; that others were not 'passing the buck' (see Community Care, 1989, for similarly intentioned legalistic disclaimers of responsibility by local authority social services administrators).[6] Nor is it difficult to appreciate this embattled stance; besides the burden on the department of publicised criticisms stimulated by the many inquiries into child deaths following abuse, the programme was witness to defensive and therefore sometimes less than honest dealings over referrals to social services. Most practitioners were hard-pressed and, increasingly, those in the statutory agencies complained of a discrepancy between resources and demand; the political and economic climate increasingly encouraged them to 'export' cases. Some, health visitors and probation officers for example, who frequently had an interface with child abuse operated formal and informal policies which, being part of an array of socially organised defences, favoured referral and/or served to dilute their responsibility. And they, too, were under the influence of official and media strictures and the anxious threat child abuse poses.

The reciprocal channelling of anxiety between agencies

The experience of child abuse afforded by the programme showed that attempts to ward off task-related anxieties generated by it are manifest at the institutional level as well as by practitioners at the personal level. It suggests that institutional defences characterise interactions between agencies (albeit through their agents) and constellate in a way which is mutually reinforcing.

This arises from the way anxiety generated by a given class of problem is channelled by the network into whichever agency is seen as specially competent and responsible in that area. Child abuse was the most dramatic and universal example in the programme but there were others which affected each discipline in turn, as the cases and workshop discussions throughout Part II and chapter 9 testify. Doctors were invariably treated as omnipotent and omniscient (notwithstanding their disagreements with each other) whenever illness was at issue. Health visitors were deferred to, if not to the same degree, on matters of abnormal infant development and could be exploited in their role as 'normal' visitors to clients' homes. It often seemed as though marriage guidance counsellors alone held the key to intimate couple relationships, behind a veil of secrecy. Probation officers were credited with moral authority, correcting delinquents either by care or by punishment. And madness could safely be left for the non-participating psychiatric services to deal with.

The essence of all such attributions was the search for a receptacle to carry the anxiety; and when the nominated practitioner or agency failed to live up to the idealised expectation, blame and denigration were quickly fuelled by the same anxiety. It is in this way that agencies and disciplines become stereotyped (always in two forms, 'good' and 'bad'), not only by society at large but by each other. At the institutional level each agency, as we have seen, is subject to specific anxieties related to its task; but at the network level it also has channelled into it the anxieties about its area of competence that other agencies cannot contain. This incessant projective redistribution of unmanageable anxiety between agencies can only serve to rigidify the structures and practices through which their members attempt to ward it off. In the relevant service network constellated by a given case, the practitioners involved may be impelled to use institutional defences not only internally against their own anxieties but externally against each other, to the detriment of collaboration. Alternatively, as we found earlier, practitioners may form coalitions, especially against other 'third-party' practitioners with opposing views. The same process can occur between agencies in a local network. Although this was not a phenomenon we observed in the study programme, a coalition in which whole agencies became 'at one' against third parties was one feature of the so-called 'sexual abuse crisis' in Cleveland in 1987. In a book on inter-agency collaboration we cannot ignore that episode, nor the special anxieties of child sexual abuse which gave rise to it and to which we now turn.

The extra dimension of child sexual abuse

Our collective study of practitioners' cases was concluded by the mid-1980s, which probably explains why we heard little or nothing of child sexual abuse.[7] Though it is no new phenomenon—any more than physical abuse was when it belatedly claimed attention—it has been increasingly acknowledged in recent years. Generally (though not exclusively) perpetrated by men, its admission to public awareness probably owes much to the re-evaluation of gender relationships and the insistence by women that their voices be heard. Whatever the historical and socio-political antecedents of the change, child sexual abuse has become a focus for heightened anxiety in society and its helping services; justifiable indeed, but with even more primitive connotations (unconsciously and consciously sexual) than the anxiety raised by physical abuse.

Some assert that the inter-agency structures developed to protect children and manage cases in which abuse occurs are inherently flawed; that they do not serve the cause of child development and mental health (see, for example, Woodmansey, 1990). Others, the majority, acknowledge their imperfections but, seeing the administrative mechanisms as the best available, seek their improvement. They seem to recognise, sometimes only by implication, the need for containment of the confusions and powerful emotional conflict to which sexual abuse particularly gives rise. Kraemer's (1988) contribution to the debate is of particular interest in the present context. Summarising it, he says:

> One of the functions of the 'taboo against incest' is to prevent discussion of the subject—an ancient cover up. The discovery that sexual abuse is occurring on a far wider scale than was previously believed has divided society in two. In particular cases where abuse is known or suspected there is a similar partition of opinion, both within the minds of the individuals involved and between them; inducing a kind of stupidity which undermines the capacity for honesty and judgement and all but the most authentic professional skills (p. 247).

Sexual abuse has therefore added an extra dimension to the singular capacity of child abuse to induce anxiety in professionals which is met by the primitive defence of splitting—undermining collaboration precisely when it is most needed. This seemed to us so important that in the absence of material from the programme we undertook a case study of the Cleveland 'crisis'; this was particularly apposite to our theme because the judicial inquiry report (Butler-Sloss, 1988) was the first to survey processes that developed in a *network of local services* in relation to a whole class of case in which responsibility was shared—as opposed to the circumstances surrounding a single instance of abuse. Though not without its limitations—the difficulty of getting at the truth of what actually happened is certainly no less a problem for a judicial inquiry than for any other—the material provided by its version of events is particularly relevant to this book. In the Appendix we therefore examine the Butler-Sloss report in the light of the thesis developed from the present study, as an exercise in application.

The disturbing impact of sexual abuse, amply recorded in the Butler-Sloss report, is a special case in a larger class of human situations which objectify conflict and anxiety alive and essentially active in the inner worlds of professionals no less than others. Behaviour is catalogued by the report in all the relationship systems involved, including the service network, which can only be understood by taking account of defensive responses to task-related anxiety. As Kraemer (ibid., p. 240) expresses it, 'the price paid for [such] protection is a kind of stupidity in which only half the mind is able to work at a time'. In the interplay of agencies, with only 'half-minds' at work, departmental policies, priorities and interests tend to be protected at the expense of the shared task. This is not solely due to the fact that these aspects of institutional cultures may be operationally at variance. Though invariably difficult to harmonise, the objective organisational differences are ultimately capable of resolution through negotiation and compromise. But conflict is likely to arise and dispute be uncompromisingly pursued when the defence of splitting is the protective mechanism, and to the extent that the largely unconsciously determined institutional defences embodied in agency practices are not of mutual emotional value. When institutional defences are (or seem to be) more compatible, the same defensive mechanism of splitting can lead to dangerous coalescing against 'incompatible' third parties.

A dimension is added both to anxieties and to defences by child sexual abuse. And in a field so characterised by uncertainty, the implications of 'not knowing' (always a potent anxiety as was evident in the work discussed in earlier chapters) become too fearful to contemplate. Integrity and autonomy, institutional as much as personal or professional, can be threatened by uncertainties which in reality should be seen as relevant and inescapable. Meanwhile, preoccupation with the rules and such less concrete issues as professional status serve to obviate the need to think about the unthinkable: sexual abuse with its compulsive and repulsive aspects.

SUMMARY AND IMPLICATIONS

The occasions when inter-professional collaboration runs into difficulty are legion; we and our colleagues studied some of them in this training-cum-research programme. Less publicised than those concerning child abuse, where they are writ large, the impediments to collaboration which we identified have a similar quality nonetheless. They turn out to involve dynamic processes within the person stemming from the mode he has developed of managing many-faceted anxiety, and the resulting psychological manoeuvres that affect his interaction with others in all the relationship systems of which he is a part.

There is ample evidence to show that the painful impact of anxiety on the human psyche and the measures taken to ward it off can inhibit individuals' capacity to think with all their minds, leading at times to what can only be considered as a kind of madness. Practitioners and managers in the caring professions, in their work with and on behalf of clients and patients, are bound to find themselves in situations where events external to themselves seek out and speak to raw sense data from the past.[8] As is now clear, they will use their respective groups and institutions in an effort to avoid the impact. Collaboration is impeded by these powerful and largely unconscious psycho-dynamic factors. They are necessarily resistant to change since change threatens established ways of perceiving and understanding and, more fundamentally, it also threatens the identities practitioners and their agencies have found themselves impelled to assume. Personal, professional and institutional boundaries are employed to protect them.

The learning system

Though the collaborative exercise from which this book is derived is not in itself a transferable model for inter-professional training, it did confirm that the struggle to modify defences against anxiety in a learning system dealing with the work that stimulates it can enhance practitioners' development and self-esteem through improved task performance. Their capacity to collaborate with others is thereby extended. A large proportion of participants can be affected given that, though they are bound to resist it from time to time, they are able to share responsibility for the learning function, the primary task. As Dicks (1967) pointed out in relation to marital tensions, problems generally contain the seeds of their own solution.

Even so, the understandable urge towards 'inter-agency training'—the basis on which our multi-disciplinary programme was initiated—requires examination. The reader will be the judge of our belief that the evidence points to benefits to be gained from sustained work in inter-disciplinary learning systems of the kind described. But since, by definition, such systems must be established outside the boundaries of the participating agencies, consciously expressed and unconsciously experienced issues may be brought into them which belong inside those boundaries and can only be effectively confronted in comparable learning systems *within* each agency. These are rarely available, however. If the present work can be taken as a guide, enthusiasm for inter-agency training can represent an attempt to get help with 'back home' working problems and sometimes a flight from conflict and difficulty in that setting. In our view, it is a pre-requisite for effective inter-agency training that the agencies concerned should first establish learning systems of their own, in which their practitioners and managers are enabled to contain, understand and master their main task-related anxieties, and identify and moderate their defensive use of institutional structures.

Some agencies and disciplines, particularly in the field of health care, have hardly any tradition of such learning systems and will need to find motivation before they can incorporate them in ways appropriate to their settings. In other agencies, such as social services and probation, a tradition does exist of regular supervision, for example, but it is commonplace to find that this has either lapsed altogether or become an arena for anxious case management rather than for reflective understanding. In the absence of internal agency learning systems, there should be no surprise if recommended developments in in-service and inter-agency training (especially for work with child sexual abuse: Butler-Sloss, 1988; DHSS/Welsh Office, 1988) are slow and uncertain adjuncts of improvement in inter-agency collaboration. And since conservatism is an inherent ingredient of change, change must in any case be expected to take place differentially—to be greater or faster in some parts of the field than others. As all are part of potential service networks and some agencies carry disowned burdens on behalf of others, the tendency to scapegoat or isolate 'resistant' organisations has to be countered.

What is true of inter-agency training is also true of collaboration itself. Neither administrative measures nor organisational change, uninformed by the considerations we have outlined, and certainly not admonition will be successful in improving collaboration—especially when dangerous situations arise. The intrinsically complex tasks of inter-agency structures designed to promote collaboration are rendered even more difficult if not impossible to the degree that they become vehicles for displacing and externalising problems that belong elsewhere—in the members and their organisations.[9]

It could just be that the developmental threat posed to society by becoming aware of the sexual abuse of children will prove sufficient impetus for the emergence of a shared view about evolutionary changes required in its caring systems. But for this to be so calls for an appreciation of what is involved for change processes to be initiated *within* institutions, a pre- requisite of improved collaboration *between* them. The way of 'reading the situation' evolved here sees this as essential to foster modification of socially organised professional defences against the inescapable anxiety arising from group membership of agencies and from the tasks society delegates to them.

EPILOGUE

In Part VI of his seminal paper, *The unconscious*, Freud (1915b) foresaw dissatisfaction with his work on the subject and the doubts that would be cast on the way he had delineated the derivatives of unconscious processes. He went on:

> Our answer is, however, that we have no other aim but that of translating into theory the results of observation, and we deny that there is any obligation on us to achieve at our first attempt a well-rounded theory which will commend itself by its simplicity. We shall defend the complications of our theory so long as we find that they meet the results of observation, and we will not abandon our expectations of being led in the end by those very complications to the discovery of a state of affairs which, while simple in itself, can account for all the complications of reality (p. 190).

It goes without saying that we do not equate our work with Freud's. But we enter the same defence to objections about complexity; and we have had the same aim: to make theoretical sense of our observations and experience. A more comprehensive and well-rounded formulation of processes involved in inter-professional and inter-agency collaboration will certainly be made. Whether there can be one that accounts for 'all the complexities of reality' is, however, doubtful—except in as much as it builds in the principle of uncertainty. It is in the nature of open systems to be unpredictable as they develop.

Emery and Trist (1972), in their exploration of social ecology, have pointed to the evidence that rapid and accelerating social and technological change is giving rise to 'turbulent fields' in post-industrial society. They also trace the gradual emergence of values leading to a new guiding principle in society, namely that welfare and development at every level are interdependent, the emphasis being on the realisation of potential for the individual and for society.

But a notable feature of turbulent fields is the contradictions observable within them. As contraction has followed expansion in the statutory services and caring professions (including the education service which underpins them), shifts in values and attitudes to and within the field of care can be seen reflecting just such contradictions. For example, there has been a growing recognition that collaboration, interdependence and the interplay of differences are as requisite for the development of institutions as they are for individuals, couples and families. But these values have been articulated at the same time as an increasing insistence on the finite nature of resources in the face of escalating demands. Reductionist attitudes vie with those encouraging attention to process and the interplay of the inner and outer worlds of people in difficulty (Woodhouse, 1990). Contrasting and conflicting approaches to personal problems may, as Sutherland (1980, p. 15) warned, 'reflect a situation not so much of stimulating differences within a healthy enterprise as one with serious and potentially dangerous contradictions'.

A survey of the field of care reveals contradictions which seem to negate the evolutionary trend linking welfare and development, for which the historical evidence is so persuasive. But we need to keep in mind that the caring services are society's attempts to deal with what its members most fear in and for themselves. They reflect the inherent tension between autonomy and dependency, care and control, love and hate. Anxiety activated by rapid change and the accompanying experience of loss and uncertainty tends to induce regression and the employment of the more primitive defences such as splitting and denial at every level. These defences are manifested in oscillating and contradictory attitudes towards those to whom the compassionate function is delegated. Yet over ever-widening areas of human affairs, including man's relationship with his natural environment, the fact of interdependence becomes inescapable and increasingly a determinant of priorities. Dependence and independence are ceasing to be relevant alternatives. Evolutionary processes are never linear, however; the outcome is always uncertain, and the caring services cannot be insulated from developments in the wider arena. Their unpredictability puts a premium on the continuous review of psycho-social processes through adaptive learning systems that increase our understanding of collaborative problems.

Notes

1   Some half-dozen cases were brought more or less explicitly to challenge the relevance of psychodynamic concepts and the interactive stance with which we and the TIMS were identified. These offered valuable opportunities to examine differences.

2   Our assessment that this kind of change was evident in the work of the majority of practitioners, though in varying degrees and differentially as between disciplines, was confirmed by their individual evaluations at the end of the programme.

3   Practitioners who are not employed in organisations are an exception which proves (tests) the rule. Many therapists in private practice make use of their colleagues and professional associations not only to discuss working problems but also for emotional support. Those who are geographically isolated make frequent reference to the want of such opportunities. See also *Fairbairn's journey into the interior* (Sutherland, 1989).

4   For those who find their personal and professional development impeded by their agency and its institutional defences, the alternative is to leave. But pressures to conform to what can be and often is an anti-developmental model provided by the institutional setting are powerful; disparity between what is projected into practitioners in institutions and their own personal and professional needs can lead to significant stress.

Another way of gaining relief, if not escape, may be by way of illness. Both these possibilities occurred during (and after) the programme. A few practitioners approached us privately to ask for referral to psychotherapy; a few embarked on a change of career letting us know that the programme had helped them understand their discomfort in their former roles.

5   In the workshops members occasionally invited collaborating practitioners from outside the programme to join the group for discussion of their shared case. As was to be expected, all these 'guests' found it intimidating to come into a strange, established group; only one (who attended a number of times) participated in a way that extended our understanding and, it must be assumed, found the experience profitable herself. It is, of course, impossible to know all the reasons for the disparity, but one was clear: the quality of relationship between the respective pairs of practitioners. One visiting practitioner found herself at odds with her co-worker and the group, withdrew and put an embargo on her material (see chapter 8); one promised to come but failed to appear; another arrived to hear that her partner in the workshop (from the same agency) had sent her apologies! This marginal evidence seems worth recording only because it tends to confirm the tendency to avoid examining the experience of joint work and the absence of a collaborative culture in the field.

6   It is of interest that when we and other participants became persuaded that a book would be appropriate, as opposed to the initial arrangement for reports to funding bodies and journal articles, social services alone stood by the 'letter of the law' and quoted the original undertakings—which it and its staff had been punctilious in fulfilling. The point in the present context is that *at the level of the service network* the department may well have been enacting not only its own uncertainty and reluctance, but also the similar (though denied) misgivings of other agencies whose practitioners did collaborate in the production of the book.

7   In two cases sexual abuse had been a feature some years previously, and in one it was a current anxiety. One of the earlier allegations was apparently of doubtful authenticity.

8   This theme, frequently made explicit by practitioners in this study, has been cogently elaborated by Garland (1991) in relation to the reactions of survivors of disasters. As noted by Menzies Lyth (1987), practitioners and therapists are not only increasingly involved with large-scale disasters—the Cleveland episode was one of them—they meet countless individual and family disasters in their day-to-day work: broken marriages, child neglect and abuse, deprivation, disability, unemployment, illness and untimely death.

9   The formally established co-ordinating structures described by practitioners in the programme and in recent literature (for example Butler-Sloss, 1988; DHSS/Welsh Office, 1988; Stevenson 1989b) are evidently not well placed to afford the kind of container within which tensions inherent in inter-agency work can be appreciated and attended to. The following are some of their characteristics:

—The groups have no continuing life; what binds them, like the service network they represent, is a particular class of anxiety-provoking clients/patients.

—They are accountable only to their member agencies.

—Leadership (the chair) is vested in a member agency.

—Agency representatives may vary.

—As open systems, member agencies are subject to powerful influences (emanating from their salient client/patient groups) of which field-level practitioners are the 'conductors'. These influences and the member agencies' socially organised defences against task-related anxiety are taken into such groups by their representatives.

—Group processes, including the tendency to enact reflections of client/patient defences and the triangular dynamic will always, if variably, be at work in their deliberations.

—The members are unlikely to have a shared understanding of the problematic phenomena such groups have to work with (for example of aetiology, individual and family functioning and dynamics).

—Few, if any, of the participating agencies will have their own built-in 'learning systems' (in social work, for example, supervision increasingly consists of little more than case-management; Dearnley, 1985).

—The subject matter and atmosphere of discussion is likely to be suffused with a threatening sense of urgency; the emphasis will tend to be on action/reaction with little time or space for the recovery of objectivity, rounded thought and lost wits.

Appendix

Defences against anxiety and responses to child sexual abuse

Some aspects of the report on the Cleveland crisis, 1987

When children suffer and even die as a result of physical and emotional neglect and abuse by parents or parent figures and what seems to be the failure of practitioners and caring agencies there is great public concern. The intensity of emotion aroused and the impulse to blame and punish is understandable if only because we identify both with the vulnerability of children *and* with the destructive impulses which as adults and parents most of us keep in check and so find intolerable, sometimes beyond belief, when acted-out by others.

Official inquiries following such events have almost invariably been judicial ones.[1] In emotive circumstances, the legal approach has been invoked to establish and analyse the facts; to search for, test and evaluate evidence. The quest is for objectivity. The task being to make judgements about what went wrong and where responsibility lay, individuals and institutional procedures are inevitably criticised; professionals and their employing bodies are to be held accountable. Ensuing reports and recommendations aim to eradicate short-comings for the future, and invariably urge better collaboration. Complex questions remain, however, which a different frame of reference may throw light on.

THE REASON FOR THE CRISIS

The crisis in the county of Cleveland was a particularly large-scale example of problems in the vexed area of child abuse in which, as before, failures in communication and collaboration between practitioners and agencies were a prominent feature. It came about because of an unprecedented rise in the diagnosis of child sexual abuse and the separation of large numbers of children from their parents which resulted. In total, 125 children were diagnosed as having been sexually abused between February and July 1987, 121 of them (from 57 families) by two paediatricians. Most were removed from their families through 'place of safety' orders obtained by the social services department in circumstances that led to protests by parents—and ultimately to a Statutory Public Inquiry under the chairmanship of a High Court judge. By the time it reported, less than a year later, 98 of the children were back at home though this did not imply that they had necessarily been misdiagnosed.

THE NATURE OF THE REPORT

Though a judicial one like its predecessors, the Cleveland Inquiry was distinctive. It was specifically concerned with the sexual abuse of children and was the first to be so, though physical abuse was included in its terms of reference; the two forms of abuse may be associated. There were no child fatalities during the episode the Inquiry had to consider and, also unlike previous ones, the matters to be investigated came to public knowledge because of parents' complaints about the way they and their children were treated by professionals and statutory agencies. Above all, it was the first inquiry to survey the workings of an entire local network of services in relation to a whole class of case—as opposed to investigating a single tragedy. The report was written speedily, but the document produced (Butler-Sloss, 1988) is comprehensive and, while restricted by its form and orientation, is notable for its insight and sensitivity.

PRE-EXISTING PRESSURES

The Inquiry learned of little complaint or overt concern about the way community services had responded to cases of child abuse other than sexual abuse. The guidelines and procedures evolved by the local Area Review Committee, the main forum for co-ordinating responses to child abuse,[2] were said by all concerned to work well. But there is a marked tendency for cases of child abuse and neglect to be divisive of practitioners and agencies and it is often difficult to distinguish between what is reported to have happened and what has actually happened in such circumstances (as was noted in the main text of this book). It is unlikely that Cleveland's ARC had been free of difficulty in fact, though the Inquiry did not bring serious contention to light.

Nonetheless, the report emphasises that the co-ordinating machinery, like the local agencies, had come under severe pressure; the volume of physical abuse cases in Cleveland was high. This, it says, was an indication of the area's social problems and meant that social workers and other practitioners were already hard-pressed in the run-up to the sexual abuse crisis. Publicised failures in child care elsewhere also weighed heavily, especially on the Cleveland Social Services Department. The report records its director's resolve that his agency 'should learn from mistakes made elsewhere which resulted in children being avoidably abused' (4.13, p. 56). The picture presented of the environment in which the Cleveland agencies and practitioners were functioning is one of strain and anxious concern. Social workers were bound to be aware of their vulnerability to blame for under-reacting in cases of child abuse, like their fellows in earlier fatal cases.

SEXUAL ABUSE: ANXIETY AND DEFENCES

The report points out a parallel between the reluctance to recognise the physical abuse of children in the United Kingdom in the 1960s and the reluctance by many to accept the reality of child sexual abuse in the 1980s, particularly within the home and family. This was reflected in Cleveland, before the crisis, by the difficulty of interesting people in the subject and the tardy response to an initiative to encourage comprehensive, inter-agency approaches to it.[3]

As the report recognises, the sexual abuse of children, though it may well be associated with physical abuse, adds an extra dimension to pressure on agencies and practitioners and can give rise to anxiety that is qualitatively different. A senior health service professional underlined this point when giving evidence about the training sessions that were eventually instituted:

> Somehow sexual abuse touches a part of the individual which perhaps physical abuse does not. Most of us can see how we could quite easily hit a child in a moment of stress . . . and emotional abuse, again I think we can all understand the damage that is done by it . . . sexual abuse has an effect on the person which is an individual response depending on perhaps your own knowledge, your own background experience, and some people find it extremely difficult to listen to us talking about it. I have sometimes had to go back and repeat the training I have given because they found it so painful . . .' (8.7.6, p. 121).

Individual differences

The quotation above vividly shows the emotional impact child sexual abuse can have when practitioners (of any discipline) are confronted by it in training groups. Though emphasising the general impact, the witness notes that the response is an individual one. We would add that behind individual practitioners' varied knowledge and personal experience lie the defences against anxiety, unconscious as well as conscious, which each person has evolved—defences which have become part of their personality. The practitioner's gender is especially significant in this field, but his or her personality is also a major variable in individual differences in practice and technique. Child sexual abuse presents problems for everyone; there is an emotional element from which no-one is immune, the effects of which may be manifest in various ways, as the report points out. Moreover, practitioners do not function in a professional vacuum, but in an institutional culture; professional and agency allegiances determine the socially organised defences which all practitioners draw on. The variable effects of child sexual abuse on practitioners in their work derives from the interplay of person and setting, and the influence on them of pressures from the wider environment.

Ambivalence and the sexual component

The report records the evidence of a child psychiatrist (not a principal figure in the crisis) that whenever a new diagnosis or treatment is described, 'a flurry of excitement develops among professionals' but in the case of child sexual abuse 'there is an added voyeuristic component arising from the universality of interest in sexual matters'. Those attempting to help in this difficult field 'would do well to bear in mind the complex forces which can affect judgement and action when dealing with emotionally powerful material' (36, p. 11). The 'complex forces' activated by sexual material must include conflict; emotional conflict between attraction and repulsion. The Inquiry report, acknowledging that the anxiety associated with child sexual abuse is often defended against ('most people have some understandable unease or distaste for the subject'; 37, p. 11) also recognises that the anxiety may be dealt with by an opposite, and reciprocal, response: 'some feel the need to manage the denial of others by demonstrating its prevalence and engaging in active campaigns to eradicate it' (37, p. 11). As examples in Part II of our main text have shown, in a relationship system such opposite defences are the more liable to become polarised, rigid and impervious to moderation the more personal and professional autonomy is felt to be under threat. They represent the two sides of ambivalence; what is rejected in the self is located in the other through the defences of splitting, projection and projective identification. The mental processes involved are unconscious.

CHILDREN, PARENTS AND PROFESSIONALS

The children involved in the crisis ranged from infants to adolescents. The Inquiry was at pains to shield them from the burden of giving evidence, but special arrangements were made for those who wished to talk, especially since the perceptions, concerns and arguments of the adults often 'seemed to have little to do with the problems of the children themselves'. So vignettes of a score of their stories are included 'in an attempt not to fall into the same trap' (1.6, p. 25). Many of these suggest problematic family relationships irrespective of any abuse; some children were grossly disturbed and in need of help. Even from the report's limited material it is clear that many had been upset by separation during the crisis and while some seemed glad to escape most, not surprisingly, wanted to be back with their families whatever the situation at home.

The report also recounts the experiences of parents, including difficulties in getting second medical opinions on the clinical diagnosis of sexual abuse. Having noted some inconsistencies in parents' evidence which were not fully tested, it summarises the substance of parental complaints: 'they were denied or unable to obtain information about their children, or what was happening or what was planned for the future; ... social workers were not interested in and not enquiring into family environment and history and ... paediatricians and social workers had concluded that the parent (usually father) or parents were abusers and, until that was accepted by one or both, were indifferent, unresponsive and lacked compassion' (2.52, p. 44).

Not all parents complained, however. A minority recounted a different experience. There were some, especially among those with established relationships with practitioners, who felt they had been shown care and consideration by the two doctors mainly involved and by social workers. A few mothers were grateful that sexual abuse they said they had not been aware of had been brought to light. Nor was the group of parents a homogeneous one. There were families well known to social services, with many family problems and much social work intervention; some were entirely unknown, others had been trusted foster parents. Overall, the Inquiry was left with a major misgiving: 'whether the parents were abusers, possible abusers or ordinary people caught up in the results of misdiagnosis, their situation of isolation and lack of support was a most worrying feature of the Cleveland crisis' (2.65, p. 46). The overall picture presented by the report is redolent of anxiety. There were two suicides of alleged male abusers.

The account of what happened shows that processes and procedures intended to protect children and promote their welfare degenerated into instruments of de-personalisation, and that practitioners distanced themselves from the relevant adults. So far as abused children were concerned, the 'caring systems' reflected the way they were treated by abusers—as objects. Towards the adults, the behaviour of the paediatricians who were the focus of attention and the more numerous social workers was inconsistent; in other circumstances they were known as caring and committed, especially when there was no suspicion of sexual abuse. This points to defences which we found characteristic of medicine and social work respectively: maintaining rigid boundaries between doctor and patient and between the presenting patient and others in the family system; in social work, keeping an emotional distance from 'bad parents' who were often hostile and accusing; and in both disciplines the resort to the 'certainties' of a reductionist stance, in place of a more integrative approach which requires toleration of uncertainty and complexity.

Experience of our interdisciplinary programme prompts the question: once there was apprehension of sexual abuse, did the practitioners most involved distance themselves from the families as a defence against the phantasised threat of loss of personal boundaries—boundaries that have indeed been lost by those who sexually abuse children? With whatever level of self-awareness, they behaved in the main as if to be open to influence meant being swamped so that personal and professional integrity was felt to be endangered.[4]

As Mattinson (1977) has pointed out, however, psychological distance proves no protection from the strongest projections. The effect of such emotional separateness from parents could only be to reinforce the dominant defences of most of them and increase their hostility, fuelling the reciprocal, persecutory situation that developed. In such a climate practitioners can scarcely sustain their capacity to listen reflectively and with discretion, on the way to the very difficult judgements and the measured assessments of individual differences which they must make and which the report calls for. These assessments must in any case often be made in the face of denial (which, the Inquiry was reminded, is a general response to allegations of child sexual abuse) or of potential collusion between parents (to which the same expert witness as well as some of the children's stories drew attention). The unconscious as well as conscious anxiety generating pressure to rescue the defenceless child had the paradoxical effect of creating what the report called 'double victims'; even very young children were almost invariably separated from their parents and families as soon as a diagnosis of sexual abuse was made (even when there was no way of identifying a perpetrator).

PRACTITIONERS AND AGENCIES: THE SERVICE NETWORK

We shall discuss the practice and behaviour of professionals and agencies described in the Inquiry report only as it seems to throw light on the way anxiety and defences against it affected events in Cleveland. We have already seen how the document exposes the polarising of defensive responses to the anxiety engendered by child sexual abuse. The personal responses of the practitioners and managers concerned will have been distributed along a continuum between denial and preoccupation, flight and fight—determined in large measure by the unconscious processes at work in their inner worlds, their interaction with clients or patients and their capacity to mediate the conflict of feelings stimulated by child abuse. But, whilst persons are instrumental, they are also influenced by collective preoccupations and socially organised defences in which they participate, within their agency settings.

In revealing the circumstances that gave the Cleveland episode its particular character and form, the report also notes responses and reactions from outside the group of local agencies, some of which aggravated the situation. Of the array of professionals involved within Cleveland, not all played a significant part. GPs, for example, were not prominent and (as in our study programme) there was a marked tendency for them to be isolated from, and by, practitioners in other services. But those in three institutions had a leading role in the crisis, especially in their interaction with one another: hospital paediatric services, social services and police. Together, they comprised the 'relevant service network'.

The doctors and their setting

According to the report, the two paediatric consultants who became the centre point for the diagnosing of child sexual abuse which reached crisis proportions in Cleveland had a single-minded and highly conscientious commitment to their speciality. And they had a strong personal investment in child protection as part of their concern for child health in a deprived and, in their view, under-resourced area. One was a well-established consultant; the other was not long in post and known to have an interest in child sexual abuse.

The doctors progressively came to be of one mind and to the view that a particular diagnostic technique was sovereign in the detection of anal abuse. As the report puts it, the presence of certain physical signs 'was elevated from grounds of strong suspicion to an unequivocal "diagnosis" of sexual abuse' (3, p. 243). They acted promptly on every such finding, in concert with the social services department but often as if oblivious of the legitimate interests of other professionals and agencies, for example, nurses in their hospital, GPs and the police. One of them expressed the belief that some child patients had been failed in the past because the diagnosis of child abuse had been missed. These doctors were generally averse to second opinions, particularly those by police surgeons, which they felt not to be in the child's best interests, but they did participate in what the report describes as not very satisfactory arrangements set up for such examinations as the crisis developed—though they were liable to dispute the results when at variance with their own positive diagnosis of sexual abuse.

An appreciation of the idiosyncratic response to child sexual abuse of these consultants and its outcome, as reported, must however take account of the institutional and professional system of which they were a part, with its entrenched socially organised defences against task-induced anxiety. Among these, closed-system thinking and the defensive use of professional boundaries are prominent. Not surprisingly, the report shows these defences to have been in operation within the health service in Cleveland. Meanwhile, being hospital based, the technical and organisational context of the paediatricians' work was one that will have placed a premium on precise diagnosis and speedy treatment, on scientific reductionism and prompt intervention. Working environments are never neutral; with inbuilt support for the authority of consultants, their professional context will have been more favourable to diagnostic conviction than to relevant uncertainty. With customary autonomy in their clinical practice, they were able to resist requests from their employing authority to ease the situation by limiting admissions. Organisationally, they were the principal gatekeepers of their department's external boundary. As such, they were able to diagnose and admit children as sexually abused who were originally referred with signs and symptoms of other conditions, i.e. without complaint of abuse by the children or anyone else. Thus they were in a position to allay their fears of failing children at risk even though the input of cases led to massive work-loads for themselves and for others (for example the children's wards became stretched to breaking point; social workers were also put under considerable strain); their reaction against second medical opinions potentially at odds with their own can also be seen as a response to the same anxiety.

Whatever part their personalities played (with which we are not concerned), it could be tempting to assess the paediatricians' recorded behaviour primarily as an embodiment of the defensive omnipotence fostered by medical training and embodied in health service and hospital organisation.[5] To do so would be to ignore the further influence on them of powerful projections of omnipotence by those in other disciplines as part of their own defences against anxiety arising from child sexual abuse. Some of the evidence recorded in the report indicates that authority in respect of child sexual abuse was lodged by others in the doctors and their medical diagnosis. The tendency to blame the messenger rather than the perpetrator in such circumstances was thus given added scope (see Kraemer, 1988).

Social workers and the social services department

The atmosphere of anxious concern in Cleveland revealed by the Inquiry report and the increasing pressure on practitioners and agencies prior to the sexual abuse crisis bore particularly on the social services department because of its statutory responsibilities in the field of child care and protection. Well before the episode, child care and support to vulnerable families had been given priority over all other tasks in the department. As well as additional resources to improve levels and standards of social work practice and administration locally, three new consultant posts had been provided with a county-wide remit of policy co-ordination and service development. These posts were concerned with fostering and adoption, child-care practice and child abuse. Local recognition of sexual abuse of even young children was already growing, and the role of child-abuse consultant achieved further prominence in the department following publication in 1985 of the official report on the death of Jasmine Beckford, with its censure of the social workers and social services department involved in that notorious case.

This background material specific to the social services department establishes the psychological as well as the organisational context of the child abuse consultant and her work which attained prominence during the Cleveland episode. Here, as in our own study, 'bad parenting' had clearly become a major and threatening preoccupation for social work practitioners and their agency. This laid the foundation for what followed.

If we focus on the social services department as a relationship system, its behaviour during the crisis as described in the Inquiry report portrays a group in the grip of a collective collusion which, in a psychological sense, meant the establishment of a predominantly unconscious and therefore unreflective agreement. A situation is revealed in which prevailing rules and procedures were unsuccessful in containing task-induced anxiety which, being unmastered, worked against rather than in aid of task performance. What Bion (1961) described as 'basic assumptions' flourished and, in their grip, individuals lost or surrendered personal and professional autonomy. It was as if not only the child abuse consultant, but most social work practitioners and managers became as one with the paediatricians; distinctiveness and the capacity to appreciate difference was lost.

Social services and the paediatricians

Conflict and hostility developed and was integral to the Cleveland crisis and we return to this aspect of it presently. Here we note from the report that 'the suggestion of conspiracy and collusion [between one of the paediatricians and the child-abuse consultant] denoting bad faith and some sort of impropriety [was] raised from time to time during the evidence to the Inquiry, as it was before it began. It [was] alleged (by a Member of Parliament), taken up by the media and the police and never withdrawn ... there has not been a shred of evidence to support any collusion, conspiracy, bad faith or impropriety' (4.188, p. 83).

But there clearly was an accord. It was one we judge to have derived from institutional and inter-institutional factors (aside from personal ones) which were dynamically related and mutually reinforcing.

The roles of both professionals were integral to strategies developed by their respective organisations in the socio-economic conditions prevailing in Cleveland, in pursuit of tasks assigned to them. Both were innovative appointments reflecting institutional policy and attitudes. More overtly so in the case of the social services department, this was also true of the health authority whose representative told the Inquiry that, at the time of her appointment, the particular interests of the recently joined paediatrician were seen as 'a bonus in that the South Tees population contains many communities which are among the most "deprived" in the Northern Region' (8.5.1, p. 111). Both practitioners will have been selected on grounds of technical competence and a professional approach deemed to fit in with the institutional culture. And (as our study showed) not only are child health and child protection complementary tasks, the socially organised defences against anxiety developed as a corollary of these tasks tend also to be complementary and can lead to coalition between practitioners. Here the coalescing occurred *at the service agency level* as well as that of the individual.

While both doctor and social worker apparently held similar strong views about what the response to child sexual abuse should be, and the report conveys that their personalities were also compatible, our focus here is on the systemic interactions for which this created an opening. Given the threat posed to social workers and their agency by 'bad parenting', the child-abuse consultant would have afforded a readily available channel through which to project omniscience and certainty into the doctors who became identified by social workers and their agency with their own primary task. The doctors, *fortified by these attributions*, could in turn regard the social services department with its crucial statutory powers as an extension of themselves. Each set of practitioners came to perceive the other as their agents.

Collusion did not occur in a judicial but in a psychological sense and it had implications beyond the boundary of the relationship between the two individuals against whom the allegation was made.

The phenomena we are attempting to understand more comprehensively are captured in the report's concluding comments on social work practice. Having noted that the public climate had changed by 1987 because of media focus on child sexual abuse, including assertions about the number of children affected, and that the new techniques adopted by the two paediatricians resulted in authoritative statements that children had been abused in this way, it continued:

> Social workers did not regard themselves as competent to question the basis of the medical diagnoses from a consultant paediatrician whom they treated with the

respect due to that status. Few felt able to query the basis of the diagnostic findings on the basis of a co-equal professional relationship ... In many cases the social workers were not only presented with a diagnosis but also a firm request for a place of safety order from the consultants, and after the 29th May they had the instructions received from the director of social services. [N.B. He was censured earlier in the report for failing to test the advice of the child abuse consultant. He, too, accepted the validity of the paediatric diagnoses and acted to prevent his staff and department being criticised for failing to act on such serious allegations. Later, as the crisis mounted, he took remedial steps, for example, to secure second opinions and validation of further diagnoses. In our terms, he became able to extricate himself from the institutional collusion and act independently in the service of his agency task.]

Under the guidance of senior staff and in the absence of any specific complaint by a child or allegation by an adult and without wider assessment, social workers treated the diagnosis of sexual abuse as a matter which in all cases and all circumstances required an immediate emergency intervention to protect the child's health and safety. The procedures and practice failed to recognise that child sexual abuse has different characteristics from physical abuse. It requires cautious measured intervention which will allow the risks of a false positive finding to be balanced against those of a false negative ...

They adopted a procedure where there was no assessment of the individual circumstance of each case or any alternative to an application to a magistrate. The attitude of key managers and the child-abuse consultant suggested that the way to resolve the conflict was to "suspend disbelief". Often in suspending all critical appraisal and without their general skills in assessment being properly utilised, they saw their task narrowly as securing the protection of the child ...

This passage of the report goes on to emphasise that there had been no evidence that 'any social worker has acted other than in good faith' (4. 189, pp. 84-5). But there could be no clearer statement of the propensity, under intense anxiety, to fall back on the bedrock of a narrow definition of primary task.

The record of the corporate behaviour of the social services department in Cleveland becomes the more comprehensible when, to the consciously experienced threat posed by parental failure, is added the kind and quality of unconscious phantasies to which child sexual abuse is liable to speak in any practitioner, especially those who have to work directly with it. They relate to the psychic world of the very young child and to incest; a primitive world that can be activated in any individual and is associated with the longing to possess and be possessed by the parents. These are longings against which the strictest taboos have been almost universally established.

The report emphasises that many social workers involved in the crisis were inexperienced, but it was evidently not solely experience or the lack of it that differentiated them with regard to the dependency most of these professionals exhibited in their relationship with the paediatricians, and their associated sense of powerlessness. Nor do we believe it was primarily their position in the hierarchy of the professions that led to acquiescence. More important was the fact that their interaction with the doctors in the prevailing climate left insufficient mental and emotional space in which to adopt a questioning attitude; boundaries were lost. The difficulty for them lay in distinguishing the difference between a challenge to medical diagnoses—which, as non-medicals, they were not competent to make—and questioning the child-care implications of these diagnoses, which was their province and responsibility. To have exercised such authority would, however, have required them and their managers to occupy the tense, uncertain middle-ground between two extreme defensive responses to child sexual abuse—denial of it and aggressive assault on it. This emotional task of mediation is an onerous one, but a pre-requisite of the 'cautious measured intervention' which the report rightly advocates. Drawing on Bion's work again, it would have entailed bringing together primitive and sophisticated mental states which is the essence of developmental conflict. As the experience discussed in Part II of this book suggests, this is invariably discomforting and can be a further source of anxiety. Our evidence, however, is that such conflict has creative potential if ways can be found to contain work-related anxiety and to facilitate its understanding and mastery.

Change, the police and child abuse

The emerging recognition of sexual abuse of young children, often within the family, has confronted a range of practitioners, their managers and their institutions with the need for change. But change and loss are inseparable and, because it speaks to innate conservatism, resistance to change is the general rule (Marris, 1974). Established beliefs and ways of construing experience are challenged. The doubt and anxiety that accompanies an excursion into the unknown are carried into the life of the groups to which individuals owe emotional and contractual allegiance and influence their interaction.

A major theme of the Cleveland Inquiry concerns the dilemma for practitioners and their agencies posed by the challenge to established practice from new awareness and information about child sexual abuse. The report chronicles disarray at both personal and institutional levels; small wonder since these relationship systems are interdependent. Because sexual abuse tends to objectify forbidden primitive sexual phantasies in the person's inner world, defences against associated anxiety are likely to be tested; they may then become more rigid or shift to cruder forms. And, just as these personal defences are activated and sometimes exacerbated in the practitioner by exposure to sexual abuse through the professional task, so too are the agency's characteristic socially organised defences. The institution's rules, procedures and structures tend to become more entrenched, less subject to internal scrutiny, because of their reassuring defensive emotional significance for its members. This was the scenario for all practitioners and agencies involved in the Cleveland crisis but, from the report's account, none were more threatened by change and development in the field of child abuse than the police.

The police have a variety of roles, variously compatible, but here we are concerned with their traditional task: to investigate and prosecute crime. Child abuse is crime; violent physical assaults on children and sexual abuse constitute serious crime. Like other professionals in Cleveland, the police conveyed that earlier procedures and inter-agency collaboration had been effective as regards physical abuse. The report records a principal point in police evidence to the Inquiry: that arrangements for dealing with child sexual abuse were also effective before the arrival of the social services child abuse consultant. Relationships with the social services department and between police officers and social workers at field level were said to have been good hitherto. Describing the position up to 1987, it continues:

> Previous arrangements, which had existed for a number of years, appeared to be [satisfactory] for those cases of sexual abuse in which the police had a clear and traditional role to play—sexual offences involving teenage children most frequently perpetrated by adults from outside the family. However, with increasing awareness of the problem of the sexual abuse of younger children within the family, the need for a more complex and sensitive type of inter-agency intervention and co-operation required alteration of existing arrangements. Cleveland Constabulary were slow to respond to this need and, as in time other agencies moved to meet this new challenge, there was difficulty in carrying the police along with the new arrangements ... we heard evidence that some professionals involved had known each other for twenty years or so ... New faces with new ideas would inevitably have difficulty in initiating change (6.11-16, p. 89).

One voice at least was raised within the organisation on the need for change in the police approach to sexual abuse within the family and to inter-professional collaboration. It appears not to have been heeded. It came from the organisation's community relations rather than its criminal investigation branch—some of whose members, along with other senior figures in the force, expressed reservations about multi-disciplinary working in abuse cases.

The report items two main concerns of the police. The first was that they had great experience in investigating sexual offences against children; social services did not. The second, later to impinge on working relationships with the two paediatricians, concerned medical examinations. While willing to accept the evidence of any suitably qualified doctor, the police felt they must be free to invoke a police surgeon when they considered it appropriate. They had been used to the collection and presentation in court of forensic evidence by such specialised doctors and relied on them. The social services department, increasingly preoccupied with the sexual abuse of younger children (many too young to give evidence in criminal proceedings), saw no need for the provision.

A divergence of priorities becomes apparent. For the police, the need to secure a sound basis for criminal prosecution took precedence; for social workers and social services, child protection—for which care or wardship proceedings under civil law were the preferred remedy. Later, as the crisis developed, social workers were to protest when the police were slow to act in respect of alleged perpetrators of child sexual abuse. The report notes that the difficulty of the police in pursuing investigations was exacerbated by precipitate medical and social work responses following a diagnosis of sexual abuse, and it is clear that these practitioners did not always keep the police and their task in mind. For their part, the police felt at risk of being left without the kind of evidence that would 'stand up in court'. But overall the report concludes that 'undoubted strains in the system' (6.27, p. 9) prior to the crisis were insufficiently recognised by the police at the Inquiry, which was 'given little confidence that the force had been willing or committed to dealing with the problem of child sexual abuse *before* [our italics] the arrival of the social services child abuse consultant in 1986' (6.24, p. 90).

This is one of the points at which the significance of gender becomes salient. The child-abuse consultant was described in evidence by a senior police officer as a very strong-willed and determined woman. The report notes that she indeed expressed disagreement forcefully—for example, about the employment of police surgeons. But leading figures in the highly structured, hierarchically organised and predominantly male institution of the police force (no basic grade or women officers featured in the report) blamed the female social work consultant for its problems. And she was to be joined as an object of blame by the female paediatrician with whom they believed she colluded—to their detriment as well as that of the families embroiled in the crisis.

Meanwhile, the technical problems the police confronted in bringing charges against alleged sexual abuse offenders were not communicated to the other agencies and therefore were not collectively addressed. In fact, each of the parties, doctors and social workers as well as the police, used professional and institutional boundaries defensively in their several ways; they all contributed to this most common hindrance to creative interaction. In psychodynamic terms the symbolism of these inter-agency phenomena is inescapable. It was as if the service network was re-enacting not only the abuse of female by male, but also the disastrous failure of co-parenting by male *and* female which child sexual abuse in the family represents. Meanwhile many of the real parents and children felt ill-used by the professionals.

The regret if not resentment by the police that long established and 'comfortable' working relationships had been disturbed; the lack of commitment to the problem of child sexual abuse; the failure to acknowledge a warning voice within the organisation about the need for change and collaboration; the reluctance, even in retrospect, to recognise 'strains in the system' all point to the operation of a characteristic socially organised defence—that of denial. It not only reflected resistance to change and support for the status quo, but, being rooted in the agency's culture, must also have served as a defence against the anxiety engendered by the sexual abuse of young children. The police are no more immune to its disturbing effects, conscious and unconscious, than other practitioners.[6]

The documented material suggests, too, that the difficulties the police experienced resonated with persecutory anxiety inherent in their prosecutory task, that of 'laying the blame'. Blaming [7] and denial, both related to splitting, emerge as salient defences (these are no doubt the same primitive defences employed by many if not most people should they become the object of police attention and accusation). Reviewing their complaints about the child-abuse consultant, the Inquiry, in its final conclusions, took the view that the police 'should not have allowed personalities to stand in the way of an objective assessment of the situation and the need to resolve it' (9, p. 244). But police attitudes seem to have been permeated by a powerful and largely unconscious collective defence against task-induced anxiety, inimical to the objective assessment and problem resolution the Inquiry found to be lacking.

THE CLEVELAND CRISIS AND THE TRIANGULAR DYNAMIC

The Cleveland crisis provided a striking example of collaborative difficulties in tripartite relationship systems (see chapter 9). In any local network of services it is the clients or patients they have in common who are 'third parties'; they are at the apex of the collaborative triangle. It is they who bring the network into being and the nature of their problems and difficulties (real or suspected) define its composition. The nature and orientation of the Inquiry precludes detailed examination of cases from the varied groups that comprised the population of parents and children involved in the crisis. Evidence of the psychodynamics of their marital and family relationships, defences against anxiety and interaction with the different practitioners who worked with them cannot be gleaned from the report. But a general comment can be made.

The report notes that, even at the height of the crisis, some good collaboration was achieved, if only in a few instances; but, apart from the small group who were known to have accepted that their children had been abused and were relieved by the intervention, most parents were ill-used by the service network—including those who were abusers and denied the fact. All however will have experienced the anxieties peculiar to child sexual abuse, which will have affected their relationships with each other and with practitioners. Irrespective of the reality of sexual abuse in any given case and of who abusers might or might not have been, the spectre of forbidden incest is raised even by the possibility of the offence; this of itself speaks to oedipal phantasies and the importance of containment in triangular relationships.

With these volatile forces as 'raw material', the dimensions of the triangular dynamic as it affected the Cleveland crisis can now be discerned. Mutual trust amongst the service network was undermined by a combination of factors built up before and intensified during the episode, but the Inquiry found that a 'major source of dispute between the police and the other [two] agencies was the diagnosis of anal abuse on the basis of the anal dilation test and the subsequent evidential value of this test' (6.73, p. 98).

The report highlights an early case heralding overt conflict. The police had made an arrest based on such a diagnosis (of both anal and vaginal abuse on this occasion) and on what proved to be a misleading initial disclosure to a social worker by the child. The need to withdraw proceedings embarrassed the police and, as one officer put it, left them with 'egg on their face' (6.32, p. 92). Access by their senior police surgeon had been requested but was restricted by the child-abuse consultant; he was later excluded from the case by the female paediatrician. Unlike the non-medicals, this doctor was in a position to challenge the validity of the clinical procedures, and consistently and vehemently did so from then on. The police 'were much influenced by his strong condemnation of [the paediatricians'] methods' and increasingly inflexible in requiring his involvement. 'They were in fact asking for the senior police surgeon to examine for the purpose of providing a second opinion on the diagnosis of the paediatrician or, as must have been increasingly obvious in the light of [his] declared views, to discount the diagnosis' (6.73, p. 98). The police were indeed faced with receiving very serious allegations, mainly against parents, and often then being unable to act effectively. The Inquiry felt that, with the reliability of the diagnoses in doubt, their quest for a second opinion was reasonable as was their inclination to rely on this particular doctor whom they had come to trust. However, 'with the knowledge of the depth of feeling exhibited . . . in his dispute with [the paediatricians], senior officers should have reflected upon the wisdom of relying thereafter exclusively upon his advice' (6.75, p. 99).

It is most unlikely that police managers were without the wits to appreciate what was happening—any more than the director of social services was when he omitted to question the advice of his child-abuse consultant, or the paediatricians when they failed to consider the wider implications of the significantly large number of children they diagnosed as sexually abused. But wisdom and common sense—the senses working in harmony—had evidently deserted them all.

Medical opinion was divided and, with divergent tasks and different priorities as they perceived them, police and social services moved 'in different directions bound to bring them into conflict' (6.75, p. 99), as the report puts it. By contrast, social work and paediatric tasks—child protection and child health—were felt to be complementary. The two institutions concerned and not just practitioners entered into a sustained coalition. Differences between the groupings that evolved were threatening to the perceived interests of each and were therefore fiercely contentious.

At the manifest level, the fissures in the service network opened up along lines determined by the institutional vulnerabilities of its constituent organisations. These vulnerabilities could be ascribed to the differences in tasks and responsibilities, in philosophies and values and in the status and working conditions of practitioners. But latent in such vulnerable states were the socially organised defences against anxiety inherent in work with child sexual abuse and the collective psychological needs of the members of the Cleveland agencies. These were needs to which their leading personalities gave such distinctive and fateful expression.

Thus, the service network was reduced in scope. There being effectively two irreconcilable camps in relation to 'third party' families, the unconscious as well as conscious tendency of at least some of the parents to split practitioners and agencies will also have exacerbated the divisions. The report observes that few complaints were made against the police; 'this was less than surprising because it was clear from the parents' evidence that, by the time the crisis had been reached, police officers were displaying or expressing the doubts and reservations they held concerning the medical diagnoses' (2.59, pp. 45-6). With the agencies in such a stance, practitioners were inauspiciously placed to address a central and often perplexing conflict: the rights and needs of children versus those of their parents. Rigidly defined and increasingly impenetrable professional and institutional boundaries precluded flexible working alliances between practitioners to meet the demands of different circumstances and particular cases. Like members of a conflictful family triangle, they lost the capacity to be bounded and separate and yet interdependent. And, as we noted above, they were liable to re-enact with unconscious symbolism the tragic drama of child sexual abuse itself.

THE INQUIRY'S CONCLUSIONS

Interconnected issues arising from the investigation and analysis of evidence are summarised in the Inquiry's final conclusions. These acknowledge the complexity of the phenomenon of child sexual abuse and the problems faced by professionals in balancing conflicting interests and needs in what was recognised as an 'enormously important and difficult field' (15, p. 244). Practitioners, especially social workers, have been under critical scrutiny in past inquiries and concern is expressed by this one that they might be demoralised by attacks on them and 'hesitate to do what is right' (17, p. 245). Meanwhile there are generative conflicts of feeling and deep-seated ambivalence in society, whose instrument such inquiries are, towards those assigned to perform its compassionate function by attending to people who fail, and fail as parents. Their 'thankless task' was clearly recognised: 'social workers need the support of the public to continue in the job the public needs them to do. It is time the public and the press gave it to them.' And the report continues:

> whilst it was important to try and identify what went wrong, it is equally important not to let that identification impede progress, in Cleveland and elsewhere. We make criticisms of individuals. Those criticisms must not be permitted to obscure the wider failings of agencies; nor would we wish to suggest that the identification and management of sexual abuse within the family is easy. It obviously is not (17-18, p. 245).

Alongside this reparative and balanced view it must be noted that the dichotomy between agencies and their members is shown to be false by a psychodynamic frame of reference. Agencies do not exist and cannot be considered apart from the individuals that comprise them. Institutions reflect the psychological needs of all their members, including the need for defences against anxiety which are socially organised—whether by social workers, doctors or police.

By implication, but perceptively, the report places the relevant hierarchy of open systems—families, practitioners, agencies and local co-ordinating machinery—in the context of the larger system that embraces all of them: 'How society acknowledges the existence of, recognises and then handles child sexual abuse poses difficult and complex problems' (19, p. 245). Some issues did not come before the Inquiry and were therefore not addressed but were deemed important, 'specifically the nature of abusers and the reasons for the sexual abuse of children; the effectiveness and appropriateness of the strategies used once the problem has been identified; and the response of society and agencies to those who abuse' (19, p. 245). Some matters stemming directly from the Inquiry require further thought and discussion: the possibility, under existing provisions, of extending social work effort to avoid the need for removing children from home; the needs of adults who were sexually abused earlier in their lives; and help for abusers in the wider interests of child and family.

Like its report, the Cleveland Inquiry's recommendations are wide-ranging. Mainly concerning the practitioners and agencies at the centre of the crisis, they reflect very different orders of consideration. The first recommendation concerns the need for accurate data on identified abuse and for an epidemiological approach to the problem. And, in line with its predecessors and its judicial character, the Inquiry emphasises legal, administrative and procedural matters. At the same time, the approach is catholic and often challenges attitudes which, as we have seen, are intimately connected with underlying personal and institutional defences against anxiety. The section referring to children, for instance, urges that the individuality of children should not be lost: 'the child is a person not an object of concern' (2, p. 245); and the first recommendation relating to parents of children believed to have been abused is that 'the parents should be given the same courtesy as the family of any other referred child. This applies to all aspects of the investigation into the suspicion of child sexual abuse, and should be recognised by all professionals concerned with the family' (3, p. 246).

Social services, the police and the medical profession are each the subject of a prescriptive section. As noted, procedural and organisational changes are to the fore, but otherwise the agencies are addressed differently. The vulnerability of social work practitioners arising from their child abuse tasks is emphasised: they 'need structured arrangements for their professional supervision and personal support. The work is stressful, and it is important that their personal needs are not overlooked' (4, p. 247). This reference to staff supervision is exclusive to social workers, no doubt in recognition of their statutory responsibilities in this field. But in fact all practitioners involved, irrespective of discipline or status, are exposed to conscious and unconscious anxiety by their different roles and tasks. The professional traditions and culture of some institutions—medical and police among them—tend to make this inadmissible and do not facilitate work-related learning and 'containing' systems analogous to those recommended for social workers.[8] Our experience is that other practitioners need them no less, not only as persons but in aid of task performance.

It is with this in mind that the Inquiry's views on strategy for promoting inter-agency co-operation and the related issue of training have to be considered. All the recommendations about the former point to the importance of task-boundaries and their management.

The evidence before the Inquiry showed that, in Cleveland, practitioners and agencies got 'hung up' on the medical diagnosis of sexual abuse. In fact, says the report, 'no single agency—Health, Social Services, Police or voluntary organisation has pre-eminent responsibility in the assessment of child abuse generally and child sexual abuse specifically. Each agency has prime responsibility for a particular aspect of the problem' (8, p. 248). So practical issues and detailed arrangements need to be recognised and worked out at local level in careful discussion between the respective agencies. The report's examples concern the level of suspicion of abuse that should trigger notification to the police that an offence appears to have been committed; when and what to tell parents when medical signs of abuse have been detected; when social workers should hold back from seeing parents until they have been interviewed by the police. All are surely liable to be contentious issues given the varying cultures and perspectives of agencies limited by their respective tasks.

Meanwhile, managers and chief officers are charged by the report with ensuring that their agencies eschew unilateral changes in policy, and they are not relieved of the duty of maintaining their organisations' co-operation with others because of the existence of local co-ordinating machinery. Its observations evidently led the Inquiry to be apprehensive that inter-professional collaboration may lead to a 'dilution of responsibility' (cf. chapter 5). Early on, the report had been highly critical of the Area Review Committee and the Joint Child Abuse Committee that succeeded it. They 'proved for the most part an ineffective mechanism to co-ordinate the work of the key agencies ... There was some evidence ... to suggest that representatives may have had more concern to protect what they saw as departmental interests than to commit themselves to the prime purpose of establishing an effective co-ordinating mechanism ... The role of the Joint Child Abuse Committee throughout the Cleveland crisis demonstrates the ambivalence that its constituent members had towards it' (3.64-65, p. 54). The Inquiry seems to have little confidence that such structures have a major part in promoting collaboration. Its recommendations concerning JCACs are limited to the review of arrangements for identifying and monitoring suitable training for professionals working with child sexual abuse, and to insistence that members must have authority and responsibility properly to reflect their agencies' views and bind them to implement decisions.

The central element in the proposed collaborative strategy is the recommendation that practitioners and agencies be able to call on multi-disciplinary Specialist Assessment Teams of approved doctors, social workers and police officers to undertake the assessment of difficult cases. Their job would be assessment, not treatment or planning for the future; that would rest with the referring agencies or case conferences. It is emphasised that the special duties of SAT members should be complemented 'with other less demanding work' to 'avoid stress and ensure a balanced perspective'. The establishing of such teams 'will have the advantage of building a reservoir of experience in a difficult area ... [and] foster teamwork and co-ordination of activity without undermining primary professional responsibility or agency function' (8, p. 249). This acknowledges the potential for distortion from endemic anxiety, and the need to recognise and maintain differences of function and responsibility. However, members would not be working in teams except in a piecemeal way and, as Stevenson (1989b) has pointed out, as a second-tier structure with the sole function of assessment the SAT proposal does not address the basic need for better mutual understanding at field level and in the continuing work of monitoring and intervention. Moreover, there is no avoiding the triangular dynamic and the fact that it is on the boundary between different functions and responsibilities that agency-specific anxieties and defences are most likely to be manifest and to generate conflict; and it is in difficult cases that clients' conscious and still more their unconscious divisive propensities are most likely to lead to 'complementary acting-out' on the part of practitioners in the Assessment Teams and their agencies.

'Training', says the report, 'is one of the major needs shown by the Cleveland experience. We recognise that training requirements are different for each profession' (9, p. 251). In placing strong emphasis on training and improvement of professional skills, the Inquiry was enlightened in its response to what was found to be lacking in Cleveland—in all the major professional groups. Our own work and that of other professional educators shows that understanding linked with personal change promotes consciously creative ways of managing anxiety and reduces reliance on less mindful ones. However, the Inquiry was primarily concerned with the wealth of specific information relevant to the different disciplines to be assimilated in this 'rapidly developing and difficult area' (9, p. 252). Its recommendations, necessarily only in outline, are for this kind of teaching on child sexual abuse from the student stage, through in-service provision to specialist training for experienced professionals with immediate responsibility for children suspected of being abused and their families, and they include inter-agency training.

Such comprehensive proposals also offer an opportunity to give practitioners the care they themselves need in coping with distress, destructiveness and conflict. In our view, the structured supervision and support systems advocated for social workers, and needed in fact by all practitioners if appropriate forms of provision can be found, should not be seen as separate from training. Far from inducing dependency or being, as some would see it, an expensive luxury, they are integral to staff development which envisages practitioners not as passive recipients of information but as autonomous participants in a learning system greater than themselves. In this sense, training is also a vehicle for research. In sustained programmes that take learning seriously, practitioners are able to make important *contributions* to knowledge (in this context about the genesis of abuse) out of their continuing experience with clients and patients and the observations they are in a position to make of family and marital interaction. The Inquiry's recommendations on training offer scope for advance—if their perspective can be extended.

Notes.

1   There were more than twenty such inquiries between 1974 and 1988.

2   The development of local co-ordinating machinery, at the behest of central government, was largely a result of the findings of earlier child abuse inquiries. The Area Review Committee had been superseded by new machinery (Joint Child Abuse Committee) in Cleveland prior to the crisis, in response to recommendations in a consultative document of 1986, revised and published as *Working together* by the Department of Health and Social Security and the Welsh Office (1988).

3   This accords with our TIMS colleagues' experience when setting up workshops for practitioners working with unemployed clients or patients. They too met the phenomenon of denial, especially in one locality where unemployment was in fact high. They came to recognise this as a defence against the anxious and conflictful personal feelings engendered by being 'employed to help the unemployed'—particularly in places where such clients were prevalent, welfare services were stretched to the limit and practitioners' own jobs could be in jeopardy through cuts in public expenditure (Mattinson, 1988).

4   Dr Sebastian Kraemer has described similar experiences in the paediatric department of an inner-city hospital, where other considerations seem to 'become irrelevant when sexual abuse is on the agenda'; the more the reality of children's suffering is confronted 'the more *business-like* [our italics] we become ... one can take maybe ten per cent of it; more and one loses touch with reality'. But when such abuse is not at issue, 'one is freer to attend to parental difficulties and depression' (paper read at the James Robertson memorial meeting, Tavistock Clinic, November 1989. See also Kraemer, 1988).

5   Omnipotent feelings originate in the most primitive phases of development and the earliest months of life: 'a conviction that whatever tricks the mind may play can achieve the desired result—freedom from anxiety' (Herman, 1989, p. 12). Doctors and their institutions are routinely the object of the helpless patient's projections and are liable to adopt the defence in their practice and organisation. It is easy to see that defensive omnipotence is liable to flourish when practitioners confront the reality of helpless suffering in abused children. And omnipotence tends to negate the concern required for reality-based co-operation with others.

6   Our attention was drawn to another police authority which instituted organisational change aimed at protecting the best interests of children and reducing the potential for inter-agency tension by establishing *all-female* units to deal with child abuse. The operation of socially organised defences (denial and splitting) may be deduced from the

fact that the women concerned, and their units, were reportedly kept at a distance by colleagues, not least through such colloquial designations as 'the smutty squads'.

7   'The hostility created by the blame is likely to make the relationship yet more insecure and hence increase the lack of trust which helped to give rise to the blaming in the first place' (Mattinson and Sinclair, 1979, p. 94).

8   It is as though to acknowledge the need for this kind of developmental opportunity, through which anxiety can be mastered and defences against anxiety modified, is to open the door to weakness or admit to incompetence. The reverse is usually true. The problem is exemplified by the following anecdote: one of us had occasion to talk with two police constables who had been on duty during a disturbing and traumatic event. They had received a notice informing them that, if they felt the need, they could discuss their experiences individually with a psychiatrist. Both had indeed felt 'shaken' (as had their families) but did not intend to take up the offer because they believed that admitting to stress would count against them and debar them from such special duties, which carried status and for which they had undertaken special training. On the other hand, they said they *might* have accepted discussion in a group. We know of some recent initiatives elsewhere in which police are, in fact, regularly doing this.

Bibliography

Arden M (1985). Psycho-analysis and survival. *International Journal of Psycho-Analysis, 66:* 471-80

Balint E (1959). Training postgraduate students in social casework. *British Journal of Medical Psychology, 32:* 193-9

—— (1967). A study of the doctor-patient relationship using randomly selected cases. *Journal of the Royal College of General Practitioners,* B 13: 163-173

Balint E and Norell J S eds (1973). *Six minutes for the patient: interactions in general practice consultation.* London: Tavistock Publications

Balint M (1954). Method and technique in the teaching of medical psychology, II: Training general practitioners in psychotherapy. *British Journal of Medical Psychology, 27:* 37-41

—— (1964). *The doctor, his patient and the illness* (second edn). Tunbridge Wells: Pitman Medical

Bannister K, Lyons A, Pincus L, Robb J, Shooter A and Stephens J (1955). *Social casework in marital problems.* London: Tavistock Publications

Bateson G (1973). *Steps to an ecology of mind: collected essays in anthropology, psychiatry, evolution and epistemology.* St Albans: Paladin Frogmore

Bettelheim B (1983). *Freud and man's soul.* New York: Alfred A Knopf; London: Chatto and Windus

Bion W R (1961). *Experiences in groups.* London: Tavistock Publications

—— (1962). *Learning from experience.* London: Heinemann

—— (1963). *Elements of psycho-analysis.* London: Heinemann

Bowlby J (1973). *Attachment and loss. Volume II: separation, anxiety and anger.* London: The Hogarth Press and the Institute of Psycho-Analysis

—— (1979). *The making and breaking of affectional bonds.* London: Tavistock Publications

Brannan J and Collard J (1982). *Marriages in trouble: the process of seeking help.* London: Tavistock Publications

Britton R (1981). Re-enactment as an unwitting professional response to family dynamics. In *Psychotherapy with families,* Box, Copley, Magagna and Moustaki eds (1981). London: Routledge and Kegan Paul

Brook A and Temperley J (1976). The contribution of a psychotherapist to general practice. *Journal of the Royal College of General Practitioners, 26:* 86-94

Butler-Sloss E (1988). *Report of the inquiry into child abuse in Cleveland 1987, Cmnd 412.* London: HMSO

Capra F (1982). *The turning point: science, society and the rising culture.* London: Wildwood House

Clayton M (1963-5). *Annual reports of the Medical Officer of Health.* Coventry

Clulow C F (1982). *To have and to hold: marriage, the first baby and preparing couples for parenthood*. Aberdeen: Aberdeen University Press
—— (1985). *Marital therapy: an inside view*. Aberdeen: Aberdeen University Press
Clulow C and Vincent C (1987). *In the child's best interests? Divorce court welfare and the search for a settlement*. London: Tavistock Publications
Community Care (1989). 755: 3
Community Nursing Review (1986). *Neighbourhood nursing—a focus for care*. London: HMSO
Cooper B (1971). Social work in general practice: the Derby scheme. *Lancet, 1:* 539-542
Corney R H and Clare A W eds (1982). *Social work and primary health care*. London: Academic Press
Courtney M J F (1979). Balint groups for general practitioners. In *The human face of medicine. Fourth International Balint Conference*. Tunbridge Wells: Pitman Medical
Dearnley B (1985). A plain man's guide to supervision—or new clothes for the emperor. *Journal of Social Work Practice, 2:* 1.52-65
Dept of Health and Social Security and Welsh Office (1989). *Working together. A guide to arrangements for inter-agency co-operation for the protection of children from abuse*. London: HMSO
Dicks H V (1967). *Marital tensions*. London: Routledge and Kegan Paul
Emery F E ed (1981a). *Systems thinking, volume one*. Harmondsworth: Penguin Books
—— ed (1986b). *Systems thinking, volume two*. Harmondsworth: Penguin Books
Emery F E and Trist E L (1972). *Towards a social ecology: contextual appreciation of the future in the present*. London: Plenum Publishing Company
Erikson E H (1965). *Childhood and society*. Harmondsworth: Penguin Books
Foreman J A S and Fairbairn E M (1968). *Social casework in general practice*. Oxford: Oxford University Press
Freud S (1915a). The unconscious. *Standard Edition, 14*. London: The Hogarth Press and the Institute of Psycho-Analysis
—— (1921) Group psychology and the analysis of the ego. *Standard Edition, 18*. London: The Hogarth Press and the Institute of Psycho-Analysis
Garland C (1991). External disasters and the internal world: an approach to understanding survivors. In *Handbook of psychotherapy for psychiatrists*, Holmes ed (1991). London: Churchill Livingstone
Gilchrist I C, Gough J, Horsfall-Turner Y, Ineson E, Keele G, Marks B and Scott H (1978). Social work in general practice. *Journal of the Royal College of General Practitioners, 28:* 675-86
Goldberg E M and Neill J (1972). *Social work in general practice*. London: Allen and Unwin
Gosling R H, Miller D H, Woodhouse D and Turquet P M (1967). *The use of small groups in training*. Hitchin: The Codicote Press/Grune and Stratton, Inc. and the Tavistock Institute of Medical Psychology
Graham H and Sher M (1976). Social work and general practice. *Journal of the Royal College of General Practitioners, 26:* 95-105
Guntrip H (1971). The ego psychology of Freud and Adler re-examined. *British Journal of Medical Psychology, 44:* 305-18
Harwin B G, Cooper B, Eastwood M R and Goldberg D T (1970). Prospects for social work in general practice. *Lancet, 2:* 559-61

Heisler J and de Groot M (1984). Counselling in surgeries. *Marriage Guidance, Winter Issue:* 13-16

Herman N (1989). *Too long a child: the mother-daughter dyad.* London: Free Association Books

Hicks D (1976). *Primary health care.* London: HMSO

Home Office/DHSS (1979). *Marriage matters.* London: HMSO

Home Office (1984). *Probation service: statement of national objectives and priorities.* London: HMSO

Hornby S (1983). Collaboration in social work: a major practice issue. *Journal of Social Work Practice, 1:* 35-55

Huntington J (1981). *Social work and general medical practice: collaboration or conflict.* London: Allen and Unwin

Irvine E E (1959). *The use of small group discussions in the teaching of human relations and mental health.* London: Association of Psychiatric Social Workers

Jackson D (1957). The question of family homeostasis. *Psychiatric Quarterly Supplement, 31:* 79-90

Jantsch E (1980). *The self-organising universe: scientific and human implications of the emerging paradigm of evolution.* Oxford: Pergamon Press

Jaques E (1951). *The changing culture of a factory.* London: Tavistock Publications

—— (1955). Social systems as a defence against persecutory and depressive anxiety. In *New directions in psycho-analysis,* Klein, Heimann and Money-Kyrle eds (1955). London: Tavistock Publications; New York: Basic Books

Jefferys M and Sachs H (1983). *Rethinking general practice: dilemmas in primary medical care.* London: Tavistock Publications

Jordan N (1968). Some thinking about 'system'. In *Systems thinking, volume two,* Emery ed (1981). Harmondsworth: Penguin Books

Koestler A (1964). *The act of creation.* New York: MacMillan

Kraemer S (1988). Splitting and stupidity in child sexual abuse. *Psychoanalytic Psychotherapy, 3:* 3.247-59

Kubie L S (1970). Problems of multidisciplinary conferences, research teams and journals. *Perspectives in Biological Medicine, 13:* 405-27

Laing R D (1960). *The divided self.* London: Tavistock Publications

Lawrence W G (1979). Introductory essay. In *Exploring individual and organisational boundaries,* Lawrence ed (1979). Chichester: John Wiley and Sons

Lyons A (1973). Therapeutic intervention in relation to the institution of marriage. In *Support, innovation and autonomy,* Gosling ed (1973). London: Tavistock Publications

Marris P (1974). *Loss and change.* London: Routledge and Kegan Paul

Martin F (1977). Some implications from the theory and practice of family therapy for individual therapy (and vice versa). *British Journal of Medical Psychology, 50:* 53-64

Mattinson J (1975). *The reflection process in casework supervision.* London: Institute of Marital Studies

—— (1979). The deadly equal triangle. In *Change and renewal in psychodynamic social work: British and American developments in practice and education for services to families and children* (1980). Massachusetts: Smith College School of Social Work; London: Group for Advancement of Psychotherapy in Social Work

—— (1988). *Work, love and marriage: the impact of unemployment.* London: Duckworth

Mattinson J and Sinclair J (1979). *Mate and stalemate: working with marital problems in a social services department*. Oxford: Blackwell; paperback (1981), London: Institute of Marital Studies

Meacher M (1979). *New methods of mental health care*. Oxford: Pergamon Press

Medawar P B (1969). *Induction and intuition in scientific thought*. London: Methuen

Menzies Lyth I (1969). Pleasure foods. In *The dynamics of the social: selected essays, Volume II* (1989). London: Free Association Books

—— (1970). The functioning of social systems as a defence against anxiety. In *Containing anxiety in institutions: selected essays, Volume I* (1988). London: Free Association Books

—— (1974). A personal review of group experiences. In *The dynamics of the social: selected essays, Volume II* (1989). London: Free Association Books

—— (1985). The development of the self in children in institutions. In *Containing anxiety in institutions: selected essays, Volume I* (1988). London: Free Association Books

—— (1986). A psychoanalytic perspective on social institutions. In *The dynamics of the social: selected essays, Volume II* (1989). London: Free Association Books

—— (1987). The aftermath of disaster. In *The dynamics of the social: selected essays, Volume II* (1989). London: Free Association Books

—— (1988). *Containing anxiety in institutions: selected essays, Volume I*. London: Free Association Books

—— (1989). *The dynamics of the social: selected essays, Volume II*. London: Free Association Books

Miller E J and Rice A K (1967). *Systems of organisation. The control of task and sentient boundaries*. London: Tavistock Publications

Miller E J and Gwynne G V (1972). *A life apart: a pilot study of residential institutions for the physically handicapped and the young chronic sick*. London: Tavistock Publications

Parsloe P and Stevenson O (1978). *Social service teams: the practitioner's viewpoint*. London: HMSO

Parton C and Parton N (1989). Child protection, the law and dangerousness. In *Child abuse: professional practice and public policy*, Stevenson ed (1989). London: Harvester Wheatsheaf

Patten J and Jervis M (1989). Radical reform and golden opportunities. *Social Work Today, 20*: 26.12-13

Pincus L ed (1960). *Marriage: studies in emotional conflict and growth*. London: Methuen; paperback (1973), London: Institute of Marital Studies

Pines M ed (1986). *Bion and group psychotherapy*. London: Routledge and Kegan Paul

Prigogine I (1976). Order through fluctuation: self organization and social system. In *Evolution and consciousness*, Jantsch and Waddington eds (1976). Reading, Massachusetts: Addison-Wesley

Rapoport L (1965). The state of crisis: some theoretical considerations. In *Crisis intervention: selective readings*, Parad ed (1965). New York: Family Service Association of America

Ratoff L and Pearson B (1970). Social casework in general practice. *British Medical Journal, 2*: 475-7

Ratoff L (1973). More social work for general practice? *Journal of the Royal College of General Practitioners, 23*: 737-42

Ratoff L, Rose A and Smith C (1974). Social workers and general practitioners: some problems of working together. *Journal of the Royal College of General Practitioners, 24:* 750-60

Roycroft B (1987). Presidential address to the Association of Directors of Social Services. *Social Services Insight:* 2 October 1987

Rice A K (1965), *Learning for leadership. Interpersonal and intergroup relations.* London: Tavistock Publications

Rosenfeld, J and Caplan, G (1954). Techniques of staff consultation in an immigrant children's organisation in Israel. *American Journal of Orthopsychiatry, 24:* 42-62

Searles H F (1955). The informational value of the supervisor's emotional experience. In *Collected papers on schizophrenia and related subjects* (1965). London: The Hogarth Press and the Institute of Psycho-Analysis

Seebohm F (1968). *Report of the committee on local authority and allied personal social services, Cmnd 7303.* London: HMSO

Sheppard M (1986). Primary health care workers' views about social work. *British Journal of Social Work, 16:* 459-68

Skynner A C R (1964). Group analytic themes in training and case-discussion groups. In *Institutes and how to survive them,* Schlapobersky ed (1989). London: Methuen

—— (1976). *One flesh: separate persons. Principles of family and marital psychotherapy.* London: Constable

Stevenson O (1989a). Reflections on social work practice. In *Child abuse: professional practice and public policy,* Stevenson ed (1989). London: Harvester Wheatsheaf

—— (1989b). Multi-disciplinary work in child protection. In *Child abuse: professional practice and public policy,* Stevenson ed (1989). London: Harvester Wheatsheaf

Sutherland J D (1955). Introduction. In Bannister, Lyons, Pincus, Robb Shooter and Stephens, *Social casework in marital problems.* London: Tavistock Publications

—— (1962). Introduction. In *The marital relationship as a focus for casework.* London: Institute of Marital Studies

—— (1980). *The psychodynamic image of man: a philosophy for the caring professions.* Aberdeen: Aberdeen University Press

—— (1983). The self and object relations: a challenge to psycho- analysis. *Bulletin of the Menninger Clinic. 47(b):* 525-41

—— (1989). *Fairbairn's journey into the interior.* London: Free Association Books

Tagore R (1985). *Personality.* London: Macmillan

Vickers G (1968). *Value systems and social process.* London: Tavistock Publications

—— (1983). *Human systems are different.* London: Harper and Row

—— (1984). *The Vickers papers,* Open Systems Group, Open University eds. London: Harper and Row

Watzlawick P (1967). *Pragmatics of human communication.* New York: Norton

Will D and Baird D (1984). An integrated approach to dysfunction in interprofessional systems. *Journal of Family Therapy, 6:* 275-90

Wilson S and Wilson K (1985). Close encounters in general practice: experiences of a psychotherapy liaison team. *British Journal of Psychiatry, 146:* 277-81

Winnicott D W (1949). The ordinary devoted mother and her baby. In *The child and the family* (1957). London: Tavistock Publications; New York: Basic Books

—— (1956a). Primary maternal preoccupation. In *Through paediatrics to psycho-analysis* (1978). London: The Hogarth Press and the Institute of Psycho-Analysis

—— (1956c). Paediatrics and childhood neurosis. In *Through paediatrics to psycho-analysis* (1978). London: The Hogarth Press and the Institute of Psycho-Analysis

—— (1986). *Home is where we start from*. Harmondsworth: Penguin Books

Woodhouse D L (1962). Some implications for casework practice and training. In *The marital relationship as a focus for casework*. London: Institute of Marital Studies

—— (1967). Short residential courses for post-graduate social workers. In Gosling, Miller, Woodhouse and Tourquet, *The use of small groups in training*. Hitchin: The Codicote Press/Grune and Stratton, Inc. and the Tavistock Institute of Medical Psychology

—— (1977). Referral from general practice to specialized agencies. *Proceedings of the Royal Society of Medicine, 70:* 498-502

—— (1990). The Tavistock Institute of Marital Studies: evolution of a marital agency. In *Marriage: disillusion and hope,* Clulow ed (1990). London: Karnac Books for the Tavistock Institute of Marital Studies

Woodmansey A C (1990). Approaches to child abuse. *Journal of Social Work Practice, 4:* 2.2-29

Index